MW01611209

Tributes

"In a time marked by doubt and disillusionment, Woman-A Godly Creation *offers a path to restoration and hope. Important women in Dick Toliver's life have opened his eyes to the many female virtues, and he brings his experience to life in his latest work. Be prepared to recognize and embrace this greatness through many historic and present day examples in these inspired pages."*
Dr. Charlene E. McGee Smith, PhD.
Author and Educator

"As a man, husband, father, and grandfather, Colonel Richard Toliver really "gets" women. His inspirational message can serve to empower young women to love themselves, set high goals, and believe that they should never allow themselves to be treated with less than the respect that they deserve. This book will also serve as a valuable resource for parents, educators, and anyone who facilitates the growth of young women."
Louise J. Privette, MC, NCSP
School Psychologist

"Richard Toliver has enlightened and illuminated the greatness of women in this book and brought this quality to the forefront in multiple, exciting passages. As teachers and educators, we have the Divine purpose of being on the front line of instilling in young minds self-worth and an awareness of their greatness. This book is a great teaching tool and should be added to every high school library."
Shirley Tolbert Jones
Retired Teacher
Prince William County Public Schools, Dumfries, VA

"Profound and valuable; every woman deserves a copy of this book!"
Sarah Whitmore
Financial Planning Executive

"This is an extraordinary, well-written, descriptive book. You will be greatly inspired by examples of heartbreaking adversity and suffering, followed by amazing recoveries and successful personal and professional achievements. Dick Toliver lets you live vicariously through his eyes with a riveting mix of adventure and spiritual convictions."
Major General Irene Trowell-Harris
Retired Veteran of United States Air Force
and Air National Guard

WOMAN
A GODLY
CREATION

By Richard Toliver

SAGUARO PUBLISHING COMPANY
Goodyear, Arizona

Woman–A Godly Creation
By Richard Toliver

Published by
SAGUARO PUBLISHING COMPANY
10914 S. San Ricardo Drive
Goodyear, Arizona 85338
Email: rtoli@cox.net
Website: www.agodlycreation.com

Production Coordinator: Qualitypress.info
Interior Design by The Printed Page
Cover design by Alonzo McDowell
Courtesy of Greensky Media Group

All Rights Reserved.

This book, or parts thereof, may not be reproduced in any form or stored in a database or retrieval system without the prior written permission of the publisher.

Unless otherwise noted, scripture quotations are taken from the Holy Bible, New International Version®, NIV®. Copyright © 1996 by the International Bible Society. Used by permission of Zondervan. All rights reserved.

Additional scriptures taken from The Ryrie Study Bible New American Standard Translation, NAST®. Copyright ©1978. Used by permission of Moody Bible Institute. All rights reserved.

DISCLAIMER

Many of the historical stories, summaries, references, and photographs were taken from the abundance of information on the Internet. In particular, Wikipedia was used extensively to document and validate historical stories and timelines. Where necessary and when possible, credit has been given to other authors and writers posted on the Internet or in Wikipedia summaries. Information regarding active duty and/or retired military persons was obtained as public information from the websites of DOD and the respective branches of the armed services.

To the best of my ability, the personal stories in this book are accurate and true. In some cases, names were changed at the request of the persons involved, or to protect the privacy of others with whom they may have been related or with whom they were associated. The direct quotes used have only been modified to correct spellings, verb use, and punctuations.

Copyright © 2014 by Richard Toliver
First Edition: January 2014

ISBN-13 • 978-0-9840991-2-2
ISBN-10 • 0-9840991-2-3

Library of Congress Control Number: 2013922302

Printed in the United States of America

Dedication

*This book is respectfully dedicated to women worldwide
who faithfully and graciously embrace their God-given greatness.*

Richard Toliver

Acknowledgments

I want to express my profound gratitude to the many women and others who participated in completing this book. I especially appreciate the women who provided their candor, stories, and selflessness in face-to-face, telephonic interviews, and or in completed questionnaires. You gave me confidence to write the true stories recorded herein, and you inspired me to conduct considerable research for the others. I owe a great debt of gratitude to an exhaustive list, but fear I cannot do justice to all of them. Yet, I do want to recognize some who deserve special mention. An omission of anyone is not deliberate, and I trust that I'll be forgiven for this shortcoming.

First, I want to thank my editors who worked faithfully and tirelessly during the two years in completing this book. Peggy Toliver, my precious wife, read, critiqued, and edited every chapter of the book, sometimes repeatedly, to ensure I stayed on point. Her patience was priceless. Frances Porter and April Hall are greatly appreciated for reading the entire final manuscripts and providing outstanding comments, edits, and suggestions for improvements. Many others provided editorial support for specific chapters and sections of the book. These included Sheila Johnson, Sarah Whitmore, Louise Privette, Irene Trowell-Harris, Beverly Kavouras, Sylvia "Sparks" Byrnes, Betty Locke, Dorothy Mcewen, Ginger Thrope, Anita Mamy, and Stephen and Rita Wade.

I am especially grateful for the scores of women who completed the questionnaire used to gather inputs for the book and/or allowed me to share their personal stories: Violet Bower, Linda Brown, Deborah Carper, Kia Cottrell, Mahama Grayson, Phyllis Hayhurst, Jean Holloway, Julie Hurowyj, Mary Jane Jojola, Shirley Tolbert Jones, Renea Toliver Lewis, Diane Martin, Meredith McCleary, Renata Mills, Frances Porter, Rogina Ruffin, Zella Toliver Rye, Charlene

Smith, Stephany Snowden, Bernadette Stepne, Gail Toliver, Ann Towns, Casey Walker, Sara, Sandy, and Stephanie Walton, Floyd and Patricia Whitaker, Desiree Williams, Heather Wilson, Erika Woods, and Carol Young.

I owe a great amount of gratitude to Tony and Yvonne Rose of Amber Communications Group, Inc. for their wise counsel, encouragement, and support at critical junctures in the development of the draft. Also Beverly Black Johnson, founder of Gumbo for the Soul Publications was very instrumental in helping to define the post-production outreach efforts.

Finally, I want to express my deep gratitude to my family and others for allowing me to share openly many events and circumstances in our lives. I pray such honesty will confirm to the readers that God is faithful to forgive, restore, and transform anyone who turns to and trusts in Him. That is the ultimate good news of this book.

Contents

Introduction

Scores of others have written books about the greatness of women, so what makes this book different? What is my credibility, and what makes this book worth the read? I humbly offer the following:

Most of the crucial lessons in life that I learned came from women. The first came from my late mother who had only eighteen years to instill in me how to appreciate women and how to be an honorable man. She died when I was just twenty-two years old, but the lessons she taught guided me throughout my life.

The second woman that impacted my life was my eighty-year old sister who has been a lifetime confidant, friend, supporter and teacher.

The third set of "lessons" came from my Godly wife of fifty-one years, who has been a true soul mate, outstanding mother, supporter, and best friend.

Finally, I had a saint for a mother-in-law who blessed our household for twenty-seven years before she passed away at age ninety-eight.

In addition, I am blessed to have the love and respect of six daughters, two biological and four by adoption or through a loving mutual acceptance. When coupled with many other unique life's experiences, I feel compelled to honor women as God's great creation.

God used women to instruct and reveal to me many of the things I needed to know to be a total person. Although I grew up without a father's guiding hand, women pointed me to the greatest "father" of all—God. What I missed from the absence of an earthly dad, God worked through women to teach me how to appreciate, love, and to respect a woman. They taught me how to be the best that I could be as a man.

I used available history and personal interviews to collect real-life stories to encourage, inspire, and to motivate women of all ages to embrace their God-given greatness. These attributes are part of a divine master plan, and they are infused in women at the moment of their conception. Hopefully these truths will help women accept nothing less than the best in life for themselves. I also have an over-arching motivation to testify about the greatness of God's work as manifested through women. Having been blessed to "see the light," I have a passion to share it with others.

When I initially began this book, I jumped in with both feet by interviewing a cross-section of women to give credence to my topic: *Woman-A Godly Creation.* The responses gathered corroborated my premise; however, I realized something was missing. While I had a general appreciation for women, I did not have sufficient knowledge of the historical impact they have made. Thus, I paused to research the history of women from the beginning of time. The result was an eighteen-month journey delving into the available written accomplishments of women and discovering just how God used them to advance humanity.

Much has been written about the ancient greats such as Alexander, Aristotle, Julius Caesar, Socrates, Voltaire, Gandhi, and Einstein. Conversely, the history of great women is more difficult to obtain. Fortunately, I found that Biblical history provided a good point of departure. A careful study of Biblical history confirms that God established the model of greatness in women during the creation of the universe. He continued to use women at critical or pivotal times throughout the progress of humanity.

My desire to write this book was driven by the several hundred years of collective female influence in my life. My experience has been filled with critical observations of women over the past sixty years. These observations were sometimes deliberate, subtle, unintentional, and at times, made from a distance. Some were made across the treacherous divide of racial prejudice and at great personal risk. Other observations were gained from my travels in many parts of the world. Still other observations were made in the crucible of survival during combat. I have also been privileged to interact with women from various ethnic groups such as Hispanics, Asians, Pacific Islanders, Europeans, and Africans. Others came from Southwest Asia, the Middle East, and the Caribbean. Remarkably, the attitudes, culture, images, and nuances of women have reinforced my appreciation of their greatness as God's magnificent creations.

My primary goal in writing this book is to help young women *and* young men truly appreciate the beauty, character, and total embodiment of their greatness established at the creation of the universe. In today's world, this greatness is too often trounced upon by a myriad of negative attitudes, callous behavior, ignorance, and pure ungodliness. Even more grievous, many women give up in despair and accept far less than they deserve for themselves. In their quest for love, too many become single parents and subject their children to dead-beat men, child-abusers, and other perpetrators. Many others fail to appreciate their own self-worth and accept the opinions of men who are not qualified or who are not worthy to affirm their greatness. Because of these tragic relationships, I want to reach young women and encourage them to appreciate their value and to stand firmly in their creative greatness. I want to encourage them to fiercely insist that whoever dares enter their space do so with the utmost of appreciation, honor, and respect.

My concurrent goal is to shake the apathy, callousness, and complacency in men and others who fail to recognize the tremendous blessings we have in this world because of women. I want to help revive the "chivalry of old" when men esteemed the value of women instead of wallowing in the mire of their own inadequacies and insecurities.

Despite worldwide poor treatment, abuse, negligence, and efforts to relegate women to a lesser status, no one, nor any circumstance can alter their intrinsic magnificence. Regardless of how hard man and the world tries, they cannot improve upon God's creative greatness in women! The roles of women have changed dramatically all over the globe during the past fifty years. Men should not fear or try to diminish this rise in the prominence of women. Instead, men need to celebrate, honor, and revere the progress women have made.

The book is in two parts. **PART I** underscores the premise that women are indeed a great creation. The initial chapter explains my divine inspiration from God. Next, the book established the foundation of God's intentional purpose of women throughout history. Given that foundation, women are then encouraged to embrace their greatness through the application of spiritual keys, practical tools, and comments from other women. The succeeding chapters address the manifestation of a woman's greatness through relevant, real-life stories of those who graciously shared their experiences for the benefit of others. The section continues with chapters of women in the military, nurses, a personal story about four women in my life, a message for men, and acceptance of God's plan for humanity. **PART II** provides the results of my research as a chronology of short stories of great women throughout history—from Biblical times through the 20th century.

The majority of this book focuses on women; however, I hope that men will also accept the challenge to be all that God created *them* to be in support of women. I do not expect my opinions to change the world, but I do want to try to make the society in which we live just a little bit better. It is my fervent hope that those who read this book will be motivated to reach out to the women in their lives and let them know how much they are appreciated and loved. This is my hope for my daughters, granddaughters, and great granddaughters. It is my hope for a better world.

Richard Toliver
December 2013

Prologue

Manifestations of Greatness

Two major sub-themes are pervasive throughout this book: (1) The *creative greatness* of women has been used by God since the genesis of time to further the progress of humanity, and (2) Sometimes, God allows the *fire of adversity* to prove and sharpen the creative greatness of women to confront many challenges in their lives.

The Creative Attributes of Women

I marvel at God's plan for the procreation of life on this earth for all species, especially humans. Herein, I believe, is the greatest purpose for His creation of women. In the beginning, God placed the seed of humanity in man. But without the unique anatomical, biological, emotional, and physiological attributes of a woman, man's seed would have been useless, then and now. Moreover, the Lord established this immutable process for *all* life on earth!

As a result, I believe a woman's ability to conceive, nurture, and give birth to a child is her greatest attribute. However, for many reasons, not all women can or will become mothers by physical birth. Nevertheless, motherhood is an *act, behavior,* and *commitment* rendered from a strong mind, kind heart and loving nature. It is a God-given instinct that cannot be suppressed or denied. Yet, God still allows the woman to have the free will to bear children. Above all, *love* trumps *blood;* therefore, countless women are serving as loving mothers to children born of other women.

Power That Overcomes Adversity

Every woman who has lived for any period of time will tell you that adversity is a part of life. Adversity is caused by many different circumstances, experiences, or unforeseen events. Some of the greatest adversities in life are caused by the loss of loved ones, broken relationships, divorce, debilitating illnesses, persecution, professional hardships and social ostracism. Often, adversity results from the actions of another person in a woman's life. Other difficulties are caused by circumstances beyond human control for which no one can be blamed. Yet, hope springs forth from suffering. Often, adversity is used to refine one's faith. Resolve and strength can be gained by persevering under fire. Regardless of life's experiences, God has always worked to bring some good out of trial and tribulation, joy from sorrow, and peace in the midst of turmoil. I have witnessed such manifestation of greatness in women while they were in the midst of grave adversity.

PART I
THE GREATNESS OF WOMEN

CHAPTER ONE

In the Beginning

The Creation Story

I first heard the biblical story of the Creation when I was in the sixth grade. During an Oratorical Contest, Nettie Nelson, a young girl from my neighborhood gave a rousing rendition of the *"Creation"* by the black poet, James Weldon Johnson. Nettie was about eleven years old, but her performance captivated my attention. Her description of God creating the expansive universe and the beautiful earth was particularly intriguing. I was especially moved when she said God surveyed all that He had created and declared it to be good. She stated that God was still lonely, so he said, *"I'll make me a man!"* Next, she painted a picture of God kneeling down beside a river and scooping up a handful of clay. He rolled it around in His hands and shaped it into an image of Himself. Thus, man became a living soul when God blew the breath of life into his nostrils.

Wanting to know more, I later read about the creation in our family Bible and discovered the rest of the story. The Lord finally said:

> *"It is not good that man should be alone; I will make him a helper suitable for him."..... "So the Lord God caused a deep sleep to fall on the man, and he slept; then He took one of his ribs, and closed up the flesh at the place. And the Lord God fashioned into woman the rib which He had taken from the man, and brought her to the man."* Genesis 1:18,21-22

The creation story was an exciting vision for my youthful mind, and I was filled with awe and wonder. I imagined the universe as it evolved and visualized earth as a pristine planet unmarred by human hands. I had wanted to be a pilot since I was seven years old, but now I was anxious to soar high above the earth and see it from thousands of feet in the sky.

Inspired By God

> *"The heavens declare the glory of God;*
> *the skies proclaim the work of his hands."* Psalm 19: 1

Fifteen years later, my dream became an exhilarating reality when I became a pilot in the United States Air Force. The years that followed were filled with vivid scenes as I flew all over *"America the Beautiful"* and other parts of the world. From the vantage point of six miles above the Pacific Ocean, the vast expanse of water was overwhelming in every direction. My small existence in the universe was put in proper perspective when I flew above the deepest part of the Pacific Ocean that was six miles below the surface of the water! Later, when flying over the Alps of France and Italy, I beheld the indescribable beauty of majestic snow-covered mountains totally untouched by man. At other times, my flights across the Mediterranean Sea and its emerald-like islands underscored the "gathering together" of the earth and the waters in their creative places. On the ground, I have also been blessed to behold the indescribable tapestry of God's magnificent paintbrush while standing on the rim of the Grand Canyon and at the foothills of the Rockies.

Despite the expansive, magnificent evidence of God's creation, it took three catastrophic events in my life before I finally "saw" His greatness right before my eyes. The first involved two combat tours in Southeast Asia, seven years a part. The second was a lightning strike while I was flying an F-15 jet at 20,000 feet. The last event was a rocket seat ejection approximately six seconds before my crippled jet made a seventy foot fiery crater in the ground. The lightning strike proved to be the Lord's "creative two-by-four" and my wake-up call.

The ejection, four years later, finally made me realize that my "skill and cunning" account was woefully overdrawn. It finally got my attention and renewed my appreciation of who the great creator of the universe really is. At age thirty-eight, I had become blind to these truths and lost sight of other important things in my life. First and foremost, this "turning point" caused me finally to *see* God's greatness through my precious wife and family. In particular, His goodness was evident in the women He had already blessed me to have throughout my life. This dramatic awakening was well overdue, but I humbly accepted it. My vision also cleared up on many other things, and I began to see *all* people and things in a different light.

Years later, when I re-read and meditated on the scriptures about the creation, an epiphany slowly emerged: First, the heavens and earth had been created simply by God *speaking* them into existence. Secondly, when making man and woman, He chose to use His hands to create them! Thirdly, God did not need to take a rib from man but I believe He had a great purpose in mind. By taking a rib from man, God instituted and blessed the *oneness* in the union of a marriage between a husband and wife. He also wanted man to realize that he had no part in the creation of woman; it was God alone who performed this miracle. Furthermore, God did not intend for man to dominate or rule over the woman! Instead, He expected man to appreciate His great work and to embrace, honor, and love her.

In writing about women, I reiterate that their *"greatness"* is really about God and how He advanced humanity through them. Women have been great instruments of God for all time. Just as He works through the imperfections and weaknesses of men, He works through the frailties and shortcomings in women. Thus, the great works that women have done and continue to do are all about the greatness of God.

Historical Prominence of Women

Biblical Evidence

The evidence of the greatness in women is firmly rooted in biblical history, and I am amazed at how God established His plan for mankind through multiple and significant roles for women. Furthermore, the Lord has persistently raised up women through the centuries to carry out His specific purposes at critical times in history. Some years ago, I read a passage written by Alan Redpath (1907-1989), a well-known British evangelist, pastor, and author. Pastor Redpath said that nothing on earth takes place unless the Lord allows it. Inherent in these words is the assurance that nothing is happenstance. Therefore, I believe God's purpose for women was intentional and that He wanted them to have significant impacts throughout history. The Lord never fails, and His ways are always perfect. Since Adam, the history of man is inextricably impacted by the way God used women to execute His perfect plan for *all* of humanity.

The Old and New Testaments are replete with scores of outstanding examples of the Lord's use of women of all races, creed and color. I am pleased to present in this book a number of exciting examples to underscore this fact. However, my overarching premise is still emphasized throughout this book: every woman is *A Great Creation* of God!

First Century to the Middle Ages

Since earliest history, women were considered intellectually inferior to men and only recognized for their creative ability to bear children. Historians focused on the exploits of men and presented them as the heroes of their eras. Much of the history of man is well-recorded in scores of books that reside in libraries all over the world. To gain a greater appreciation of early century women, I had to delve into the works of ancient historians, biographers, orators, philosophers, poets and playwrights, and religious archaeologists.

Societies were largely patriarchal during the time of Jesus, Greek, Jewish culture, and the Roman Empire. Women were generally considered subordinate to men, and they were not allowed to attend school, control property, or hold political office. Instead, women were expected to be obedient wives who worked in silent seclusion as caretakers of the homes and children. Conversely, Egypt was one of few exceptions. Egyptian women enjoyed a legal status almost equal to men. They were educated, free, and a few even reigned as pharaohs. The Egyptian women also had inheritance rights, were able to acquire wealth and political power, and make choices about who they married. The status of Egyptian women survived through the period of ancient Greece to the emergence of ancient Rome. By then their status had begun to influence the Greek and Roman societies as is evidenced by the relationship between Julius Caesar and Mark Antony with Queen Cleopatra VII, who ruled in her own right.

The emergence of Greece as a worldwide empire resulted in great changes in mores and society. The roles of women changed dramatically, and they exercised economic and political power with skill and confidence. Others became competent professionals in athletics, literature, medicine, music, philosophy, and a multitude of crafts. Traditional social barriers began to break down and women who possessed real economic power used it to gain their freedom and equality. Despite the predominance of male-dominated cultures and societies in the early centuries AD, God confounded man and continued to use women in the furtherance of His purpose. As the world evolved, women ruled kingdoms in the ancient provinces of Europe and Asia. Ultimately, they served as leaders and made decisions that impacted the spread of civilization from North Africa, Europe, across the Atlantic, and onto the continent of North America. Eventually, their history was duly recorded in documents from about the 18th century forward.

The period of history from about the 5th to the 15th centuries is generally called the Middle Ages. Women of this era filled the roles of wife, mother, peasant, artisan, nun, noblewoman, and other important leadership roles. They made wide-ranging contributions to business, culture, politics, religion, and war. History books are filled with exciting stories of famous kings and noblemen, but as the old adage states: *"behind every great man, there is a greater woman!"* In the Middle Ages, these women were queens, princesses, and mistresses who shared the powerful positions with their husbands and lovers. Some held very important sway over their sons. Still others reigned as queens in their own rights while others served as Mother Superiors of large convents. In addition, Christian convents provided an alternative to the subservient roles for the majority of women in the Middle Ages.

As with men in this era, the lives of peasant women were difficult, and they shared in the poverty of that class. Women from poor families tended to marry in their early twenties and their life expectancy was significantly less than that of male peasants, especially during the birth of children. Peasant women not only had to care for the children, but they had to continue their daily work, both in the home and on the land. As a result, many women from poor families did not live past the age of forty.

Women from rich families generally married when they were teenagers, but their marriages were usually based upon political or other advantages for the bride's family. After marriage, the bride was under the control of her husband, and producing a male heir within a rich family was considered paramount. Accordingly, many women spent a considerable amount of their married life pregnant despite the dangers in childbirth and poor medical care. An estimated twenty percent of all women died in childbirth with the most common being young women.

In researching the role of women during the Middle Ages, I discovered that the magnitude of their contributions and influence on society was overwhelming. Nevertheless, huge volumes would have to be created to do justice to those women and to better educate the generations of today. I have been greatly enlightened and inspired by just a limited study of these women; but Hopefully, you will conduct a more intentional study of this significant part of history available on the Internet and other forms of media.

The 18th and 19th Centuries

The period of the 18th and 19th centuries was a time of transformation as Europeans brought their attitudes, cultures, and mores across the Atlantic to the Americas. The predominant subservient roles for women that were sanctioned by church, law, custom, history, and society were about to be dramatically changed. These changes were forged by the challenges faced by early settlers who came to America. Such hardships included extreme weather conditions, limited food and water supplies, diseases, death, and numerous other problems. In many cases, these conditions caused significant loss of life or near total extinction. Several years passed before the settlers gained a foothold in their new colonies and established the foundation for what would one day be called the United States of America. Out of necessity, the attitudes toward women had to change to ensure mutual survival of the former Europeans. The demands of building and safeguarding communities, farming, and raising the children required a **shared** responsibility between the men and women. Later, changes in the attitudes and roles of women continued to emerge because of national growth, industrialization, rising expectations of women, and wealth accumulation.

During the American Revolution in the last half of the 18th century, the contributions of women on both sides caused increased recognition for the importance of women's education. The traditional domestic behavior of women now held greater significance since they faced a war that affected all aspects of their civil, domestic, and political lives. They participated in the war by boycotting British goods, spying on the British, following armies, washing, cooking and tending soldiers. Women also delivered secret messages, and some even fought disguised as men. All the while, women continued to labor at home to feed and care for their families and the armies.

After the American Revolution, the growth of town and village schools increased, female schools were created, and books that addressed the changing roles for women were published. By the early 1800s, the influence of some well-known writers who were considered liberals began to advocate greater economic and educational opportunities for women. Some even suggested women be allowed to participate in government; however, the conservatives, including the clergy, were strenuously opposed to these new ideas. A few gains were made in the education of women, but the European ideals and methods were still entrenched in the colonies.

As late as the mid-19th century, most women still lived a life slightly better than slavery. They did not have the option of choosing a career, whether or not to marry, or deciding to have children. Women still received less education than men, and they were obliged to obey men and rely upon them for subsistence. When women did get married, everything they earned, owned, and inherited automatically belonged to their husbands. The few exceptions were wealthy widows or spinsters; however, those who remained single suffered social disapproval and or pity. If a woman did risk cohabitation with a man, the social penalties were simply too brutal to endure. It would take another one hundred years and the accumulation of wealth before the status of some women shifted from that often depicted in the plantation life of the 19th century.

Women of Color

Biblical history substantiates the prominent roles given to *Women of Color*, (or dark-skinned women) since ancient times. Just as God "chose" the Jews for His glory and purpose, He firmly established *Women of Color* as an intricate part of the lineage of humanity. When considering the accomplishments and exploits of women from the 16th through the 21st centuries, *Women of Color* historically were ignored or intentionally omitted. In particular, the true legacy of African American women in America can never be told completely because of the limited documented history about them. A careful review of available recorded history confirms that *all* women are great creations of God and that *Women of Color* are part of His master plan for the entire human race. While expressing my profound appreciation for these women, I want to make it clear that my intention is not to alienate women of other races, creeds, or colors. I am confident that the truth will be evident throughout this book.

Women of the 20th Century

At the turn of the 20th century, America, as a republic, was just 124-years-old. However, over the next 100 years, our country and world experienced a quantum leap over the impediments of cultural, economic, educational, military, political, and social barriers. The creative and ingenious application of science and technology enabled America to rise from its cradle of infancy to become the leading world power in less than fifty years. This advancement was made possible by the birth of aviation, medical breakthroughs, diminished contagious diseases, two world wars and other conflicts, progress in civil and women's rights, space exploration, and the conquering of scores of other frontiers.

Despite incredible human achievements, the 20th century still found women outside of the political and social inner circles in America. Women still could not vote, serve on juries, hold elective office, or manage their own wealth. Furthermore, the wide range of gender discrimination kept them shackled as secondary citizens. Susan B. Anthony, Sojourner Truth, and many others had led the women suffrage movements in the 19th century. Yet, the dedicated and forceful efforts of women suffragists, at both state and national levels, had to be continued well into the new century to move the mountains of obstruction. A major breakthrough took place on August 18, 1920 when the Nineteenth Amendment (Amendment XIX) to the United States Constitution became law throughout the United States. This hard-fought milestone prohibited any U.S. citizen from being denied the right to vote on the basis of gender.

Armed with the right to vote, the power and the status of women in America changed dramatically in the decades that followed. Though not totally equal, women moved confidently into the labor force, politics, multiple professions, and most other cultural and social arenas. After World War II, America and the world saw a significant wave of feminist activism that forged additional changes in the traditional roles for women. Some of these were less strident and visible than others. All of them, however, required persistent and unrelenting efforts towards equality with men. Today, women around the world have appropriately staked their claim to full participation in every aspect of a nation's affairs—in economic, educational, military, political, and public service.

The Value of History

Since knowledge is power, the foregoing brief summaries of the historical prominence of women may serve as an inspiration to women today. In particular, I hope young women will draw strength to believe in themselves by knowing and embracing the greatness of women from past generations. Women of the past have established a solid foundation of commitment, determination, and resolve in using their God-given attributes for the betterment of human kind. I strongly encouraged women everywhere to embrace their imbued creative greatness by the application of spiritual keys, practical tools, and comments offered in the chapters that follow. Hopefully, you will also be inspired by the relevant, real-life stories of those who graciously shared their experiences for the benefit of others. I further trust you will be motivated to strive for excellence in all your pursuits after reading the chapters on women in the military, personal stories about four women in my life, the message for men, and the acceptance of God's plan for humanity. I have documented a selected list of great women from biblical times to the 20th Century in Part II of this book. These selections are intended to give you solid evidence of my consistent premise: Women have been great instruments of God for all time. Finally, the epilogue culminates the full circle of over 4,000 years of greatness in women in a very unique way. It has been my honor and privilege to write this book for you, the reader, and for ultimate glory of God.

CHAPTER TWO

Embracing Your Greatness

The State of the World

One of the most perplexing challenges that face our nation today is the widespread erosion of its moral and spiritual foundation and the corresponding apathy of its people. These grievous conditions are caused by intentional assaults upon our traditional core values, disintegration of families, ineffective education for the poor, and the alarming economic disparity between the "haves" and "have-nots." While we are a nation of plenty, too many people are trapped on islands of despair and hopelessness. An alarming number of our youth still suffer from the crippling effects of poverty, disease, drugs, illiteracy, and violence. High school dropouts and teenage pregnancies remain at epidemic levels, especially in minority communities. So what on earth have these things to do with the *greatness of women*? I believe that if America is to reestablish its greatness as a nation, women will have to take a crucial role in its restoration. God has historically worked through women for His greater purpose for humanity. Thankfully, He is still doing that today, and I have great faith in what women continue to do for this nation that I fought for and dearly love. I intend to stay in the fight with them!

Throughout the world today, the image of women has been woefully distorted and exploited by every form of media and social outlet. But in the context of the Godly role of women, their actual contributions to humanity need to be better appreciated and recognized. For the sake of our daughters, granddaughters, and great granddaughters, there needs to be a tidal wave of change in attitudes and perspectives in how women are presented. Young women in particular need to be more appreciated, affirmed, and held in greater esteem. They need to believe in themselves and know that they are indeed great and special. Women have the God-given power to change the world's view of who they really are. Like the *Women Suffrage Movement* over a century ago, women must decide that they have had enough and that they are going to change things. I am not ready to concede that America and the world are doomed to continue down the destructive path of the exploitation of women. Instead, I encourage women to use their creative greatness that God designed in them to work for the betterment of themselves and their children. Despite the notion to the contrary, there are still enough good men desiring to get involved in a meaningful way.

Spiritual Keys

The suggestions that follow come from over fifty years of witnessing the sad failures of people who searched for fulfillment, happiness, and love in all the wrong places. You already know some of the heart-breaking evidence of these broken and scarred lives. They include "highly successful" women such as Janice Joplin, Karen Carpenter, Marion Jones, and Whitney Houston. Women were not alone in these vain pursuits. The men include President Bill Clinton, Kobe Bryant, Jesse Jackson (Senior and Junior), and Tiger Woods. The sad truth is these horrific events didn't have to happen. Learn from these mistakes; you do not have to fail! So how do we get this train rolling down the right track? As a caring father, big brother, friend, and a sinner saved by the grace of God, I offer four critical spiritual keys: (1) Recognize and embrace your God-given creative greatness, (2) Have faith in God, (3) Trust God, and (4) Pursue wisdom.

Recognizing Your Creative Greatness

I believe the first step in embracing your creative greatness is to seek to know who you truly are as a woman. This requires you to explore truthfully who you are deep down inside, where only you speak and think to yourself and perhaps to God. Some of you need to really look into the mirror until you accept, appreciate, and love the person looking back at you. As you search, stop believing what someone else said about you. Resist accepting the lies that media presents as the perfect image of how a woman should be or look. Have sense enough to know that skinny women in beer and vodka commercials are beyond the pale of reality!

If you want to be successful in life, you must truly believe in your total worth as a creation of God. The woman who is searching to know herself must appreciate her ethnicity, facial features, DNA, genes, size, and every other part that was chosen by God hundreds, perhaps thousands, of years ago. He didn't make a mistake! Each of you is exactly what God wanted you to be. When the timeline of eternity was created, God established a place on it for every living creature to be born and an appointed time to die. No matter what external measures are taken to alter, makeover, or mutilate your outward appearance, God's work cannot be improved upon. When girls, young ladies, and women grasp these truths, they are well on their way to saying, *"YES!"* Every girl, young lady and woman can then declare in confidence that she is:

"...fearfully and wonderfully made...[your] frame was not hidden from Him...
[you] were skillfully wrought in the depths of the earth...His eyes have seen [your] unformed substance
...and the days that are ordained for [you] are written in His book."

Psalm 139:14-16, Paraphrased

Let me cut to the chase. In clear, plain language, this means that a woman's body is her most prized possession. It is the "crown jewel" that should never be squandered on a man who is not ready to lay down his life for her or their future children. Society has so cheapened the view of women through the exploitation of sexual images in every conceivable way. The consequence is that many young women entering the age of consent have never really appreciated what it means to preserve their precious treasure. Yet, a well-preserved body is the greatest gift that a woman can present to her husband in marriage.

God meant for sexual intercourse to be a true act of "oneness" between a man and his wife. If both the man and woman have not committed to a love relationship with God, they will never experience the true bliss and ecstasy for which sex intimacy was intended. There may be a plethora of prior or ongoing sexual encounters; but the sad truth is, these are mostly empty and short-lived experiences. God's creative plan for sexual enjoyment and procreation has not changed, no matter what the world says about it. Therefore, with the collective, intentional efforts of caring parents, responsible communities and churches, and sincere educators, there is still hope for a positive change.

The Essence of Faith

The next step in getting to know yourself is to develop an unwavering faith that God created you for a specific purpose. You must have faith in Him to **believe** and **act** upon that truth, but it is up to you to seek to know what that purpose is. Sometimes it may take a few trial and error excursions. But as difficult and uncertain as this challenge may be, I am confident that all things are possible with God. As you search for meaning in your life, you can hold onto a faith that is:

"The assurance of things hoped for, the conviction of things not seen." Hebrews 11:1

This scriptural truth holds value when a person decides to take a leap of faith, regardless of the circumstances he or she faces. It doesn't matter how much negative baggage you may have accumulated or how much you have suffered from abuse, exploitation, or neglect. Your inner soul can never be destroyed. No matter how many times you may have fallen down, God is still able to clean you up and transform you into a new creature. If you are a broken or scarred vessel, the "Potter" is always open for repairs. Even when the wounds have been self-inflicted, the "Great Physician" is willing to mend the broken-hearted soul. This is the essence of faith that is available to any woman who dares to believe in and trust in her great Creator—God.

Trusting God

One of the hardest things to do in life is to remain faithful during the storms of life or when others less deserving seem to prosper. Yet, that is exactly what you must do if there is to be real joy and peace during, or at the end of the struggle. Furthermore, placing your trust in a man for your happiness carries a very high risk for disappointment. If you cannot guarantee your own success, it is not likely that another person can satisfy your needs. Moreover, if you can't save yourself, why would you trust someone else to do so? Family and true friends can help, but ultimately you must take action for your own good. Again, God is the one sure hope upon which to cast all your cares. For over thirty-seven years, I have relied on a favorite scripture to overcome many doubts and uncertainties:

> *"Trust in the Lord with all your heart,*
> *And do not lean on your own understanding.*
> *In all your ways acknowledge Him,*
> *And He will make your paths straight."* Proverbs 3:5-6

There are a host of reasons to trust a God you cannot see; and there is an abundance of evidence that He does exists. For example, many people have been blessed to survive certain events that cannot be explained away by human logic. These include recovery from critical illnesses, miraculous survival of auto or vehicle accidents, and the birth of a "normal" baby when abnormalities or defects had been projected. On other occasions, Christians and non-believers alike have witnessed answers to scores of intercessory supplications offered on behalf of others. Regardless of your belief or faith, God still answers prayers and He has never failed! The answers may have been different from what was requested, but in retrospect, He is still faithful and reliable. Given such evidence, I believe that any woman can trust God with her every aspiration, desire, need, and unspoken requests. My mother-in-law shared a scripture with me many years ago when I was very discouraged, and it has been an assurance for me despite the challenges I faced:

> *"Do not fret because of evil men or be envious of those who*
> *do wrong,*
> *For like the grass they will soon wither, like green plants they*
> *will soon die away.*
> *Trust in the Lord and do good, dwell in the land and enjoy*
> *safe pasture.*
> *Delight yourself in the Lord and he will give you the desires*
> *of your heart.*
> *Commit your way to the Lord; trust in him and he will do*
> *this."* Psalm 37:1-4

Pursue Wisdom

The wisdom needed to get through life is an attribute from God that should be sought after and cherished. It is more precious than diamonds and gold. Wisdom is the ability to judge fairly and to make wise use of the facts being presented. Many people lack wisdom, yet think they are cunning and smart. But true wisdom is only obtained when one has a contrite heart and is humble enough to ask God for it. When a person makes such a request, he or she must ask in faith without doubting. It also requires the person asking to be willing to change or turn from an activity or behavior that blocks the blessings that might otherwise be readily available. God will not work through a rebellious, unrepentant heart. Therefore, the beginning of wisdom is to have a healthy respect and reverence for God.

The successful application of the preceding four spiritual keys to embracing a woman's greatness requires that she also embraces the one who created her. In addition, there are a few practical considerations that can be instructional as a woman deals with the challenges in life or when she is faced with making the right choice.

Practical Tools

It is helpful for a woman to have a few practical tools to keep her focused on her value as a human being and on her goals during the journey ahead. Many suggestions have been proposed; however, I have chosen a few keys that my late mother gave me as I grew into manhood: common sense, courage, and survival instincts. Again I want to directly address women here.

Common Sense is that ability to use simple arithmetic when encountering men who are in a perpetual search for a "conquest" or "victim." If a guy is making a load of promises or offering a bunch of "wooden nickels" without visible or tangible evidence, do the math! If what he is proposing doesn't add up, reject the offer and move on. Believe your gut feeling. If it starts to churn, step back and say "no thanks!" Common sense lets you know there are no "free lunches." Even precious life-saving water costs something.

Don't be beguiled by a smooth talker. Talk is indeed cheap, and the man who is trying to weave you into his net probably has lots of practice. Give yourself time to assess and think critically before making a decision to enter into a relationship. What many men want is your most prized possession—your body—without having to pay the appropriate cost. That price is marriage and all that goes with it—love, commitment, integrity, respect, trust, and if necessary, his life! If the man fails the common sense and math tests, have the courage to disengage sooner than later.

Courage is the inner strength that allows you to back away or sometimes run from danger. It is the confidence to accept who you are and not fear what some may say or think about you negatively. Courage enables you to stand firm on your beliefs and principles, regardless of the external pressures. It is the self-confidence that overcomes fear of failure in a relationship when you choose to guard your heart by not showing your emotions or feelings. Remember, it doesn't hurt to keep a man guessing about how you really feel about him. Have the courage to believe that if a man really wants a serious, respectful relationship with you, he will be willing to take the time for it to develop. One of the first things you'll notice is the emphasis he puts on **you** rather than himself. You'll also recognize the sincere respect that he has for you and for women in general. If you've been in a "serious" but uncommitted relationship for over six months, you are simply wasting your precious time! It doesn't take a man that long to see true greatness in a woman. If it does, he's not very bright, and you'd be wise to break off the encounter before any serious consequences occur.

Survival Instinct is the ability to have enough self-love to avoid putting yourself in danger or harm. Again, one of the greatest lessons I learned from my mother was this:

"Son, if you don't want to be tempted by the devil, stay off of his ground."

The application of this wise counsel has kept me from personal danger, harm, and temptation most of my life, and I am still applying it today. Adhering to this advice will preclude a woman from putting herself at emotional, medical, and physical risks associated with men who have careless and irresponsible behavior. With the present-day epidemic occurrences of sexually transmitted diseases, girls and women need to take extreme care to avoid being self-inflicted victims. Sexual abstinence is the surest safeguard possible.

Girls, young ladies, and women also need to be very vigilant about entering relationships with boys and men who show tendencies of being a controlling person. The occurrences of women who have been assaulted, injured or killed by their husbands or boyfriends are appalling. Insecure, self-serving control freaks are easy to recognize. They usually show their cowardly "stripes" during the first few dates or meetings. If a man starts to tell you how to dress, fix your hair, or tell you when or where to go, he wants to control you. DISENGAGE, DISENGAGE, DISENGAGE!

There is a more subtle, yet dangerous practice that men who seek to control or dominate women use. It often comes as an enticing offer to move into his beautiful home or drive his expensive cars. In this case, the man wants to exploit your most prized possession while having the freedom to discard you when he tires of you or wants another victim. I am going to use the word "never" here. *NEVER* give up your independence, job, or family to move in with a man who has not made the appropriate down payment—MARRIAGE *before* you move in! This is especially a *NEVER* if you are being asked to leave your hometown and family support environment. If you need help with the rent, even when moving to a new town, find another woman who has compatible attributes, goals, and finances.

Finally, if you are considering being a wife or mother, please think of the welfare of an unborn child **before** the pregnancy! Thousands of children who will be abused are being born every day because women decided to have children for the wrong reasons. Having a child simply because you want something of your own to love is a horribly selfish aspiration. It is always the child who suffers in the aftermath of broken relationships and harmful environments. Having a child simply because you want something of your own to love is a horrible, selfish ambition. Also, getting pregnant in an attempt to fix a failing marriage is an abysmal decision that has long-lasing, negative consequences. Almost always, it is the child who suffers from the aftermath of broken relationships; and often one or both parents struggle to recover. Too often, the child is at the mercy of abusive, uncaring husbands, boyfriends or "babysitters." Astute use of the innate survival instincts will preclude such tragedies.

Perhaps this "fireside" chat has been helpful and thought pro-voking. I want to continue by sharing four real-world confirmations of the reliability and trustworthiness of the preceding discussion.

Living Confirmation

"Jenny"

Nearly twenty years ago, a broken, scared young woman was brought to our door as a last resort to save her. I'll call her "Jenny." She had tried several times to commit suicide because of guilt and sorrow for some events that were beyond her control. In addition, she suffered from a deep personal sense of failure because most of her high school peers had graduated from college and she had never attended. Jenny could not believe that a God she didn't know could truly love her. It was an incredible challenge for Peggy and me, and we took the risk of entering into Jenny's life with a great amount of caution and trepidation. We began by praying with Jenny and by trying to convince her that God still loved her, no matter what her experiences had been. We got her involved in our Bible study and spent considerable extra time explaining what the Scriptures meant. Eventually, we were able to get her to accept and embrace her creative greatness. Today, Jenny has been happily married for twelve years to a man who truly adores her, and they have a beautiful, talented ten-year-old daughter. Through faith and trust in God, and by embracing her inner greatness, Jenny's life was saved!

"Mia"

Mia was a thirteen-year old "latch-key" girl who had a baby by a seventeen year-old teenager. Both of them remained in the home of their mothers who were single parents. At fifteen, she gave birth to a second child fathered by the same teenager. At seventeen, Mia finally married the father of the two children, but he turned out to be an abusive drug dealer. Mia hit rock bottom by the time she reached twenty. The next year, she narrowly escaped a long-term jail sentence when she and her husband were busted by the Feds for *his* drug dealing. At this point, Mia remembered her grandmother who took her to church and taught her how to pray when she was in trouble. She sincerely repented and prayed for deliverance while still in jail. God heard her plea, and with a revived faith in God and an extraordinary personal effort, she achieved victory over adversity. After a life-changing turn-around, Mia completed high school, enrolled in college, and eventually earned both a bachelor's and master's degree. Today she is an office manager of a major corporation with offices throughout the United States and overseas! Mia is also successfully guiding a daughter and son through college.

The Faith of a Dying Mother

One of the most moving and heart-rending stories told to me came from a young lady in her mid-forties, whom I shall call "Ava." Ava gave up her family, friends, and a well-paying job and moved across country in hopes of becoming the wife of a very successful man. Mr. "Right" had a beautiful, spacious home, two fine automobiles, and job security in a reputable industry. His smooth style and words eventually enticed Ava to move from her initial apartment into his home. He made promises but never delivered on the crucial one—marriage. After several intense years of a "married-like" affair, the relationship ended very poorly. Ultimately, Ava was obliged to return home to her family and friends and pick up the pieces of her life. Among those waiting for Ava was a critically ill mother who embraced her with compassion and love. Through the shared faith and prayers of her dying mother, Ava found the courage to recommit her life to God and is striving to live according to His commandments. The following are her words:

> *"My parents were so hurt when I did this thing. My heart was broken so badly that I felt myself literally losing my mind. I felt myself disengaging from reality, and I didn't care to do anything about it. I recall hearing my mother say to my sister that she didn't think I was going to come out of it. Meanwhile, my sister made an appointment with a mental institution representative to assess my condition regarding whether or not I needed their services. Mom then asked me to go to church with her; I didn't want to but because of her terminal illness I felt obliged to attend. So I went with her to a small church near our hometown.*
>
> *I really wasn't listening to the sermon until I heard the pastor speaking about heartbreak and Christianity. My mother reached for my hand, and for the first time during the service, I looked at her. She was praying! Mom was in constant pain, and I saw her health and life slipping away with each breath every day; but now she was praying for me! Realizing that my*

mother had sacrificed so much for her children, I was healed right then and there from that spirit of depression. Here was a woman who could have taken that moment to plead to the Lord, our God, to grant her a miraculous recovery. But instead, she was praying for her heartbroken daughter. I thank the Lord each and every day for the power of a praying mother!"

Three Sisters of Faith

I am blessed to be the father of three of five daughters who are still single and who are striving to live virtuous, Christian lives. So I have first-hand knowledge of their challenges in a world that cares very little about such noble character and where unscrupulous men constantly seek to exploit them. Each has confirmed that their greatest challenge in remaining steadfast is finding or establishing a relationship with a godly man who is equally committed. I am very proud of these women, not only because they are my daughters, but because they remain faithful in their walk with God. All three are successful in their professional lives and are actively engaged in helping other young people, particularly younger women. Thankfully, they are not alone in their noble pursuits. The story that follows tells of others who have chosen to follow the path of godly women. I trust the reader will appreciate the commitment, confidence, and perseverance of three beautiful young women that I had the pleasure to interview.

In early 2012, I had the privilege of participating in the rollout of the new movie, *The Red Tails*. This movie is about the extraordinary combat exploits of the Tuskegee Airmen, those great African American patriots of WWII fame. The post-movie activities featured three of the original Airmen of the local Tuskegee Airmen chapter, and several other participants who highlighted the men and women of that era. Three young ladies from *Matilda's Vintage Closet Fashion Shows* were dressed and made up like the women of the 1940s. They call themselves *"The Honey Sisters,"* and they added a tremendous authenticity to an exciting evening. As a blonde, brunette, and redhead, each could easily compete with the best looking women in Hollywood today. These ladies brought back a flood of personal memories for me.

As a boy growing up during WW II, I was greatly impressed by the men and women in military uniforms and by the general attire and appearances of people. I was especially taken by the appearance, demeanor, and dress of my mother, relatives, and other women in my life. Though very young, I appreciated the *inner* beauty of women reflected in their *outward* confidence, poise, and self-assurance. In those days, a woman did not need to flaunt her sexuality by exhibiting inappropriate clothing or behavior. Instead, her sensuality was accentuated and complimented by the clothing and make-up she wore. These were exciting times, and the women of that era were exceptional in the part they played to help win the war and preserve our freedom. The three "Honey Sisters" readily captured the beautiful essence in women of a generation long past. They caused a resounding flashback of sixty-seven years in our country! Not only were they attractive, but each exuded something more than an act or replication of the past. I discerned something beneath their outward appearance and sought to learn more about them.

During a subsequent conversation with these sisters, my initial impression was confirmed, and I told them about *"Woman—A Godly Creation."* When asked if they would be interested in helping me reach other young women who may need to be inspired by their peers, they agreed to share their story. I am delighted to share it with you.

Sara, Sandy, and Stephanie Walton were born and grew up in Glendale, Arizona. They are twenty-nine, twenty-six, and twenty-three, respectively. Sara, the eldest, was a twin born three months prematurely, but her twin sister lived only eight days. This initial tragedy painfully affected both parents and their children for years to come. Their parents and a sixteen-year old brother still reside in the home where the children grew up. The sisters attended local schools and began working after high school graduation.

The Walton family lived a somewhat normal but unremarkable life until the parents embraced the Messianic Jewish religion and led their children in accepting this faith. As the family began to read and study the *Tanakh* (Jewish Bible), they gained a deeper understanding of God and developed a sincere faith in Jesus Christ. Today, the entire family celebrates Shabbat, the seventh day of the Jewish week and the day of rest. They also celebrate the Jewish High Holy Days, *Rosh Hashanah* and *Yom Kippur*.

All three sisters were positively influenced by their parent's lives as they had lived it. Like many families, there were challenges to be faced, but they used these experiences to shape and solidify their own commitment and walk of faith. Sara was ten years old when she made a definite, personal decision to follow Christ. Sandy can't remember the exact moment she made that decision; however, she has strongly felt God's presence throughout her whole life. As an adult, she has chosen to live her life according to God's precepts. Stephanie was about six or seven years old when she was with her mother in the back yard. Her mother asked her out loud if she had ever asked Yeshua (Jesus) into her heart. She hadn't, but did so right then and there. Today, Sara, Sandy, and Stephanie consider themselves to be in "transition" and are not sure where the Lord is leading them. However, these sisters of faith are content and confident that God will lead them to a great place.

Sandy and Stephanie got the idea of impersonating women of the 1940s while watching old movies, about six years ago. They really loved the men and women of that era because of the demeanor and attitudes that were reflected in the way they dressed. Sandy stated:

> *"I miss the simplicity of the 40's. We live in a world now that is buzzing, always moving and never satisfied. Not that it was perfect then, because it obviously wasn't, but people had an integrity that we definitely don't encounter in this age. I think that something as simple as being dressed in the fashion of the 1940s reminds people of an attitude that we have lost. We get treated differently when we dress up."*

Stephanie added,

> *"...Our generation has become a mold to what people say they should be. Girls are only pretty if they have the right body or show the right body parts. Boys are only worth their strength or attitude. So I think if we can be different in the RIGHT way it may inspire people to think about the conformity in the world today."*

One day, Sandy and Stephanie walked into Matilda's Closet and met the owner, Rose, who asked them to be models in her shows. They agreed and have been involved ever since. Given their ideas and passion, Sandy and Stephanie decided to make themselves a group along with Amanda Lee, another beautiful "Bombshell" blonde. They wanted to bring a "little nostalgia and class" to the world around them. The group has appeared at rockabilly shows, car shows, nursing homes, and other events. Sandy and Stephanie are really the vintage models and are part of Matilda's Vintage Closet fashion shows; however, the night I met them, Sara had come along to meet the Tuskegee Airmen.

As the three sisters continue their walk with God, each expresses her own personal ambitions. Sara, the eldest has always had a passion for acting and filmmaking and loves the creative aspect of it. She has only been involved in the independent film market for about four years and has made many great connections. She would love to direct, produce, and write her own scripts. Her desire is to make a change in the world of movie making. Hollywood is not her main focus, but she believes that God has put her in the place where she can show Hollywood and the world God's love for *all* of His creations. Sara also wants to write about her life and others around her. She wants to tell about their personal struggles and how God can and will help anyone to get through the challenges. Sara plans to pursue her ultimate dream of acting and filmmaking. She plans to write a script in the near future that deals with the military, police, fire, and rescue personnel. In the meantime, she is currently attending Grand Canyon University in Phoenix, Arizona to get a bachelor's degree in Criminal Justice Studies. Sara is uncertain where she wants to go in this career but is considering law enforcement, K-9 operations, or forensics.

Sandy is currently a credit counselor with a money management firm, but would love to be a homemaker full time. She loves cooking and baking and feels that there is not enough time to do as much as she would like. She admits that she has never really had aspirations for a formal career, but is thankful for the job God has given her to do. Sandy believes it has been a blessing to her and hopefully others across the United States. Her ultimate ambition is to become a wife and mother who will raise her children in fear and reverence to the Lord.

Stephanie still secretly wants to be a Disneyland princess (Not so secret anymore!). Her current career path is also a Credit Counselor for *Money Management International*. But she believes her real career path is to be a wife and mother. Until then, she is content to continue her walk with the Lord.

All three sisters ultimately would like to have a man in their lives who truly loves the Lord and is committed to living that way. For each, that is the "deal breaker." They truly believe that God has been "chasing away the wolves" that they have encountered thus far. Each is also positive she will be able to know if the man is right for her by his fruit (lifestyle). Each continues to pray and trust that her desires are in the Lord's will.

I was much inspired by these young women as they gave me hope that there are still women who have rejected the so-called "social norms" of today. They also confirmed that faith-based families are still living together and striving to instill in their children great moral character and self-worth.

It is my hope that these preceding true stories will inspire and motivate young women to have faith in God and never quit striving to better themselves. Remember, failure comes not from falling down, but by quitting and giving up. My late mother taught me this lesson nearly sixty years ago by saying:

> *"Son, you have got to always have one more get up than a fall down; if you keep your eyes on the Lord, the shadows in your life will fall behind you."*

What Other Women Say

Now I want to share with you what other women said in response to the questionnaire used to gather input for this book. The responses were quite instructive and revealing, given the candor expressed by most of the women I interviewed. Some confessed that they had never really asked themselves some of the questions and that the exercise caused them to do considerable soul-searching. Thus, responding to the questions was often evocative and therapeutic. The cross-section of women included different ages, ethnicities, careers, economic and social status, and other variances. The questionnaire can be found in Appendix I of this book, and I respectfully suggest you use it to do a self-assessment regarding who you really are. I trust you'll find the following discourse helpful. I'll first state the question then provide several responses.

Woman, who are you?

"I am a wife, mother, and grandmother. I am a loving, devoted and supportive wife. I am a woman who loves the Lord; a woman of worth. I am humble, self-sacrificing, caring, and compassionate. I treat others as I wish to be treated."

"We are God's greatest creation because we add that extra value to a man's life. Our lips carry words of wisdom and truth. As a woman, I am vocal, spoken beyond words, sometimes sung, maybe screamed. I am humble to myself and others, yet tactful and classy enough to give respect and receive it in return. I am a twenty-one year old woman, and my journey has just begun."

"I am a twenty-five year-old documentarian and human rights activist from Washington State. I am currently in the Ukraine on a year and a half journey across the globe to capture life for the modern day orphans. Attending church every Sunday taught me who I was and who I will always be, which is a child of God. That in itself was enough of a foundation to guide everything else that followed."

"I am a child of God first and foremost. Like all of God's creations, there are parts of me that I freely share with others and parts that will remain private—known only to me and to my Creator. I am complex, yet simple at times, a deep thinker and gifted with the ability of discernment. I am a loving and loyal daughter, sister, aunt and friend. I have a compassionate nature that is innate, yet I do not suffer fools gladly. I am flawed, yet perfect in the eyes of my Savior."

"I am a mature, senior, intelligent, articulate, attractive, active, college-educated, well-traveled, independent, free-spirited individual striving (sometimes struggling) to accept growing old gracefully!"

Who or what influenced you the most in your early life?

"My Godly Mother, without question, was and continues to be the greatest influence in my life, especially the "formative" years. I witnessed her eternal patience, experienced her unconditional love, and undying faith in God. She is and always will be my greatest role model."

"My father influenced me a lot. He was very kind-natured and caring, and he spent a lot of time with me. I loved my father a great deal, and I remember him being a hard worker, always smiling and always having time for me."

"My mom, I watched her go through so many trials, tribulation and pain. When our family fell apart it was devastating to her when she couldn't be there for us. I'm proud of my mom; she went back to school, and with strong determination, graduated with her associate degree in Criminal Justice and is a certified executive secretary. My mother-in-law also played a role in my life. She is a God-fearing woman who blessed me with her words of wisdom."

What are/were your personal goals for marriage? Family? Children?

"Having a loving and successful marriage is a value that I hold very dear. After experiencing divorce and being on my own for many years, I finally found my second husband. I had never dated anyone in the military, but thought he might be right for me. He was a principled and romantic man who still gets a lump in his throat when he hears the Star Spangled Banner. Although we are very different people with a wide range of interests, we share common values and beliefs. I realize that

marriage takes commitment and my goal is to continually invest the needed time, energy and love into the relationship in order to make it work. Someday, I hope to have grandchildren to spoil."

"The goals for my personal life did not go as I had planned and dreamed early on. I always wanted a family of my own, as God prescribes a family to be, a husband first, then kids. I had to re-evaluate some things in my life when this didn't come to pass during the timeframe that I had envisioned. I set standards for a Godly mate and made a commitment to God my freshman year in college to remain pure. It will ultimately be God's will if I meet someone at this stage in my life. At forty-nine, I'm hopeful but not desperate."

"When I get married and have children, my goal is for our family to love God, love one another, and love others. We as a family will continually seek God and His design and plans."

What would you consider to have been your greatest challenge?

"Holding our marriage together. We have had numerous marital problems over the years. Infidelity was the worst to overcome. Sorting through those problems were some of the most difficult I've ever experienced. I was eighteen and my husband was twenty when we got married. I got pregnant out of wedlock. In those days it was called, "getting yourself in trouble." My daughter-in-law laughs about that every time she hears it, and I do too now! We've been through marriage counseling; we separated for a while; were close to divorce more than once; and there have been times that we were living together, but it wasn't much of a marriage. But, I am happy to report that we came through it all and are stronger for it. I don't think either of us ever wanted to give up on it. We always loved one another, remained friends somehow, but at times we felt trapped by the circumstances. Little did we know at times, just how much we were meant for each other!"

Have you established or do you have the criteria whereby you allow personal or professional relationships to be developed?

"My criteria for both personal and professional relationships are God-based. Everything is based on what Jesus would do and what He expects. I don't always match up, but He is my standard. I have close friendships with non-Christians, and my fervent prayer is for their salvation. I want my life to be a light, and I want to draw them to the Savior based on how I live."

"Professionally, I have always felt that I could do anything or be anyone that I wanted to be. However, my goals still have not come to fruition for me because of life obstacles. I have always been able to keep good relationships, professionally as well as personally. I have always been trusting of others, but at times I did not make good choices of friends and keeping company with others. As I have gotten older, I have gotten better where those choices are concerned."

Why do you believe young women enter into poor or ill-advised relationships?

"I believe that young women enter into ill-advised relationships for a myriad of reasons. Some are children of divorce or single-parent homes and have never witnessed a healthy relationship. Others suffer from poor self-esteem and do not consider themselves to be worthy of love and respect. Some women make compromises because they are seeking financial security and don't trust in their ability to make their own way in the world. Finally, some women believe that they are entering into a loving relationship only to discover that it is not what they envisioned it would be."

"Women enter into poor or ill-advised relationships for a myriad of reasons. It is over simplistic to cite their upbringing, but the formative years are SO critical. When the environment is broken, dysfunctional or abusive, the effects are far-reaching and life-

long. The lack of a positive male role-model causes a special level of harm. All girls crave a healthy, loving relationship from their dads. Sadly, that is not the case for an alarmingly high percentage of women today. We see and are living with the consequences of this fact in our culture, our country and our world (it is epidemic proportions in African-American communities). It is THE single determining factor (absent of God's grace and intervention) for shattered lives and dismal relationships."

What advice would you give young women today about life?

"I would advise women to begin early to dream of the possibilities and then to set a series of small, positive and accomplishable goals for themselves. I read somewhere that every child should have at least one other person, aside from their parents, who will love them unconditionally and serve as a positive role model for her. I would suggest to young women to avoid associating with negative people who drain the optimism and energy from your life. Instead, surround yourself with positive and successful people who will encourage you to be the 'best you' possible. Believe in the value of life-long learning. I have returned to school after many years and am currently earning my doctorate in counseling psychology. Initially, I thought I might be too old to pursue this dream. Then I realized that I will never be any younger than I am today, and that the best way to achieve this dream was to begin. Remember the old Chinese proverb, "A journey of 1,000 miles begins with the first step."

"The best advice to young women is to look to God for their value and worth, not man. It really is the most important piece of advice I could give. The other advice I would give is to seek God's guidance in all things and to not be swayed by the madness and expectations of our culture. As far as ambitions, all women should have some, though as I get older, they have changed, and are not based on "doing" so much as

"being". Regarding pitfalls—we all will experience them, so be prepared. The best way to weather storms is to know who is our Savior and Protector. He alone can help us THROUGH the trials of this life and He alone holds the answer for our future."

"To know yourself is to know God. It's that simple because He designed us. There have been countless times in my life when God has told me to move in a certain direction and I said, "Really, God? That's so not me." But when I obey, I then see that what He called me to was actually one of the deepest parts of my design. No matter how old you are, there are millions of layers to your spirit, your giftings, and your personality that you cannot "think up" or "force" out of yourself, but are joyfully unveiled by Christ."

"Make God first in your life and everything else will fall into place. The words you speak to yourself and to others are important. If you say 'I am going to change the world,' then you probably will. If you think yourself a failure, hopeless, ugly, lonely, short-tempered, broke, or depressed- then you will likely remain so."

"A woman should always have values, morals, and respect for themselves. Always set goals because life is like a journey and you should know where you are going. You have to set goals and go for them with determination. Have a positive attitude about what you want to do in this life."

A Word About Fidelity and Honesty

"Fidelity and honesty are Siamese twins in the marriage relationship. They are so tightly interwoven that the tentacles reach every segment. Because they are joined as one, they are not easily separated. It takes major surgery to accomplish such a feat, and the outcome might mean death to one or the other, or both. A Marriage rarely survives this broken trust. If it does, it is forever scarred, and it is never the same."

"The only way to keep fidelity in one's marriage is to seek God's wisdom then vow to be committed to your spouse. When you truly love your husband or wife with your whole soul and being, no one else can take his or her place, especially in a sexual way. For me, it was plainly inconceivable and dishonest on every front. To this day, I cannot visualize disrobing and giving my body to another man. What part of myself would I leave behind? Surely one would leave behind integrity and a broken spirit, and the trust in the marriage would lay shattered. God's word says NO!"

"For me, fidelity in my marriage has never been difficult. I have not had yearnings in my life that would cause me to look for someone outside to satisfy any needs I had. God promised to satisfy my needs, and He has been faithful to me. He gave me a husband who truly loves me and would give his life for me. I have looked at other men and commented that they were handsome, physically fit or otherwise. But never when making such comments or observations have I had a desire to break fidelity and honesty in my marriage. I am just a one-man woman. When you have the best you don't have to search out the rest."

By now, you may be inspired to keep reading about other manifestations of greatness in women. The outstanding roles that women play in the lives of others are a reflection of God's intentional design and work through them. Therefore, we can be confident, encouraged, and inspired that women have a Godly purpose in our lives. The following chapter identifies these great contributors to society as professional women, teachers, mentors, nurses, and others.

CHAPTER THREE

Other Manifestations of Greatness

The manifestation of greatness in women often can be seen in the multitude of roles they are called to perform or obliged to play out in the lives of others. These roles include mothers, sisters, grandmothers, friends, teachers, mentors and role models. Each of us has been blessed by women who fulfilled one or more of these crucial roles in our lives. In the context of the master plan for humanity, there is clear evidence that the Creator chooses how, when, where, or who is called to serve. Each person created is given certain gifts to exercise for the benefit of others. One can be confident that if called to serve, he or she is equipped by God to fulfill that chosen task. It takes faith to believe in a divine purpose and to have confidence to obey the calling. Those of us who have faith in God find the task easier by remembering that our lives here on earth are not about us. Our ultimate purpose is to glorify God! Even believers sometimes have difficulty with that statement; however, the biblical foundation for these truths is provided as follows:

> *"For we are His workmanship, created in Christ Jesus for good works, which God prepared beforehand, that we should walk in them."* Ephesians 2:10

> *"Now there are varieties of gifts, but the same Spirit…And there are varieties of effects, but the same God who works all things in all persons."* I Corinthians 12:4-6

Thus, when a woman seeks to know herself and embraces her God-given gifts, she is capable of doing great and marvelous work for humanity. Most people have witnessed the commitment, dedication, and tireless work of women across a spectrum of roles in their lives. I have chosen to highlight just a few of these from my life's experience. These include professional women, teachers and educators, pastors' wives, a living organ donor, and committed single women.

Professional Women

One of the greatest paradoxes of time is the preeminence of women despite a myriad of biases, hurdles, inequities, and stereotypical images they have faced and overcome. These barriers are entrenched in cultures, history, race, religion, and social structures. Other impediments can be insidious and less obvious, but they can affect both women and men. These include individual emotional make-ups and personalities shaped by early adverse experiences, perceived inadequacies, and/or low self-esteem. Yet throughout history, women have courageously faced such obstacles and forged paths that enabled them to reach the highest level of achievement in every professional discipline known to man. Today, women hold key leadership positions in aerospace and aviation, business, education, government, law, medicine, the military, politics, and in science and engineering. In addition, they are heads of state, entrepreneurs, celebrities, billionaires, activists, and philanthropists. Perhaps a woman's greatest attribute is that she can be engaged in many professional endeavors and still be a successful wife and mother.

A study of successful women confirms they share common God-given attributes and gifts that are innately a part of their make-up. Others have traits that are genetically predisposed or, in many cases, instilled by parents, caregivers, or others who have had their best interest at heart. Most successful women generally have deep-seated ambitions, intestinal fortitude, and the ability and determination to overcome adversity, whatever the cause. In the latter case, gender bias still continues to be one of the most prevalent barriers for women. This major hurdle is a *"glass ceiling,"* that unbreachable barrier that prevents women and minorities from attaining the upper rungs of corporate ladders despite their achievements or qualifications. Although women have fought to overcome the *"closed doors"* and *"glass ceilings,"* another insidious obstacle, the *"glass escalator"* emerged as a new hindrance to the progress of women. Now, women must contend with male peers who *glide* past them on an *invisible escalator* in female-dominated professions.

Another less talked about hurdle is the subtle, feminine resistance that some younger aspiring women encounter when interacting with older, more accomplished professional women. Conversely, some younger women resent advice or attempts at mentoring offered by those who have achieved a measure of success. The root causes for this troublesome impasse can be attributed to the negative emotions of covetousness, envy, fear, petty jealousy, or resentment. The occurrences quite often result in unnecessary "cat fights" that can be a disservice to all parties involved. The solution is sincere, effective communications that lead to helpful, positive relationships. Fathers and older men can and should be involved early in a young woman's development, but there is no substitute for substantive one-on-one female mentoring.

Despite the hurdles encountered, women will continue to prevail in their pursuits of professions for which they are well qualified. In the last fifty years, the world has seen the appreciation and recognition of women reach unprecedented heights. What an exciting time it is in history! As the father of six adult daughters, I say that is not enough; our society and the world must do more. As one who suffered many painful and unwarranted barriers in my life, I am thankful to have lived long enough to peek into the glorious future of women in America, as well as worldwide. As a grandfather and great grandfather of young women and girls, I couldn't be more proud. But until God's initial plan for women is fully recognized and accepted more readily, their progress will continue to be hampered by human limitations.

My opinion about the greatness of women is not novel. In recognition of the impact of women around the world, Forbes Magazine published a 2012 list of the most powerful 100 women in the world. From a preliminary group of over 200 candidates, the magazine selected its list from seven categories or power bases: billionaires, business, lifestyle (including entertainment and fashion), media, non-profits and non-government organizations, politics and technology. The overall ranking and each category was established by the three metrics of money, media, and impact. Candidates were also scored on their impact and reach across industries, cultures and countries, the number of spheres of influence, the people they affect, and how actively they wield that power.

The top ten in the Forbes list included Angela Merkel, the Chancellor of Germany; Condoleeza Rice and Hillary Rodham Clinton, former Secretaries of State of the United States; Dilma Rouseff, President of Brazil; Melinda Gates, Co-Chair of the Bill & Melinda Gates Foundation; Michelle Obama, First Lady, United States; and Cheryl Sandberg, COO, Facebook. Others receiving a top rating included Oprah Winfrey, Entrepreneur, Personality; Indra Nooyi, Chairman and CEO, Pesico; and Meg Whitman, CEO, Hewlett-Packard. Clearly, the impact that women are making around the world gives credence to my premise throughout this book.

The great attributes of well-known professional women are widely recognized throughout the world. Yet, there are countless outstanding professional heroines known to those with whom they interact daily down in the trenches where most of us reside. This is where the most significant and lasting impacts are made on individual lives. Many of us can identify with women in personal ways because of the investment of their energy, time, and resources toward our success and welfare. When I considered the attributes of greatness in professional women in *my* personal life, I thought about a few special women who fit such a mold. I looked beyond the outward appearances and considered the person behind the successes they enjoy today. The brief stories that follow highlight the down-to-earth attributes of women who have attained great success in their lives.

Heather Wilson

It is a distinct privilege to have known Heather Wilson up close and personal for over fifteen years. She possesses those rare attributes of being approachable and down to earth, compassionate, and having a genuine love for people regardless of race, creed, gender, or social status. Heather has an outstanding record of service to the people of New Mexico and our nation. She is a former member of the United States House of Representatives who represented New Mexico from 1998 to 2009. She was also the first female military veteran elected to a full term in Congress. Please allow me to share the following:

Heather Ann Wilson was born December 30, 1960 in Keene, New Hampshire. Her father, George Douglas Wilson, was a commercial pilot and member of the Experimental Aircraft Association; her mother, Martha Lou, was a nurse. In 1922, her paternal grandparents immigrated to America from Scotland where grandfather "Scotty" Wilson flew for the Royal Air Force in World War I. In the years that followed, her grandfather was a barnstormer, an airport operator, Civil Air Patrol Commander, and a courier pilot during World War II. Heather's father started flying when he was thirteen and enlisted in the United States Air Force after high school.

The doors of the Air Force Academy opened to women in 1976. Heather finished high school in 1978, and given the aviation influence in her life, she applied for and earned an appointment to the Academy. She established her marks early as the first woman to command cadet basic training, first woman Vice Wing Commander, and as a Distinguished Graduate (*magna cum laude*) in 1982. Heather had planned to go to flight school, but she earned a Rhodes scholarship to study at the University of Oxford in England. In 1985, she graduated from Jesus College, University of Oxford, with a Master of Philosophy degree and a Ph. D in International Relations.

Heather served in the Air Force for seven years as a negotiator and political adviser to the U.S. Air Force in England. She later served as defense planning officer in arms control negotiations for NATO in Belgium. In 1989, she was selected to be the director for European Defense Policy and Arms Control on the National Security Council.

In this very prestigious position, Heather interacted regularly with President George H. W. Bush's senior national security advisors and cabinet officials.

Heather left the Air Force in 1991 and pursued a professional career as the founder of Keystone International, Inc. in Albuquerque, New Mexico. In 1995, the newly elected Governor Johnson appointed Heather to be Cabinet Secretary for New Mexico's Children Youth & Families Department. Her formidable task was to reform child welfare laws, modernize the juvenile justice system, and improve early childhood education. It didn't take long for Heather's superior leadership and talents to emerge in a completely different environment. She soon directed her department to open a juvenile work camp and a secure facility for young, violent offenders. Next she eliminated the wait time for state-subsidized child care, revamped the foster care program, and made adoptions faster. She also spearheaded the governor's education agenda that allowed charter schools, annual testing, and more budget authority for local school boards.

I first met Heather when I was appointed as the state director for United We Stand America, the political arm of former presidential candidate Ross Perot. Over a period of eight years, I had frequent contact with her while I served on New Mexico Public Safety Advisory Commission and the Board of Regents, University of New Mexico. I was greatly impressed by Heather's incredible talents, servant's heart, and dedication to helping the less fortunate. By then she was married to lawyer Jay Hone and was the mother of two young children who often accompanied her on her travels. The latter was a clear indication that despite a very demanding job, Heather was still a caring and nurturing mother.

In 1998, the U.S. Congress, the Air Force reserves, and the state of New Mexico suffered the tragic loss of five-term Republican Congressman Steven Schiff to cancer. This unexpected tragedy opened another "providential" door for Heather, and she resigned her state cabinet post to enter the Republican special election primary. She won the Republican primary and was sworn into office on June 25, 1998, thus becoming the first woman Congresswoman since Georgia Lusk in 1946, another great woman. Heather also set a historic benchmark by becoming the first female military veteran elected to a full term in Congress and the first Republican woman ever to represent New Mexico.

Heather's prior military and government-related experience enabled her immediately to make significant contributions as a Congresswoman, not only for New Mexicans but also for Americans in general. Congresswoman Heather Wilson served in office from June 25, 1998 to January 3, 2009. Whether voting on global matters or more parochial issues, Heather had the personal courage to vote her conscious. Her integrity was non-negotiable. I especially appreciated Heather's voting record on issues related to the preservation of family, marriage, the sanctity of life, and welfare of the less fortunate in our nation. Those who knew her were confident that the welfare of her constituents and the American people filtered out any considerations for herself or special interests groups. Later in 2009, Heather ran unsuccessfully for the U. S. Senate seat vacated by retiring Senator Pete Domenici. She ran again for the Senate in 2012 to replace retiring Senator Jeff Bingaman. Once more Heather was unsuccessful, so she continued in the business world as head of the government contracting firm Heather Wilson & Company.

In April of 2013, Heather was selected to be President of the South Dakota School of Mines and Technology (SDSM&T). The South Dakota Board of Regents had the foresight and wisdom to select Heather as the nineteenth president, and first female president in the history of SDSM&T. I am confident that the people of South Dakota will be blessed by the talents of this great woman well into the 21st century. I am very happy to simply say, to God be the glory!

Stella

I met Stella in a professional setting and immediately was impressed by her accomplishment and her position as the local Vice President of a nationwide corporation. She is a very beautiful, considerate, generous, and kind person. Equally impressive was her down-to-earth attitude that made her very approachable. Stella has not allowed her great personal success to adversely affect her warm

personality. I have included Stella's short story because she has succeeded in life while facing squarely many of life's daily challenges. She
has not allowed any unfulfilled aspirations to dampen her continued
quest for a happy life. Stella is content and at peace with who she is.
I am delighted and honored to call her my dear friend.

Stella was the third of three children born of parents with a
mixed religious background. Her father was Episcopalian and had
recently been widowed. Her mother was a staunch Catholic who was
excommunicated from the church for marrying outside of the faith.
This led to not having a deep spiritual atmosphere in the home or close
relationships with church ministers. Stella and her older siblings grew
up on a small farm in Pennsylvania where everyone was expected to do
his or her fair share of chores. Being the youngest, she was sheltered by
her mother from doing a lot of manual work on the farm. Instead, she
was allowed to have horses that she learned to ride at the age of three
and enjoyed riding until her early teens. Her mother also introduced
her to books through which she developed an early love for adventure
and independence. Stella was considered a "good, well-behaved child"
and was usually taken along everywhere her parents went.

Early in life, Stella gained inspiration from her mom, books,
animals, and from the study of Latin. She was also influenced by a
rich aunt who loved and showered her with many interesting gifts.
Her aunt was a lively, uncharacteristically independent person who
left a lasting impression. Some of that personality would eventually
be reflected in Stella's independent character.

Stella's education through high school was relatively uneventful
for a small country girl. She excelled in school and served as class
president for two years. Her long-term ambition was to attend college
after high school. She was a high-energy person who was easily bored
with the routine, so she played tennis on the boys' team. Conversely,
her self-esteem suffered a bit because she couldn't dance or fit the
attractive, popular, blonde, "cheerleader" mold; however, she did
have friends of all races and social standings, including Christians
and Jews. Although Stella had a few dates with boys, her high school
proms were called "boring" experiences.

Upon graduation, Stella decided to attend the University of Virginia, thus becoming the first in her family to venture outside the state of Pennsylvania. Her mother wanted her to become a lawyer, but Stella completed college with a Bachelor's Degree in Western European International Affairs. After graduation she was unsure of what to do next, so in deference to her mother, Stella considered attending law school in California. Ultimately, she chose to pursue an advanced degree at the Thunderbird International Management School in Glendale, Arizona. At the age of twenty-two Stella moved away from family, friends, and familiar surroundings and moved to Arizona. Her decision reflected a growing desire to become an independent woman.

Stella completed graduate school with a Master's of Arts Degree in twelve months. By then she expected to receive a "sign" for the path that led to a successful career. She briefly left Arizona to interview for a job in New York. When the job did not materialize, she returned to Arizona. Eventually she was hired by a financial management firm and established the beginning of what would become a long-term, successful relationship. Her personal confidence and drive led to early successes and promotions in a very male-dominated field.

Earlier, while still in grad school, Stella met a handsome, inter-esting, and polite French professor who adored her. She had become quite proficient in French, and her first significant relationship with a man evolved. Although the professor was twenty-four years older, the two began a serious relationship that resulted in marriage two years later. Her husband had never been previously married and did not have any children. As a result, he was content to have Stella to himself and did not want children to interfere with their relationship. By the time her husband expressed a desire for children, Stella was too involved with work for such an interruption. She considered adopting a child, but her husband did not agree with that option. Thus, no children resulted from this marriage.

The first two years of Stella's marriage were considered fun. Both she and her husband were devoted to their jobs and were content with a somewhat benign relationship. He finished work by mid-afternoon yet relied on Stella to come home, prepare dinner, and attend whatever his needs were. Initially she did not mind being "superwoman" and performed her wifely duties out of what she thought was love. To the credit of her husband, they never argued or had any significant disagreements, but neither did they really "talk" to each other. Ultimately, Stella realized that her marriage had become nothing more than a relationship with a polite roommate, and it lacked the essentials to sustain a fulfilling, loving, and mutually satisfying relationship.

In 1988, Stella's father passed away, and this loss caused her to re-evaluate her marriage. About the same time, her husband's health began to fail, and she was obliged to become a caregiver to an increasingly demanding husband. This situation got progressively worse during the next two years, and it erupted into an irreparable break during a visitation by Stella's aunt and cousin. Over a dinner that went very badly, Stella's husband stated that she could get a divorce if she wanted to do so. That did it for Stella! In her words, *"When I'm done with someone, I am done with them!"* The marriage ended amicably thirty days later. Her husband retired from teaching and moved back to southern France.

The break-up of Stella's marriage caused her to spend the next several years discovering who she really was and deciding what her personal goals were. Fortunately she wasn't stuck in time and no longer felt obligated to live her life for someone else; however, she realized that some things in her life needed to be changed. Since college, Stella had been extremely driven to the point of being a "pushy" perfectionist. In the first ten years of her career, she rarely said "please" or "thank you." Winning was her driving motivation. She also harbored a certain amount of resentment from unresolved issues earlier in life.

Stella's introspection eventually resulted in her acceptance of herself as someone who had matured over time. Although still independent-minded, her priorities had changed, and she became more compassionate and empathetic towards other people. She also grew in kindness and patience. In addition, she became more judicious in her decisions and eventually was considered a very "genuine" person. Stella found it refreshing to find freedom within herself, and she enjoyed the peace and contentment in accepting who she had become. She was also free to choose companions with whom she could relate and be happy without a lot of emotional baggage.

Today, Stella is truly happy with her life. She gets pleasure out of pausing to "smell the roses." She also stops her car for a family of quails, and enjoys seeing a roadrunner, or the mountains turn red from a desert sunset. Success is now measured by good health and by what she is able to do to help others succeed. She is blessed to be financially secure and does not want or need more materialism. Her greatest ambition is to have a positive impact on young people in body, mind, and spirit. She is particularly interested in helping young women gain their self-esteem. Stella expects to continue in her chosen field for a few more years while considering establishing a charitable organization. Her advice to young professional women is this:

> *"It's nice to want more and better things, but it's greater to find it within yourself. When the days get tough, keep putting one foot before the other; be strong, keep trying! Reach out to friends, family, and spiritual counselors. Trust your gut; if something doesn't feel right, it's not. Have the courage to move away from evil. Don't stay in a bad or failing relationship trying to change or save another person. Enjoy each day and enjoy the ride!"*

Teachers and Educators

We live in a world today that greatly distorts the value of those who contribute to the advancement of society in every generation—teachers and educators. Our society entrusts the most critical task of childhood development—education—to teachers and administrators. Yet these exceptional servants of the human race are rarely appreciated or properly recognized for their tireless commitment, dedication, and sacrifice. Very sadly, we revere athletes, celebrities, movie stars, and countless others far more than we appreciate the unsung heroes and heroines in our schools at every level. Nevertheless, we demand and expect so much from them. As a veteran of twenty-six years in the Air Force, I see a parallel between teachers and those who serve in the military. Consider this: teaching is a *calling* that comes from a desire to serve the community, often in the toughest circumstances and environments. Teachers must be willing to "get down into the trenches and do battle" to win over the minds of their students. They must be courageous enough to risk personal danger or physical harm day in and day out, year after year. They also must be able to deal with abject disappointment and not succumb to despair. Finally, at the end of a career of twenty or thirty years, teachers cannot expect to retire wealthy or with handsome benefits. Thus the plight of a committed teacher is similar to a military careerist.

Today, many teachers are often overwhelmed by a staggering load of administrative duties, political constraints, overcrowded classrooms, and inadequate and/or outdated facilities. In addition, teachers often use their own funds for supplies and materials that amount to hundreds of dollars. These challenges are exacerbated by the attitudes and conditions with which many children show up at the school room, ostensibly to learn. Before the teacher can begin with the lessons of reading, writing, and arithmetic, he or she must first meet the child's immediate needs. These deficiencies often stem from the negative impacts of the child's home such as abuse, depression, hunger, physical anomalies, and overall learning disabilities. Add on the constraint of a six–hour day, one may get the picture of a typical day at the school. Is it any wonder why some teachers give up and flee to less stressful and more fulfilling careers?

Louise Privette—"Why I Am an Educator"

I have known Louise J. Privette for several years and know that she is a dedicated educator at Millennium High School in Goodyear, Arizona. Millennium is known for its academic excellence, rigorous curriculum, and International Baccalaureate program that prepares graduates for colleges and careers by empowering students to set and reach goals. Louise and other teachers and administrators provide extensive professional development programs based on high quality content, teaching, youth development, and advisement. Knowing of Louise's deep commitment to educating young people, I asked her to share in her own words what motivates her to remain in this field. The following is her brief story:

I was born and raised on the south side of Chicago and attended Horace Mann Elementary School. I recall sitting in the auditorium within clear view of a plaque dedicated to this great educator. The words inscribed on the plaque have haunted and inspired me to this day:

"Be ashamed to die until you have won some victory for humanity."

Although my parents did not earn college degrees, they were voracious readers, modeled a love for learning, and were my first teachers. If my father caught me leafing through a fashion magazine, he would ask why I wasn't reading something more worthwhile. Throughout my life, I have been blessed with a number of wonderful teachers who provided encouragement, served as positive role models, and worked tirelessly to meet their students' individual needs. They contributed to humanity by providing the world with the builders, engineers, homemakers, farmers, fire fighters, doctors, clergy, and yes—teachers!

My interest in psychology began in my early teens. At the age of fourteen, I began reading my brother's psychology texts and fell in love with the field. While kids my age watched Mary Poppins, I begged my mother to allow me to watch movies like *The Three Faces of Eve* and *The Snake Pit*. Although my mother is not a psychologist, she is one of the most intuitive people I have ever met. Watching these movies together and reading great literature led to in-depth discussions regarding the human condition. I believe that this early exposure to psychology influenced my beliefs about human health and agents of change.

I have held a variety of jobs, beginning in high school, while working my way through college. My jobs included working as a waitress, at a dry cleaner, in retail stores, and in a factory. These experiences gave me an early opportunity to work with a diverse group of people. The experiences also kept me humble and helped me gain a better understanding and empathy for people from all walks of life.

My father questioned my need to earn a college education, believing that I would probably marry before finishing with a degree. Although I felt hurt and angry at the time, it was probably the best thing he could have said to me. The gauntlet had been thrown down, and I was determined to prove him wrong. I graduated *summa cum laude*, in less than four years, with a Bachelor of Arts in Psychology from Arizona State University. I immediately entered a Master of Counseling program, also at Arizona State University. After earning my graduate degree, I took additional coursework in order to earn my national certification as a School Psychologist. Fortunately, my father lived long enough to witness these accomplishments, and was immensely proud of me.

Today, I am certified as a teacher, guidance counselor, and school psychologist. Although I chose school psychology over teaching, I do not subscribe to Shaw's belief that *"He who can, does; He who cannot, teaches."* I believe that teaching is a noble profession, and I recall with a mixture of gratitude and reverence the teachers who have made a difference in my life. I further believe that good teachers never believe they have arrived. Instead, they are always engaging in self-reflection, consulting with others, seeking ongoing training, and engaging in best practices so they can help their students reach their full potential. I believe in the value of life-long learning, so I have returned to school after many years. I am currently earning my doctorate in counseling psychology; and after completion, I hope to join the ranks of those who teach in higher education. Initially, I thought I might be too old to pursue this dream. Then I realized that I will never be any younger than I am today, and that the best way to achieve this dream was to begin. Remember the old Chinese proverb, *"A journey of 1,000 miles begins with the first step."*

In addition to the traditional duties of a school psychologist, I have had the pleasure of working with students in a variety of roles and settings. This has included sponsoring the National Honor Society and working alongside students to build homes for Habitat for Humanity. I have seen the joy on the faces of young children when we delivered a turkey with all the trimmings, stockings stuffed with toys and candy, and a Christmas tree to needy families. I have marveled at the brilliance and humility of academically gifted students that I coached in Scholastic Bowls and rejoiced with them when they took home their first-place trophy. My duties have included working on various crisis teams. I have also grieved with students while counseling them to deal with the losses of parents, family members, fellow students, and teachers. I have cheered for special needs students while watching them cross the finish line at Special Olympics and hugged them as I placed a medal around their necks. I cannot imagine any field other than education that would enable me to have such rich experiences, and I hope that I've had an influence on hundreds of children.

I have not been blessed with biological children, but I have experienced the thrill of a proud parent when my stepson received his diploma from Arizona State University. My husband and I were equally proud when the foreign exchange student we hosted received the highest achievement award in Trigonometry.

My heart dances whenever former students contact me to share their accomplishments. When special education students overcome insurmountable obstacles and graduate from college, a team of educators walk invisibly up the steps of that stage to receive their diplomas with them. Those who have chosen the field of education realize that we will never achieve monetary wealth, but we have untold treasures from the students who have enriched our lives. I may not ever achieve the fame of Horace Mann, but I hope that my life as an educator will enable me to win numerous small victories for humanity.

Mrs. Jones—School Teacher and Military Wife

I believe everyone should have a "Mrs. Jones" as a teacher somewhere in his or her life. I have known Shirley Tolbert Jones for over fifty years, and she is one of the most inspiring and motivating persons I know. In addition to being an exceptional classroom teacher, she is a devoted military wife, outstanding mother, and faithful friend. Shirley has positively influenced scores of lives all across America and overseas. She is a compassionate and giving person to countless people regardless of race, gender, religion, or station in life. "Mrs. Jones" is the most positive person you'll ever meet; however, I caution anyone who wishes to meet her: Whatever you do, do not enter her presence while "down in the mouth!" If your "pity party" exceeds fifteen seconds, you'll immediately get an attitude adjustment! Shirley has many attributes that exemplify greatness; however, one of her greatest is that of a teacher who reaches out well beyond the classroom.

Shirley was born in Mobile, Alabama. She was raised largely by a devout, Christian grandmother who planted the seeds of faith and the value of a moral conscience in her early years. By the time she was just four years old, a positive self-awareness was already established. Shirley accepted Christ into her life at the age of eight, and she has adhered to the moral values learned at home and church. That spiritual foundation served to define who she has been throughout her life, and it gave her self-confidence and a desire to live a pleasing life in the eyes of "Her Great Creator."

Shirley possessed a sharp young mind and finished high school at the age of sixteen. Barely seventeen, she enrolled at Tuskegee Institute (University) and began a study in science. Her effervescent, outgoing personality readily attracted many students who became life-long friends. Although younger than most, her peers sought her out for advice and guidance when needed. Shirley always exhibited an ever-present, infectious smile, but she also could cry with those who needed consoling or were grieving a personal loss.

The four years Shirley spent in college were a real growing experience that provided many wonderful memories. She learned to interrelate with others and also discovered a lot about herself. Whenever encountering a setback or stumbling block, she simply turned the occasion into an additional growth opportunity. During her sophomore year, she was one of three female students enrolled in an organic chemistry class. The foreign professor openly stated that *"women didn't belong in his class, but should be home having babies and washing bottles."* As horrific as that attitude and these words were, Shirley simply thought, *"Mister, you have underestimated my will and ability: no one decides where I belong!"* With fierce determination, Shirley set her eyes on the prize. She successfully completed one of the most difficult courses taught by a bigoted professor. Two years later, she graduated with a BS degree in biology and chemistry. She had grown from a child into a mature, self-assured young woman with a clear purpose for her future.

While still a senior at Tuskegee, Shirley felt prepared to explore several opportunities after graduation. Accordingly, she decided to join the Peace Corps and applied for an assignment overseas. She recognized that her success in life would be measured by doing things for other people, even if it took her to a far off land. Thus, she committed to using her college experience and knowledge to help the less fortunate in another part of the world.

As Shirley waited for her Peace Corps assignment, she accepted her first teaching position at a high school in Fredericksburg, Virginia. Although very different than her familiar surroundings, she was excited to launch her teaching career as a biology teacher. She soon became so energized by her impact on students that she enrolled in a master's program at Howard University. She didn't know it, but the Divine hand of God was just about ready to alter her plans!

Shortly after arriving in Virginia, Shirley went on a blind date, but didn't consider it to be a lasting event. Conversely, it took U. S. Marine Lieutenant Fred Jones just one evening to recognize the rare gem that would fit perfectly into his life. Fred, however, had a problem: he was soon scheduled to graduate from the Marine Corps Basic School at Quantico, Virginia. Shirley had accepted a Peace Corps assignment to Jamaica. They had become close friends in a very short time, but three weeks after their initial meeting, they said good-bye and headed off in different directions, so it seemed. A string of unsuspected events resulted in the two meeting again before going their separate ways. This last "chance" meeting proved to be providential preparation for the unforeseen changes to Shirley's well-thought-out plans.

The Peace Corps training was delayed for a year, so Shirley returned to Mobile and was hired to teach Physical Science and Chemistry at a junior college. This delay also provided the couple an opportunity to continue their friendship from a distance, and the relationship grew beyond what each expected. When they met the next time, God's plan for their lives took hold and their paths were redirected toward each other. Exactly one year after their initial meeting, Shirley and Fred were married! Instead of serving in the *Peace Corps*, her mission field would now be played out in the *Marine Corps!* Teaching and affecting lives in a positive way was Shirley's calling; now her classroom would become a world stage!

As a brand new bride and a husband deployed to Vietnam, Shirley faced immediate and new challenges. Always a student of learning, she adjusted to the tasks ahead. With a "can do" attitude and God on her side, she knew all things were possible. So she rolled up her sleeves and faced the new challenges head-on. She quickly learned how to cope with the uncertainties and succeeded in her new role as military wife and new mother of Fred's young son, Eugene, while still teaching school.

The mid-1960s were very difficult times for military men and women as major social changes were taking place all across America. While our men and women were fighting the war in Vietnam, many other citizens were fighting for equal rights at home. Despite these hostilities and uncertainties, Shirley's character, positive attitude, and deep faith enabled her to face life with determination and resolve. These attributes equipped her well while Fred served his country in Vietnam. Like thousands of other wives, she awaited Fred's safe return home.

During the 1960s and 1970s, our nation was still coping with racial bias and social change across every spectrum of our society. Vestiges of racism still persisted, particularly in the Deep South as well as overseas. When Fred Jones was assigned to various bases, his family often would be the only African American family in the assigned unit. Shirley did not allow racial bias to define who she was or to be a barrier for her happiness. She had learned many coping skills and survival tactics when faced with inhibiting racial prejudices. She and Fred approached each difficult circumstance with fortitude and togetherness.

The Jones family grew with a second son, Byron, and a daughter, Dedra. Later, Fred was assigned to a Marine base in Albany, Georgia. Upon arriving, Shirley inquired about a pre-school for her young daughter. She was told by an arrogant Marine officer that there wasn't one, and if she was interested in a pre-school program, perhaps she should start one. Shirley accepted the challenge. By now, she had considerable experience as a professional classroom teacher and administrator in several diverse settings. Within a very short time, she developed and initiated the opening of school programs for pre-school and kindergarten children. These educational programs served the children of the Marine Corps and the Albany community for twenty-five years!

Shirley's innate attributes, positive attitude, and great moral character continued to be a tremendous asset to Fred as he progressed through his career. By the time he reached grade of full colonel, they were stationed in Okinawa, Japan where Fred served as a Group Commander with the First Marine Air Wing. Shirley's leadership and management skills were called upon, and she was elected President the Marine Officer's Wives Club. Under her leadership, the group grew to over 500 wives. Many of these women were wives of officers who held a higher rank than Fred, but Shirley was the unanimous choice to lead the group.

Fred retired after thirty years of an illustrious career in the Marine Corps. Many of their peers and subordinates, who were counseled and mentored later, became senior officers and enlisted leaders in the Marine Corps. Countless students over Shirley's twenty-eight years as a teacher went on to become successful and contributing members of society at home and abroad. She was twice published in *"Who's Who Among America's Teachers."* Some of the most achieving students were eligible to recommend teachers who had the most impact upon them. Two of Shirley's successful college students bestowed this honor upon her while they attended college. In addition, Shirley's colleagues also nominated her for the *"Agnes Meyers Outstanding Teacher Award."*

When I interviewed Shirley, we reflected back over her life. When asked for parting thoughts for young people today, she had these words to say:

> *"Don't ever let another human being try to define who you are. Always know that you have been created for a purpose; everyone has been given a conscience to guide them. You are your own best friend, the one who stares back at you from the*

mirror; trust your God-given instincts. If you are in doubt about a path to choose or about what choice to make, seek a mentor or role model out for advice. There is always someone to help that will have your best interest at heart."

Shirley has a short and simple message for young men:

"Know or research what it means to be a real man! Take responsibility for your actions and behavior. First, learn to respect yourself. If a man does not respect himself, he is not likely to respect the women in his life. Seek to learn what God requires of men with respect to women."

After retirement, the Joneses settled in northern Virginia, but not before their three children became imminently successful adults. Their oldest son, Eugene, retired as Captain from the Navy after 29 years. Son Byron is a Department of Defense Dependent Schools teacher and has been residing in Okinawa, Japan for twenty years. He is the only non-Asian Sanshin Sensei teacher certified to teach Okinawan folk and classical music. Byron is currently studying for his Grand Master license. Dedra, the daughter, is employed by the United States Marine Corps and resides near her parents in Dumfries, Virginia. The Joneses continue to be active in their church and community. Both, Mr. and Mrs. Jones, still counsel, mentor and teach, not only men and women in nearby Quantico Marine base, but also any young person who crosses their path. Unquestionably, the world is a better place in which to live because "Mrs. Jones" is a great teacher for life.

The Pastor's Wife

To appreciate and understand the role of a pastor's wife, one must first appreciate the godly role of a *pastor*, or a *"shepherd of the flock."* In the final days of Jesus Christ, He charged his disciple, Peter, to care for and *"feed my sheep."* Present-day usage of the word is still rooted in the Bible, and it refers to the spiritual feeding of the congregation of a church. Given the changing culture, mores, and values of our society today, I don't know of a more difficult job than that of a pastor. He must be able to stay focused on his commitment to God and to tending the needs of those in his charge. The pastor is often called upon to deal with every human emotion during the cycle between life and death. The temptation to lose sight of his or her role is sometimes daunting; but staying steadfast in the word of God is the only protection against the fall. The biblical instruction for a pastor is that he or she must be:

> *"...above reproach, the husband [or wife] of one [spouse], temperate, self-controlled, respectable, hospitable, able to teach..."* I Timothy 3:2

As a combat fighter pilot in the Air Force for twenty-five years, I know what it means to stay focused on the mission at hand. Any letdown or distraction in the heat of battle can be fatal. Likewise, if a pastor loses focus, he or she is in immediate danger of falling into Satan's deadly trap. That said, I can truthfully say the role of a pastor is much tougher than any part of my career, including flying combat in Vietnam. Similarly, I believe the role of a pastor's wife is sometimes even tougher than that of the pastor himself. Biblical guidance is again provided for a pastor's wife in the following scriptures:

> *"A wife of noble character who can find?*
> *She is worth more than rubies,*
> *Her husband has full confidence in her*
> *And lacks nothing of value.*
> *She brings him good, not harm,*
> *All the days of her life."* Proverbs 31:10-12

Any pastor's wife has an awesome responsibility as a wife, mother, homemaker, and caretaker of the home, husband, and children. She also must be able to share his emotional, physical, and spiritual burdens on a daily basis. At the end of the day, the pastor's wife must be able to counter these overwhelming demands and carve out a bit of precious time for herself with the man she married. Whether or not one is a person of faith, you may agree that a pastor's wife or spouse is to be sincerely applauded. I have known scores of ministers and their wives over the past fifty years, both personally and professionally. The two stories that follow are about two pastors' wives that I have been privileged to know in the past ten years. Hopefully, you'll find them inspiring.

Violet Brown Bower

I met ninety-nine year old Violet Brown Bower three years ago when she moved in with her daughter and son-in-law, Patricia and Floyd Whittaker. She began attending Apollo Baptist Church in Glendale, Arizona. Amazingly, at 102 years old, she attends church every Sunday. Violet is alert, intelligent, and is an exemplary model of commitment and faith in God. She eagerly tells everyone she meets, *"God is so good and has never let me down."* Likewise, Violet readily expresses her great love for the Lord with *"all of her heart, all of her mind, and all of her soul."* She exudes a remarkable peace of mind and contentment and says, *"I'm ready for the Lord whenever He is ready to take me home."* This century-old mother was a preacher's wife and local missionary worker for nearly sixty years. I had the privilege of interviewing Violet and would like to share from her own words what it was like to be a pastor's wife for fifty-five of their sixty-three years of marriage. It is an amazing story of what God can do using what she says is "just an ordinary" person who loves the Lord.

Violet Vivian Brown was the fourth of ten children born to Ralph Hannibal Brown and Sarah Jane Snyder in Clarksburg, West Virginia. The Brown's home was warm and loving, and the older children helped with the younger ones since that was the way things were done in those days. Ralph was a Sunday school superintendent at the local church and took the older children to church every Sunday. Sarah mostly stayed at home to care for the younger children. The Brown children had the positive influence of their father until his death at age sixty-two. They were blessed to have their mother in their lives until her death at age 100!

The Brown family suffered a major tragedy when Violet's younger brother was struck and killed by a careless motorcyclist while walking in the neighborhood with her. Instead of becoming bitter, the family became even closer by caring for one another. While growing up, Violet had a natural love for children and dreamed of becoming a school teacher. This did not materialize because the family didn't have sufficient finances to meet the additional expenses for her to go to high school.

When Violet was sixteen years old, another tragedy struck the family. An older sister, Cora and her husband, Archie Jackson, had a four-year old son who became sick and died. The Jacksons lived in Akron, Ohio but returned the child's body to Clarksburg for burial. After the funeral, Cora begged Violet to move to Akron with them to help console her. After being persuaded by her mother, Violet reluctantly left home and went to live in Akron, Ohio.

Shortly after moving to Akron, Cora and Violet applied for work at the local tire factory. Cora was accepted and received a notice in the mail, but decided that she really didn't want the job. Since the country was in the Great Depression and jobs were hard to come by, the sisters decided that Violet should take Cora's place. This was before Social Security identification requirements, so at sixteen, Violet passed as seventeen and took the job. About a year later, Violet's parents moved to Akron and she moved back in with them to help support a family of seven. Violet worked for nearly seven years as "Cora Jackson!" Her conscience was assuaged somewhat since she used her earnings to support the Brown family.

By now, Violet had grown into a lovely, young redhead who stood slightly more than five feet tall. She and her friends were caught up in the age of the *Great Gatsby* and the *Charleston* dance craze. In fact, she met Harlan, her future husband, at a dance hall one night. Harlan was a curly-haired, handsome young man that Violet thought was an Italian. At the time they met she thought she didn't want anything to do with him. Nevertheless, the two began to date steadily, but she resisted Harlan's advances for about a year until she reached the age of twenty-one. Violet and Harlan were married on May 7, 1932. Violet still worked as Cora Jackson, but Harlan knew her real name. Later, a job change at the factory uncovered the ruse and she was fired on the spot!

The young couple was happily married, but neither of them was "saved," that is, neither had made a commitment to God by establishing a personal relationship with Jesus Christ. Violet's sister, Judy, and her husband, Todd, were concerned for Violet and Harlan. They encouraged them to attend the Ellet Brethren Church with them and her parents, Ralph and Sarah. Violet began to do so, but Harlan always found some excuse to avoid joining them. Each week, Violet asked Harlan to accompany her to church, but when he became upset about her decision, she stopped asking in order to abstain from brow beating him. During a revival in March, 1940, Violet made a personal profession of faith and was baptized at the Brethren Church, and church participation became a family affair. Harlan continued his refusal to attend church with Violet and often vowed to lock their doors if she insisted on going to church. Despite this rash threat, Violet persisted in church attendance, and the doors were never locked when she returned home.

What happened next is an amazing example of the how the Lord sometimes uses a faithful and committed wife to get the attention of a wayward husband. Violet's sister and brother-in law, the Browns, and the church members prayed each week for Violet's husband. Later, Harlan confessed that he was miserable because he considered his life worthless. Poor Harlan didn't have a chance against the power of prayer! Sometime later for some unfathomable reason, he bought Violet a Bible. In November that year, he shocked her by getting up and getting dressed. When she asked him where he was going, he said, *"To church with you!"* Later, Harlan said that he had been convicted several days earlier and knew that, like Violet, he needed to accept Jesus as his Lord and Savior. He did so that very morning. In December of 1940, at the age of thirty-four, Harlan was baptized! By then, Violet was twenty-nine, and they had a six year-old daughter named Patricia. There was great rejoicing for this event, but no one could have possibly imagined how God would work during the next fifty-five years in the lives of Violet and Harlan.

The Bower family remained at the Ellet Brethren Church and began to serve the Lord by teaching Sunday school. Harlan began to study his own Bible and sought to know what the Lord required of him. Later, they participated in starting a rescue mission in the slums of Akron. It was started in a vacant storeroom that was soon remodeled and named *"The Haven of Rest Rescue Mission."*

From 1947 to 1957, Harlan and Violet allowed the Lord to direct their steps in initiating or "planting" two new churches in Ohio and baptizing converts to Christianity. Harlan preached, taught, and baptized. Violet was just as busy teaching Sunday school, children's church, and caring for their family. Their daughter, Patricia, took piano lessons and played at most of the services. A second daughter, Sandra, was born in July of 1945. In 1955, Harlan officiated in the marriage of Patricia to a young Air Force man, Floyd Whittaker. Violet had been Floyd's Sunday school teacher at one of the churches started in Ohio by the Bowers.

During the seventeen years of service in Ohio, Harlan and Violet led scores of children and adults to the Lord. They rolled up their sleeves and got physically involved in building, pouring concrete, cleaning purchased facilities, and whatever else was required to meet the needs of their flock. Violet did whatever was needed to assist Harlan in pasturing. After leading souls to Christ, they baptized many in the baptistery of churches, or in small creeks, rivers, and suitable ponds. As a team, they were firmly committed and focused on carrying out Jesus' *Great Commission:*

> *"Therefore go and make disciples of all nations, baptizing them in the name of the Father and of the Son and of the Holy Spirit, and teaching them to obey everything I have commanded you. And surely I am with you even to the very end of the age."*
> Matthew 28:19-20

In June 1957, the Bowers finally took a vacation out west and stopped off for a few days in Phoenix, Arizona. Harlan and Violet sensed some prospects for a new church, so they decided to return later. In October 1957, Harlan resigned as pastor in Ohio; they sold their house, auctioned their furniture, departed for Phoenix, and arrived about a week later. After getting settled in their new home, Harlan and Violet were soon active in a church in the nearby community of Sunnyslope. Beginning as guest teachers, it wasn't long before the Bowers were asked to pastor a very small (five people), struggling church in Cave Creek. Following the suggestion of Violet, they used the children's church to build up the congregation. With Violet teaching the children, it wasn't long before the church needed to expand to accommodate the growing Sunday school classes and regular church services.

From 1957 until Harlan retired in 1972, their ministry of planting and growing churches continued. They participated in their second daughter's wedding in September 1964 when Sandra married Billy Adams. A significant moment of their ministry came in March 1971. Harlan had prepared one sermon, but changed his mind and decided to preach about baptism. About that time, the front door opened and a man and woman entered and sat down in the back row. The song leader told Harlan and Violet that the couple was Paul Harvey and his wife, Lynne "Angel", who owned a home in Cave Creek. This was *the* Paul Harvey, the conservative American radio broadcaster for the ABC Radio programs, the *Paul Harvey News* and *The Rest of the Story*. Harlan proceeded to preach his sermon on baptism and realized that the Holy Spirit had been involved that day. After the sermon and during the closing song, Paul and Lynne came forward to the altar. Harlan talked to them about their salvation, and Paul wanted to be baptized. He was baptized the next Wednesday in the Sunnyslope baptistery! In a 1972 Guidepost, Paul gave a wonderful testimony of his life, about being *"led"* to the country church, and ultimately about being baptized. He spoke about how joyful his life had been since he began to live for God.

Harlan and Violet finally retired from active ministry in 1972. They continued as members of Sunnyslope teaching Sunday school. They celebrated their fiftieth wedding anniversary May 7, 1982. It was a very happy and wonderful time as many old friends came that they had not seen for years. Their two daughters, their husbands, and many of the grandchildren sponsored or helped with the event.

Harlan passed away in 1995 after sixty-three years of marriage. When asked what it was like to be married to a pastor all those years, Violet readily said she had been blessed. She was very happy when Harlan was called to the ministry and felt it was her role to be supportive in every way. She never got tired of being a pastor's wife because there was always something to do in the church—teaching children, working in the nursery, giving aid to the needy, and praying for and consoling the downhearted.

Violet continued to serve until well into her nineties. She lived alone and took care of herself for sixteen years after her husband died. After a fall put her in the hospital for several days, Patricia and Floyd, her daughter and son-in-law, insisted that Violet move in with them. Today, she spends time crocheting booties for newborn babies. When I asked her what is the most challenging thing that she's ever faced, she said, *"Giving up my freedom of caring for myself."* When asked what she would tell young people today, she said:

> *"Get to know Jesus as your Lord and Savior. Know that God loves you. Love God with all your heart and with all your mind, and with all your strength; He will never let you down."*

Violet is a marvelous example of God's amazing greatness manifested in an ordinary person. Meeting and getting to know a woman over 100-years-old who speaks clearly and emphatically about serving God has been a special inspiration to me. I trust that everyone who reads about Violet Brown Bower will be motivated to really get to know what his or her purpose is in life. Her faith in God is simple, yet profound; and she is a great model to emulate. The Lord has honored her with a very long life that is reflected in the following Scripture:

> *"The length of our days is seventy years, or eighty if we have the strength; yet their span is but trouble and sorrow, for they quickly pass and we fly away. So teach us to number our days aright that we gain a heart of wisdom."* Psalm 90: 10, 12

Frances Porter

Frances Holt Porter is the wife of Pastor "Jim" Porter of Apollo Baptist Church in Glendale, Arizona where my wife and I have attended for ten years. She has been a pastor's wife for thirty-nine years and recently retired after seventeen years as a classroom teacher. Frances is the mother of two adult children, a daughter, Rachel, and a son, Michael. She is also grandmother of Rachel's two small children. She sings in the choir, teaches Sunday school, works in the nursery, and directs the children's choir for special programs. My wife, daughter, and I have had the privilege of being part of the "flock" of Apollo. Thus, we have appreciated and witnessed the outstanding teamwork of Frances and Pastor Porter as they have ministered to a plethora of needs of the congregation.

It is commonly said that *"Behind every good man is a good woman."* Another adage speaks of *knowing* the tree by the fruit it bears. I believe the same can be said about the work of a faithful, focused, and dedicated *godly* pastor. Pastor Jim Porter reflects that kind of commitment, dedication, and total support from his wife, Frances. Furthermore, she is a true partner in his ministry. She shares in the myriad of needs and competing priorities within the church— tending to the sick, injured, and dying; participating in funerals, and meeting the deep emotional needs of others. At the end of the day, it is Frances who meets the pastor's needs through the privacy of a solid relationship and a peaceful home. I'd like to share a little bit more about Frances.

Frances is the oldest of four children born to Don and Elsie Holt in Coushatta, Louisiana, a small rural town near Barksdale AFB. Her father served there in the United States Air Force, and this was one of many places where Frances lived while growing up. Her parents have been married for sixty-two years. This union has provided a solid example for Frances and her siblings. Her parents were the most influential people in her life. They were faithful in taking their children to church but did not proselytize them. Nevertheless, the children learned the valuable difference between "right and wrong" by observing how their parents lived in their home. They also stressed the importance of education and insisted that their children strive to do well in school. The Holts lived at several bases in the States, England and France. These positive exposures helped Frances develop self-assurance and self-sufficiency; however, the frequent leaving of friends was very difficult for her.

When Frances was in the eighth grade, the family settled in Tucson, Arizona for her dad's assignment at Davis-Monthan AFB. This stationary life was greatly appreciated as she was able to reach outside herself and make lasting friends. She finished high school in Tucson in 1970, and her stellar academic performance resulted in receiving scholarships to all of the universities in Arizona. By then, Frances wanted to leave home to flex her wings of independence, and the selection of a college was left up to her. She chose to enroll at Northern Arizona University (NAU) in Flagstaff. This location satisfied her desire for independence, yet it was still close enough to get home in a hurry if the need arose.

Initially, Frances was unsure of the course she wanted to pursue. She first considered mathematics because of its logic and "black and white" results. She later took an aptitude test, and the results indicated that she would make a good nun. A nun's habit was black and white, but since she's not Catholic, this option was thought to be a flawed conclusion and was not considered. Ultimately, she chose music education and teaching since her inherent gifts were in these areas. While at NAU, Frances continued the practice of attending church regularly and offering her services wherever needed. During this time, she finally made a deep personal commitment to her faith. In her words she said, *"All doubts were finally removed"* and she *"Accepted Jesus' salvation."*

With her educational goal and profession of faith issues settled, Frances, who loved romantic novels and stories, was unknowingly ready for the next great venture in her life. During her junior year, while washing dishes at a Baptist Student Union event, she met young Jim Porter from Boulder City, Nevada. Jim was also a junior and was pursuing a degree in chemistry and physics. Although Frances was very involved in church activities, Jim was generally a "Sunday only" worshiper. Nevertheless, a serious relationship soon blossomed, and the two became engaged in 1973. They set a marriage date to follow their graduation in 1974.

In the interim, Jim became a committed Christian and decided that he was "being called into the ministry." Since they both were committed to the Lord and to each other, Jim's decision did not alter their plans. Frances considered this to be God's work and did not flinch at the thought of being a minister's wife. When the two separated for the summer break in 1973, Frances felt an old independent streak surface. She did not suffer from the time apart from Jim, and given her romantic expectations, she wondered why there was no "wow" factor for the pending marriage.

As the plans and wedding date approached, Frances's concern grew into serious doubt several days before the wedding. She wondered if this was really what the Lord wanted her to do. Jim, however, was certain that Frances was meant to be his wife. To the great credit of both these young people at the time, they had the courage and good sense to pray together about this dilemma. They both have said that God gave them certainty and peace about their decision, and the wedding went as planned. Today, thirty-nine years later, the validity of their decision still stands!

After graduation and the wedding, Jim and Frances departed for Fort Worth, Texas where Jim enrolled in the Southwestern Baptist Theological Seminary. For the next four years they experienced all the "joys" typical of couples in a seminary environment—a sparse apartment, long hours of studying, many meals of hot dogs, pork & beans, and macaroni & cheese, and learning to live within one's means. Nevertheless, the young couple enjoyed being newlyweds and really getting to know one another. This was also a time of affirmation. They both knew that they were meant for each other and felt that God's hand had been intentionally involved. Although Frances suffered a miscarriage during this period, she and Jim did not waver in their faith and trust in the Lord. Jim graduated in 1978 and the Porters returned to Arizona.

Jim began his pastoral mission in Bethel Baptist Church in Mesa. At the outset, he established the foundation for Frances to be an effective pastor's wife. He insisted that she be allowed the freedom to be herself and serve in the ministry of the church as she felt led to do. Thus, they got off to a great start, and Frances served along with Jim while relying totally upon God to direct her path.

After six years of marriage, their daughter, Rachel, was born in 1981 and brought tremendous joy into their lives. In 1982, the Porters were called to pastor Apollo Baptist Church in Glendale. Frances continued to serve faithfully as Jim's wife and as an active member of the church. Their son, Michael, was born in 1984 and added to their joy as a complete family. As Jim's ministry prospered and the Porter children grew, Frances felt led to reestablish her career as a classroom teacher. Again, she followed her spiritual leaning to do what she was gifted to do rather than what someone thought she should do. Teachers, like other professionals have to acquire the initial qualifications to teach in classrooms and continue their professional development. In addition to being a wife and mother of two children, Frances's decision resulted in fifteen years of service in Christian schools.

During the past thirty-one years at Apollo Baptist Church, Frances has been a tremendous pastor's wife, a great mother, a tireless church worker in numerous capacities, and now a doting, loving grandmother. As in all lasting marriages, the Porters have gone through all the emotions, rough spots, and pitfalls, but Frances has never doubted her decision to marry Jim. Clearly, she feels that God has mightily blessed her. Despite her imperfections, she believes He consistently placed a hedge of protection around her throughout her life. Regardless of the demands, she had complete confidence in God and just accepted the challenges as coming from Him. She never felt short-changed by being a pastor's wife or having to share him so much with others. In fact, Frances considers her Jim to be her best friend and *her pastor!*

When asked about fulfillments in life, Frances cites the positive contributions she has made in the lives of countless children in the church and in schools. Today, she is content with the life the Lord has allowed her to live. She works to grow even closer to Him and continues to look to Him for guidance in all she does. With Frances at Jim's side, Apollo is in great hands and my family prays often for continued blessings throughout their lives.

Hopefully, you have been encouraged by the foregoing short stories about Violet Brown Bower and Frances Porter. As a husband, I am so grateful for God's provision of just the right woman in our lives. This is especially true because He works through the earthly *imperfections* of both the man and woman to create the *perfect* union. The imperative is that such a union is only possible when God is at the center of the relationship. While I know my life has been totally blessed by my wife, I believe God gave the pastors' wives a special measure of grace.

Military Wives

Although countless stories have been written about the commitments, dedication, and sacrifices of military men and women, nothing can compare to the military wife or spouse. These are the true patriots who keep the home fires burning and the lamps lit in widows when their loved ones go off to war or on many temporary assignments during a service career. Military wives and families are called upon to meet a myriad of challenges head-on with courage and fortitude during the absence of husbands and fathers. In recent times, the military service member is a wife and mother to those left behind. Regardless, the military spouse is the one left to care for the children or take an injured child to a hospital emergency room. At other times, they must attend the meetings at school or the children's recitals, get the car or the plumbing fixed, or sometimes handle the entire household move! These Herculean demands and expectations often leave military wives in tears, and more than a few give up and call it quits. Only through faith, prayers, and by the grace of God, marriage and families survive. I am thankful to say that I am one of the fortunate ones.

Lucimarian Tolliver Roberts

Like so many other great women in this book, I found it very difficult to adequately characterize the late Lucimarian Tolliver Roberts in just a few paragraphs. Even her own published book, *My Story, My Song—Mother-Daughter Reflections on Life and Faith*, left readers avidly wanting to hear more about her. When I think of her as wife, mother, grandmother, and dear friend, my heart is filled with many precious memories that date back over fifty years. She was an extraordinary military wife and an exemplary model for wives of any personal or professional endeavor. Her loss is still grieved by those who knew and loved her, but we are deeply grateful that God allowed such a *Great Creation* to dwell amongst us.

Lucimarian and I are not related, but we shared the same last name with different spellings. She was born in Akron, Ohio during the Great Depression on an unpaved street with an outside privy. Despite the hardships of poor black families during those days, Lucimarian was the first of her family to graduate from college. While attending Howard University in the early 1940s, she met and married Lawrence E. Roberts who later became one of the famed Tuskegee Airmen.

Lawrence was inducted into the U. S. Army in 1943 and later earned his pilot's wings at Tuskegee, Alabama. He was commissioned a Second Lieutenant and went on to serve at bases in the United States, post-war Japan, and during the Korean War. Despite Lawrence's outstanding credentials and performance records, there were no flying jobs open to black pilots where the young Roberts family was assigned when he returned to the states. At another base, the Roberts encountered blatant bigotry from the squadron commander. Often the commander held social gatherings in his home for foreign students while excluding the Roberts because of their color. Such racism was even more asinine given the fair-skinned, beautiful good looks of both Lawrence and Lucimarian. Nevertheless, the Roberts took the high road and refused to allow bitterness and resentment to overshadow their lives. At times like these, Lucimarian's deep faith and love for playing the piano, enabled Lawrence and the family to forge ahead. As difficult as these encounters were, she shielded the ugliness from her children and enabled them to grow up without any lingering emotional scars.

In 1959, the Roberts brought their exemplary character to Tuskegee Institute where I and many other aspiring officers became immediate beneficiaries. The Roberts arrived with three children, Lawrence E. II, Dorothy, and Sally Ann. Robin, their fourth child, was born at John A. Andrew Hospital during the Roberts's assignment at Tuskegee. Many years later, the world would hear about the Roberts family. Then a captain, Lawrence joined other original Tuskegee Airmen as the ROTC Commandant of Cadets. I am thankful for the mentoring and teaching that we received from those Tuskegee Airmen, such as Lawrence Roberts while he served at Tuskegee. The tutelage under these legendary patriots was one of the greatest experiences of my life. Their mentoring, counseling, and teaching helped me throughout my professional career.

I was also particularly impressed by Lawrence's wife and family. Lucimarian was a beautiful wife with well-mannered children. Their open display of a healthy, loving relationship was very real and encouraging. She was an obvious asset in furthering the career of her husband. Despite these attributes, Lucimarian had suffered racial discrimination, insults, slights, and often exclusion from the social functions of the units or bases where they were assigned. Yet, her commitment to Lawrence and to nurturing their children was evident by the success of their family. Having come from a broken home, I particularly admired the Roberts family and purposed in my heart to have one like them one day!

The Roberts left Tuskegee in 1961, and I graduated and was commissioned into the Air Force in February 1963. The Roberts and Tolivers were reconnected thirty-five years later. In August 1998, I read about Robin Roberts in the Parade Magazine and discovered that this beautiful, young television personality was none other than the "baby" of Lawrence and Lucimarian! What a pleasure it was to locate and speak to Lawrence after so many years and to share in the joy of the success of his child. My wife, Peggy, and I made plans to visit the Roberts's during homecoming at Tuskegee in November 2004;

but very tragically, Lawrence died suddenly on October 12. Despite grieving the loss of her husband, Lucimarian graciously continued a renewed relationship with me and provided the information I sought for my book.

I kept in touch with Lucimarian and stayed informed about the welfare of her family for the next several years. When Robin suffered a bout with breast cancer in 2007, Lucimarian and I frequently chatted, and my family prayed fervently for Robin's recovery. Lucimarian had a very special gift of caring for others besides her immediate family. While she was in New York with Robin, she took the time one day to call me during the completion of my book, *An Uncaged Eagle.* It was a cold and dreary day, but Lucimarian's phone call, encouragement, love, and timing were priceless. It was a blessing from heaven that lit up my life!

In April 2012, Robin and Lucimarian launched their co-authored book, *My Story, My Song.* Peggy and I were privileged to be invited to Biloxi, Mississippi for the private book signing the day before the public presentation in nearby Gulfport. For the first time since leaving Tuskegee, we met face-to-face with Lucimarian and her three beautiful daughters, Sally Ann, Dorothy, and Robin. At eighty-seven, Lucimarian was a resounding hit and blessed everyone with her charm, grace, and love. Seeing the incredible greatness of mother and daughters together in such a setting was a blessing I'll never forget. It would be the last time the world would see them as they were that weekend. Lucimarian suffered a stroke in July and died peacefully in her Pass Christian home August 30, 2012.

As a man of faith, I am confident that Lucimarian was highly favored by God. No doubt her candid expressions of faith have reached millions, believers and unbelievers alike. As a faithful military wife and loving mother and grandmother, no one could have done it any better than Lucimarian. Perhaps the greatest testimony of her greatness is reflected in her family. Lawrence retired from the Air Force as a full colonel after thirty-two years of service and was buried with full military honors. Sally Ann co-anchors the highest rated local morning news program in New Orleans, Louisiana. Dorothy is the Director of South Mississippi Regional Center, Mississippi Department of Mental Health. Robin is co-anchor host on the renowned television show, *Good Morning America.* Lawrence II is a successful businessman in Houston, Texas.

Lucimarian dedicated much of her adult life to church and community affairs by serving on numerous boards and commissions. Her many awards, honors, and recognition include the 2011 NAACP Medgar Evers Lifetime Achievement Award, the 2011 Mississippi Medal of Service, United Way of South Mississippi, and an American Association of University Women Honoree. I pray that Lucimarian will rest in peace until the "last trumpet" sounds calling all of God's children to a just reward.

Beverly Kavouras

Until February 2013 I had never heard of Bev and Larry Kavouras who live on a farm in Kansas. Frequently military veterans discover a letter or story that touches the hearts of those who have served our nation. Such was the case with a "farewell letter" written from the heart of Bev Kavouras, more than twenty-three years ago. After reading Bev's letter, I knew immediately that I wanted to include it in the section of this book about *Military Wives.*

Bev Kavouras is the wife of a twenty-year career Air Force fighter pilot. She has been married to retired Lieutenant Colonel Larry Kavouras since 1970, and they have raised two fine sons. She juggled officer wife duties, raised the children, paid the bills, minded the household, and made sure the home fires kept burning. Larry flew F-4 and F-16 fighter jets his entire Air Force career. He then flew for American Airlines for many years and is now retired. The Kavouras' eldest son, Nick, also flew the F-15 and the F-22 fighter jet during his Air Force career. Their youngest son, Todd, flew the B-52 bomber in the Air Force and is currently the operations officer for the Kansas Air National Guard bombing range.

After staying home with her children for nearly twenty years, Bev entered the working world. She didn't finished college due to the numerous moves in the military and her many family obligations and other commitments. Nevertheless, she has had a varied, rewarding career in many different areas, including the printing industry as a typesetter and graphic designer. Bev also has been a Human Resources Training and Development Manager at Kansas University School of Medicine in Wichita, Kansas. In addition, she has been a USDA Farm Services Technician in McPherson, Kansas, and is currently the Operations Manager for a Financial Services firm in McPherson.

Bev has always loved to write, garden and cook, and she continues to pursue these hobbies in her spare time. In addition to her two sons, she now has two daughters-in-law, three grandsons, three grand dogs, and many friends and family—old and new. Bev and Larry have returned to their roots and live on a farm in Kansas; and they enjoy keeping in touch with family and friends.

Bev's letter is beautifully written straight from the heart of a military wife. She truly understands what it means to love her family and country and be willing to give all she has to give. Her letter captures the compassion, courage, dedication, and fortitude of military wives, regardless of the branch of services. I believe it honors every woman who has stood by her man unflinchingly in the most perilous times. Bev graciously gave me permission to share her letter with you. I consider it a privilege to do so.

March 30, 1990

"Dear Mr. F-4 Phantom,

Your days are numbered. In a few short days you will be leaving the Kansas Air National Guard forever to go to the bone yard in Tucson, Arizona—the plane cemetery. I know it's sad for you, but it's sad for me too. Just thinking about this good-bye has made me think back and reflect on all the years we've had together.

In the fifteen years that we've shared my husband, I've spent many hours waiting on you to bring him home from some faraway place. I've watched proudly as you and he did a flyby at an air show, river fest, or parade; and I've cursed your loud engines as my babies cried from your noise.

You took our family to live in many far away places that we may have never seen if not for you. We lived in Florida, Arizona, North Carolina, West Germany and Kansas. You took my husband to many more than that—England, Spain, Turkey, Italy, Norway, Hawaii, Thailand, Alaska, Korea, Philippines, and nearly every state in the union, to name a few.

I first became acquainted with you in 1972 and it was love at first sight. My husband was learning to fly you so he could hurry over to help fight the war in Southeast Asia. What a job you did there! You were on the news nearly every night and a familiar sight in most Americans' living rooms. You were a very welcome sight to many marines and army ground personnel there who were fighting the mud, heat, the enemy, exhaustion, homesickness, and fear. They would shout for joy when they saw you coming to their rescue—their black, mud-streaked faces turning to all white teeth and smiles. I would have hated to see you dive towards me when you were mad. Your smoking, loud engines made you look so mean, and you could be when you wanted to. Your noise and size were greater than any other modern fighter. Sometimes you didn't make it back, but it was rarely your fault. The bullets just came too fast or someone didn't turn you quickly enough. You protected my husband well, and my children and I thank you for that.

After the war, there were many temporary duty assignments away from home where the two of you would go off together. You and my husband would go away to fly in dogfights with the newer planes, (F-5's, F-15's and F-16's) and he'd still win, with you strapped to his seat. You may not have been able to turn as tight or as fast, but the two of you were old friends and worked as a well-oiled cog, a part of the team. They had the new paint jobs—you didn't. They had the fancy radar—you didn't. They had the better maneuvering capability—you didn't. But you and he still won!

We had many happy reunions where we moms, wives, babies, and kids greeted you, Mr. F-4, our husbands and fathers on the ramp. We were all tears, goose bumps, and smiles to see you home safely again. I will never forget the 36-ship take-off of F-4s we had here at McConnell AFB, Kansas for a change of command. The town's people thought there was a war! One by one, you taxied out to take off in sets of two ships at a time. By the time you were all airborne, which seemed an eternity, the sky was black with smoke. F-4s filled the air and I don't think there was a dry eye or an unmoved person to be found in this city.

You know, sometimes I even felt jealous of you or mad at you. Even after a six week T.D.Y. of nothing but flying you, talking about you in the Officers' Club after flying you, being with others who flew you and getting up in the morning to do it all over again, my husband would come home and still talk about you, with his hands in the air describing in every detail what you'd done together. Never mind the beautiful candlelight dinner, how much the kids had changed, or the ever-faithful dog lapping at his heels...he still had you on his mind.

I felt at times that if it weren't for you, I wouldn't have spent a year alone raising a child or fixing broken water pipes alone or getting kids over the chicken pox alone. At times, I think you even knew him better than I did and possibly were the only one who could understand him. There's a mystique and a mythical quality that you and the men who fly you share that cannot be understood by most other people. I also think he was the happiest after he'd been with you. But I didn't mind so much. That is a given. That is the way life is when you are married to one who flies you. You were something to be proud of. You had it all. Besides, we wives probably got back at you a bit when we made you look a little silly taxiing Santa Claus in from the North Pole for all the kids. You were no war machine on those days; you were the sleigh that brought squeals of delight to young and old alike.

Just think, Mr. F-4, of all the places in the world and all the events that you've been to or seen. From our aircraft carriers to the walls of our living rooms (or our "I Love Me" walls)—you are, or were there. On our children's t-shirts, clothes, hats, posters—down Main Street of my own hometown—you are, or were there. You were the best of the best, a Thunderbird, and the best they'll ever have. You've been the main attraction, the tear in my eyes, the goose bumps on my skin, and the vibration in my chest. You have touched my very soul at funerals, memorials, 4th of July celebrations, River Fests, air shows, and parades. And yes, you've also portrayed the missing man—the comrades who never came home. I am so proud of you, my husband, and all the wonderful hard-working folks who kept you so well-maintained that you could fly this long. I am also proud of all the men who gave their lives and yours so we could live free. I am also proud of my country, of being an American, and of the freedom that you have helped to maintain.

But now, it is time to say good-bye. There will be those who will say, "Out with the old, in with the new—progress moves forever onward," and they'll act like they don't care. But you and I know better. There is no man alive who really knew you who could not miss your uniqueness, your size, your style, your noise, or something about you. You were a class act!

So the celebration is planned. Fighter pilots, back-seaters (weapon systems operators,) their ladies, and many others will be here from all around the globe to bid you farewell. There will be songs sung, stories traded (a few stretched), reminiscing, and hands in the air demonstrating the dogfights they won. Wives will again be left out of the conversation because of you, but you know… we really won't mind. There have been fighters before you and newer fighters since, but none that can compare with you. You are one of those rare legends who stands alone—in a class all your own.

Yes, you are old and tired and are going to the bone-yard. You deserve the rest. But don't feel sad, Mr. F-4 Phantom. A lot of people the world over will be there with you in mind, heart and spirit. You will continue to fly in the hearts, souls and minds of men and women for a long time to come. I also want you to know you are breaking the hearts of new and young dreaming-to-be fighter pilots, like my sons who will never get to fly you. You will have the good fortune, however, of living on in the history books forever.

So I say good-bye, faithful old friend. I thank you for a job well done, a country well served, and I thank you for keeping my husband safe and happy for all these years. I'll miss you!

Sincerely,

Beverly R. Kavouras
Wife of Lieutenant Colonel Larry B. Kavouras

A Living Organ Donor

Mahalia—A Giver of Life

Another noteworthy manifestation of greatness in a woman is exemplified by a woman I shall call Mahalia. She gave the gift of life to a total stranger by donating one of her healthy kidneys to a critically ill young mother 2300 miles away! When I heard this story, I could see God once again working through a woman in a magnificent way. Today, a mother is alive with her children because Mahalia said "yes" to an apparent divine calling from God. The recipient of this incredible gift is the caretaker of an aging mother, and her father is a veteran of the Korean and Vietnam wars. The following are a few words about this great "giver of life."

Mahalia was born in 1962 to an African American Father and a mother from Mexico who already had three children. She was the eldest of two additional sisters born after her father moved their mother from Mexico to America. Her mother held onto her native culture and was willingly subservient to her husband in many ways. Mahalia, however, remembers being greatly influenced by her father who was a very kind-natured and caring man who spent a lot of time with her. As a result, she loved her father a great deal and remembers him as a hard worker and great provider who always smiled and had time for his three daughters.

As a bi-racial child in the early 1960s, Mahalia experienced racial prejudice at a very early age while attending grade school. One particular teacher made it a point to speak of Mahalia's mother as that "n---- lover." On another occasion, she accompanied a friend home one afternoon for an afterschool event. Caught off guard, the mother of the child could not hide her displeasure with her daughter's choice of a friend. Mahalia was embarrassed and left disappointed and hurt.

At other times, her mother and siblings were followed around whenever they shopped in department stores. Her life was further compounded when her parents got divorced while she was still in grade school. Through all of this, Mahalia, learned to shrug off these experiences and did not let them impede her ambition to learn English well and overcome the racial barriers that she encountered.

Mahalia was confronted with additional pitfalls caused by some of her family members who were involved in drugs and alcohol. Despite being ashamed and concerned, she remained close to her family and did everything possible to help them. Seeing the detrimental effects of drugs and alcohol, Mahalia decided not to be a victim and eventually overcame these impediments to become a self-confident young person. After completing high school, she attended junior college and attained an associate degree as a surgical technician. She worked in this field until reaching the age of twenty-four, at which time her life took on another dimension.

Mahalia met and fell in love with a young Navy man who was stationed in San Diego, California. His mild-manner and easy-going personality reminded Mahalia of her father. After dating for about two years, the two got married when she was twenty-six years old. Shortly thereafter, she moved to Norfolk, Virginia with her husband for his next assignment. About a year later, she gave birth to her only child, a daughter. While living in Virginia, she attended school to become a real estate agent and began a successful career in that career field.

Once again, Mahalia was faced with a loved one who was an alcoholic. Her husband often spent the weekends with his "Navy buddies" in their home consuming alcohol until they passed out. Fearing the adverse impact on her young daughter, Mahalia felt compelled to end the marriage and they were divorced after ten years of marriage. Despite the failed marriage, she considers her daughter to be her greatest achievement in life. For the next several years, she continued in real estate and was able to send her daughter off to college. During this time, she entered another serious relationship, but it eventually ended because of the man's abusive and controlling behavior. By then, she chose to live her life without any significant relationships with men.

In 2009, a major milestone occurred in Mahalia's life when she was forty-eight years old. She was watching Matt Lauer on NBC's *The Today Show* talk about live organ donors. Remembering her mother's death due to liver failure, she became very interested in the program. After a subsequent Internet search, she realized that her mother may have survived by receiving a transplant from a live donor. Her continued research resulted in finding *Matching Donors,* a non-profit organization created to give people needing transplant surgery an active way to search for a live organ donor. The most common organs transplanted from a live donor are single kidney and liver lobes. Mahalia was deeply moved by the possibility to help someone else, so she volunteered to become a live donor. One week later, she was contacted by a recipient in Arizona who desperately needed a new kidney. By fate, the pending recipient happened to be a young Hispanic single mother of two small children and two ailing parents.

While still residing in Virginia, Mahalia began the requisite testing and matching evaluation procedures. Several months later when the match was confirmed, she was flown to Arizona to begin the week-long testing and final preparation for surgery. Only her family and close friends knew what she was about to do, and all were in agreement with her selfless act of saving another's life. Thus, in 2010, Mahalia discovered her life-long purpose of being one of *God's Great Creations!*

Now at the age of fifty-one, Mahalia is a proud mother and grandmother. Through the adversity in her life, she has come to realize that her greatest gift is an unconditional and loving heart for others. Above all, she still wants to help others in any way possible, and she is very content and happy to continue in real estate. I believe Mahalia is a very special person in the eyes of God because He continues to bless her and protects her from harm.

A Great Memorial

> *"For the Lord Himself will descend from heaven with a loud shout, with the voice of the archangel, and with the trumpet of God, and the dead in Christ shall rise first...thus we shall always be with the Lord."* 1 Thessalonians 4: 16-17

As stated earlier, for most of us, death is the most difficult event that we will encounter on this side of eternity. It never seems to come at an appropriate or convenient time. When it comes unexpectedly, it hurts and leaves a multitude of raw emotions or lingering grief. All people, regardless of their faith, religion, or beliefs, struggle with the last common denominator of humanity—the end of life on this earth. I have found that only a deep faith in God assuages the sting of death and gives one hope that those we love are never lost completely. Love allows their spirits to remain with us—in our hearts, minds, and thoughts. Perhaps that is what the songwriter had in mind when he wrote the words to *"Precious Memories"* so many years ago. I have chosen to share with you the memories of a young woman I had the privilege of knowing and can attest to the greatness during her short life. She had even a greater impact after her death. Death was not victorious because those who loved her were left with many precious memories.

Dyan Jojola

Early on the morning of August 20, 2005, Dyan awakened with her characteristic bundle of energy and prepared to travel from the Isleta Reservation near Albuquerque, New Mexico to Sante Fe. There she would meet her younger brother, Tony, who would be displaying his latest blown glass wares in the city square at the Indian Market. After several failed attempts to get someone to travel with her, Dyan decided to rent a small car and travel the sixty miles alone. It seemed that everyone had something else to do. Inexplicably, even her life partner, Jemerson, decided to stay at home that fateful Saturday morning.

Dyan was very close to each of her six other siblings, but Tony, the artist, was something special. She planned to use her effervescent personality to assist him in marketing his goods. They spent the day together, and to Dyan's delight, Tony bought his little "big" sister a beautiful pair of earrings. Satisfied with the outcome of the day, Dyan departed for home around 9:00 p.m.

A short time later while entering the freeway, Dyan apparently lost control of her vehicle and was ejected when it rolled over several times. The emergency response team found her alive, but she died a short time later at a local hospital. Just three days after her fiftieth birthday, Dyan's life had tragically ended. Seven years later, as a professional associate and family friend, I am still grieved by this untimely loss of a very special and beautiful creation of God. Just who was she?

Dyan was a child of the rich Native American culture of the Isleta Pueblo, one of nineteen tribes that are established in New Mexico. The reservation is situated east along the mighty Rio Grande River that flows from southwestern Colorado in the United States to the Gulf of Mexico. Further to the east of Isleta, the beautiful Manzano Mountains frame a picturesque backdrop with its twin peaks, Mosca and Guadalupe. Dyan truly loved this place where she was born and raised, and the people of Isleta still hold these mountains, rivers, and land sacred.

Dyan was the fourth of seven children born to Bernardino "Bernie" and Mary Jane Olguin Jojola. Both grew up on the Isleta reservation. During World War II, Bernie went to the west coast to work in the shipyards while Mary Jane attended St. Catherine

Catholic Indian Boarding School in Sante Fe. After the war, Bernie like many Native American veterans, returned to his respective reservation. By then, Mary Jane had grown into a beautiful young woman, and she immediately caught Bernie's eye. Despite the strict cultural protocol and the watchful eye of the nuns, Mary Jane and Bernie managed to see each other occasionally and were allowed to attend the movies together. Mary Jane graduated from high school in 1947 and attended a local business college. Upon graduation, she was hired as a file clerk by the University of California; later, Sandia Laboratories in Albuquerque. Bernie continued to pursue Mary Jane and finally earned the trust and respect of her parents. They were married July 1948 with a huge traditional Indian wedding celebration on Isleta Pueblo.

The newlyweds moved into the partially completed home, but they were determined to finish it as soon as possible. In May of 1949, their first child, Raymond, was born. In the next seventeen years, Bernie and Mary Jane were blessed with six additional beautiful children: twins Bernadette and Linda in July 1952; Dyan, August 1955; Tony, August 1958; Mary Jane, February 1964; and Martin, November 1966. Bernie and Mary Jane were strong in the Catholic Church; and they instilled this faith in their children with a solid foundation of integrity, morality, and patriotism. All the children attended school on the reservation until reaching high school. The U. S. government insisted that Indian children attend public high school, so the Jojola children were split up into schools in the surrounding area. All were required to learn English rather than speak in their native language or dialect.

The Jojola children did well in school, but Dyan excelled as a bright and avid student. Although only five feet tall and barely one hundred pounds, she was a "take charge" person at home and at school. In addition, she was artistically creative and excelled in 4H, crafts, and current events. Dyan married shortly after completing high school, and her young husband deployed to Vietnam. Upon his return, they were unable to cope with the emotional scars of war, and the marriage failed. Refusing to give in to despair, Dyan concentrated on developing her professional career. She attended the Southwestern Indian Polytechnical Institute in Albuquerque and received her certificate in Electronics and Telecommunications. She was subsequently hired by Digital Corporation, where she worked and continued her education. Later, she attended Digital-sponsored advanced courses in computers in Boston, Massachusetts and San Francisco, California.

Dyan continued her career in computers as a repair technician for a number of corporations in Albuquerque and nearby Kirtland AFB. After several years of success, Dyan joined the International Foresters Corporation and quickly embraced their emphasis on championing the wellbeing of families and communities. She was deeply touched by the Foresters' focus on delivering lifestyle protection, innovative benefits, and community support that served families and neighborhoods. Finally she was working with an organization and people that enabled her to act out her own passion for children, the elderly, and the downtrodden.

Within a very short time, Dyan's reputation was well-known as an advocate for improving the quality of life for the people of Isleta, as well as all the Native Americans throughout New Mexico. Her tireless pursuits included a myriad of projects to improve education, health, and literacy on the reservations. Dyan was at the forefront of battles to improve and preserve the quality of land and water reserves in and around Isleta and Kirtland AFB in Albuquerque. She was also a staunch advocate for providing the reservations access to the latest technology and distance-learning education.

I met Dyan in the early 1990s when I was selected by Ross Perot to be the State Director for United We Stand America, the political organization for his second campaign for president. From the outset, she was a solid supporter of the Perot movement and saw it as an opportunity to empower Native Americans who were not involved in mainstream politics. Dyan immediately became a powerful intercessor for me and arranged visitations for the Pueblo, Apache, Navajo, and Zuni tribes throughout New Mexico. Because of Dyan's dynamic persuasion and compelling argument, an unprecedented number of Native Americans became registered voters and made up a significant number of the nearly 10,000 Perot supporters in New Mexico. Thus, Dyan made a key contribution in giving voters a third party voice in politics in New Mexico through the mid-1990s.

My successful relationship with the Isleta Pueblo, as well as many of the other tribes, was made possible through Dyan's able intercession. Often, she escorted me into gatherings normally closed to non-Native Americans. When it came to helping her community, none surpassed Dyan's unique vision, determination, focus, and sheer hard work in completing whatever task she accepted. On any given day, she would be on the phone with elected officials, speaking at a community meeting, or teaching a class on Indian culture or political processes. At other times, she would be organizing a field trip for a special event for the children from the reservation.

Dyan was a determined and effective lobbyist before state governors, the legislature, members of the U.S. congress, and numerous businesspersons. For over two years, she personally organized and produced a weekly political program on Public Access Television. This was an enormous and professional effort that reached every county and all four corners of the state. In addition, Dyan facilitated and participated in many key meetings with the All Indian Pueblo Council and traveled to reservations in support of their respective concerns. Because of Dyan's personal efforts, many youngsters from Isleta Pueblo and other reservations were exposed to aviation through the Young Eagle's Program, a national outreach to boys and girls, twelve to seventeen years old.

I had the privilege of knowing and working closely with Dyan for over twelve years. She faithfully dedicated herself to furthering the cause of education, business, and quality of life, not only for Native Americans, but also for all the citizens of New Mexico. Many of her personal efforts had national implications in government and politics. I know of no one who more epitomized the role of a selfless public servant than she did. Her community, the state of New Mexico, and all of America are the better for it today.

In August 2007, the news of Dyan's tragic death left me shocked and speechless. My wife and I had great difficulty accepting that this precious jewel of humanity was gone. We traveled to Isleta to share in the family's grief and participate in Dyan's funeral service. The church was packed when we arrived and met Jemerson at the door beside Dyan's coffin. She was beautiful in repose, and looked as if she would just open her eyes and give us that famous smile and warm greeting that was so uniquely Dyan. It was not to be, but her spirit was unbelievably present and filled the church. The service was a beautiful testimony of a young woman who seemed to know her time on earth was not intended to be long. Now we all knew why she was always in a hurry. Although she left us much too soon, Dyan's work was that of ten people!

On November 4, 2007 Dyan received posthumously the New Mexico Distinguished Public Service Award for exceptional contributions to improve public service in New Mexico. Once again, Peggy and I were invited to participate with the family, and Mary Jane insisted that I come with the family on stage to receive the award. Despite Dyan's painful absence, it was a wonderful evening, and it was particularly gratifying for the Jojola family that a fitting recognition was given to a great American patriot and servant to her people. The following year, Dyan's life and work were acknowledged by the New Mexico State Legislature and the State of New Mexico.

When preparing to write this book, I flew to Albuquerque to meet once more with Dyan's mother and my "sister" Mary Jane. We had a long talk about Dyan, and both of us felt her presence in the home in which she grew up. As always, Mary Jane was the epitome of grace and warmth, while still suffering her loss. Her final words reflected a deep, abiding faith in God and her certainty of seeing her child again:

> *"God loans a child to us. Sometimes we have to give the child back because it's about God, not us. We must let go because our loved ones belong to Him. Today, Dyan is in heaven and happy in the presence of the Lord, but we'll see her again."*

My only appropriate response was *"Amen!"*

WOMEN WHO MADE A DIFFERENCE

The Walton Sisters, Sara, Sandy, & Stephanie

Heather Wilson,
Former Congresswoman,
Currently University President

Louise J. Privette, MC,
NCSP, Ph. D. Candidate

Beverly Kavouras, Military Wife of Retired
Military and Airline Pilot

Shirley Tolbert Jones Retired
Science Teacher, Military Wife

WOMEN WHO MADE A DIFFERENCE

Lucimarian Roberts, Wife of
Tuskegee Airman

Frances Porter, School Teacher,
Pastor's Wife

Violet Bower, Preacher's Wife,
Church Planter

Dyan Jojola, Activist,
Great Public Servant

CHAPTER FOUR

Proven Greatness
Women In The Military

Brief History

The history of women in the military dates back over 4,000 years across a large spectrum of cultures and nations. As a veteran of war, I don't know of a greater proving ground for character, fortitude, and heroism than upon the field of battle. This is especially true when one is called to defend his or her homeland, way of life, or future existence. When the demands of military service are added upon their shoulders, the dimension of greatness in women exceeds that of any other profession. Although the information is limited, history still confirms women have been significantly involved in conflicts since ancient times. Their influence as rulers and warriors spanned many cultures, continents, and nations, including: China, Persia, Greece, Africa, and Europe.

Throughout history, women warriors fought and led troops into battle, and they stood up against the most powerful male leaders of their day. Yet, many of their significant contributions were willfully omitted in recorded history because the documented accounts were written by the victors in war. Despite male-dominated legends and myths, the evidence of great women could not be diminished completely.

American Women Through WW II

Thousands of American women have been part of our nation's war efforts beginning with the Revolutionary War. Since then, they have been involved in the War of 1812, Mexican War (1846-1848),

Civil War (1861-1865), and the Spanish-American War (1898). In the early wars, women often cloaked themselves in disguises to serve alongside men. When they were accepted into the military, women were given auxiliary roles and served on the battlefield as nurses, water bearers, cooks, laundresses, and saboteurs.

During World War I, over 12,000 women were allowed to serve in the U. S. Navy and the Marine Corps, and approximately 400 perished during the war. Women also worked for the American Red Cross, the United Service Organizations, in factories, offices, transportation, and aviation plants.

During World War II, nearly 400,000 women served in the U.S. Armed forces. Over 60,000 served as Army nurses, and over 14,000 were Navy nurses. In 1942, the Army created the Women's Army Auxiliary Corps that served overseas in North Africa. This group later became the Women's Army Corps (WAC) where over 150,000 women served in England, France, Australia, New Guinea, and the Philippines.

In 1942, women reserves and volunteer groups were formed so that more men could be deployed for combat overseas. The Coast Guard, Marines, and Navy reserves were called *Women Accepted for Volunteer Emergency Service* or *WAVES*. More than 84,000 worked in administrative, medical, and communication jobs. The Coast Guard women reserves were called *Semper Paratus*, *Always Ready* or *SPARS*. In 1943, the Marine Corps Women's Reserve was established largely for stateside employment. By the end of the war, eighty-five percent of the personnel at the U.S. Marine Corps Headquarters were women.

In 1943, the Women Air Force Service Pilots (WASP) was formed as a *paramilitary aviation* organization. Their predecessors were pioneering civilian female pilots who had organized separately in 1942. Approximately 25,000 women applied to join the WASP, and nearly 1,100 passed the training requirements and were allowed to serve. The WASPs were employed to fly military aircraft under the direction of the United States Army Air Forces for the duration of the war. They flew as civil service pilots on stateside missions as ferry pilots, test pilots, and anti-aircraft artillery trainers. Thirty-eight WASPs lost their lives in the service of our nation. In 1977, thirty-two years after World War II, the WASP was finally granted *veteran* status. On May 10, 2010, sixty-five years after the war, 300 surviving WASPs gathered at the US Capitol to accept the Congressional Gold Medal for their services. House Speaker Nancy Pelosi and other Congressional members made the presentation.

Women Aviators

World War II opened the doors that allowed American women to demonstrate their long-standing flying skills; however, women had been involved in advancing aviation since the first Wright Brothers' flight in 1903. The most well-known early American aviatrix was the late Amelia Earhart. Her legacy is well-documented in books, documentaries, and movies; and her tremendous exploits inspired scores of women and men. The historic records of other early women aviators are less known, so I chose to share the following briefs about a few, such as: Katharine Wright Haskell, Harriet Quimby, Bessie Coleman, and Jacqueline Cochran.

Katharine Wright Haskell

The first woman to have an impact on aviation was Katharine Wright Haskell (1874–1929), the only sister of aviation pioneers Wilbur and Orville Wright. Although not a pilot, Katharine held a key role in the personal and professional affairs of the Wright family. Just fifteen years old when her mother died, she became the mistress of the home of three brothers and her father who was a minister. Of the four Wright children, Katharine was the only one who finished college and later became a teacher while still managing the Wright's home in Dayton, Ohio.

While a high school teacher in Dayton, Katharine recruited other teachers to help her brothers with their aviation experiments. She later became an international celebrity while accompanying her brothers on a trip to Europe. Along with Wilbur and Orville, the French awarded her the *Legion d' Honneur*, making her one of the very few U. S. women recipients. After Wilbur died in 1912, Katharine took on more business responsibilities and became a key officer in the Wright Company. Katharine spent most of her life taking care of her brothers and father. Neither of her brothers ever married, and their father died in 1917. Finally at the age of fifty-two, Katharine married Henry J. Haskell, an old boyfriend from college days who was now a widower and renowned newspaperman. Two years later, Katharine contracted pneumonia and died on March 3, 1929 at the age of fifty-four.

Some may debate Katharine's significant contribution to the birth and progress of aviation; however, many historical documents confirm her intense involvement. Furthermore, her significance in aviation is better appreciated and understood in light of the typical family dynamics in America during the early 1900s.

Harriet Quimby

Harriet Quimby (1875–1912) was an early American aviator and a movie screenwriter. She was born in Arcadia, Michigan and her family moved to San Francisco, California where she became a journalist in the early 1900s. She became interested in aviation in 1910 while attending the *Belmont Park International Aviation Tournament* on Long Island, New York. There she met John Moisant, a well-known aviator and operator of a flight school. Harriet trained at Moisant's school and completed her pilot's test on August 1, 1911. She became the first U.S. woman to earn an *Aero Club of America* aviator's certificate. Harriet also became the first American woman pilot to fly at night. Moisant's sister, Matilde, became the nation's second certified female pilot.

In 1912, Harriet became the first woman to fly across the English Channel. Harriet Quimby and aviator Charles Willard were accidentally killed on July 1, 1912 while participating in the *Third Annual Boston Aviation Meet* at Squantum, Massachusetts. For unknown reasons the aircraft in which they were flying suddenly pitched down from about 1,500 feet. Quimby and Willard were ejected from their seats and fell to their deaths. Although only thirty-seven when she died, Harriet left a legacy of courage and fortitude for many young women to follow.

Bessie Coleman

Elizabeth "Bessie" Coleman (1892–1926) was the first female African American pilot to hold an *international pilot's license.* She was born in Atlanta, Texas, the tenth of thirteen children. Her sharecropper parents were George, who was part Cherokee, and Susan Coleman. Bessie's family moved to Waxahachie, Texas, when she was two-years-old, and she lived there until reaching the age of twenty-three. Bessie attended a segregated, one-room school until she completed the eighth grade. She loved to read and was an outstanding math student. Her early life consisted of school, chores, church, and the annual cotton harvest. At eighteen, Bessie used her savings to enroll in the *Oklahoma Colored Agricultural and Normal University* (now Langston University) in Langston, Oklahoma. Her money ran out after one year, and she returned home to Waxahachie where her mother had been left to raise the remainder of the children alone. The meager wages for black people in the rigidly segregated south eventually caused her to look to the north for a better opportunity in life.

At the age of twenty-three, Bessie followed her brothers to Chicago, Illinois to live and work. While working as a manicurist at the White Sox Barber Shop, she heard stories about flying from pilots returning home from World War I. Consequently, Bessie dreamed of learning to fly, but no American flight schools would admit her because she was black…and a woman. The few black nearby aviators also refused to train her. Undeterred, Bessie eventually received encouragement from Robert S. Abbott, founder and publisher of the *Chicago Defender* newspaper. She took his advice and made plans to pursue training abroad.

With financial help from the *Defender* and a banker named Jesse Binga, Bessie took a French-language class in Chicago, and then sailed to Paris on November 20, 1920. The French readily embraced this determined young black woman and allowed her to enter flight school. Bessie trained at the famous *Ecole d'Aviation des Freres Caudron* in Le Crotoy in northern France. On June 15, 1921, she became the first African-American woman to earn an international aviation license from the *Fédération Aéronautique Internationale.* She was also the first American of any gender or ethnicity to do so, and the first African-American woman to earn an aviation pilot's license. Bessie spent the next two months polishing her skills, and sailed for New York in September, 1921.

Bessie was a media sensation upon her return to the United States; however, she soon realized that she would have to earn a living as a *"barnstorming"* stunt flier. This highly competitive arena required additional training, but she still had difficulty finding an instructor to teach her. Bessie returned to Europe and obtained training from experts in France, the Netherlands, and Germany. By the time she returned to America, she was confident and eager to launch her career in exhibition flying.

For the next five years, "Queen Bess," as she was now called, was a popular attraction admired by both blacks and whites. Flying the *Curtiss JN-4* "Jenny" biplane, Bessie delivered stunning performances of figure eights, loops, and near-ground dips to cheering crowds wherever she flew. She was known for her flamboyant style and daring skills, and would go to great lengths to complete a difficult stunt. Bessie still held onto her dream of starting a flying school for young black aviators, but that reality was not to be.

On April 30, 1926 Bessie Coleman flew a recently purchased *Curtiss JN-4* in Jacksonville, FL in preparation for an airshow. Her mechanic and publicity agent, William Wills, flew with her in the other seat. Bessie did not put on her seatbelt because she was planning a parachute jump for the next day and wanted to closely examine the terrain. After a few minutes into the flight, the plane failed to pull out of a dive and began to spin. At about 2,000 feet, Bessie was thrown from the plane and died on impact with the ground. Unable to gain control of the aircraft, Wills also died when the plane crashed to the ground. Bessie Coleman was just thirty-four years old.

Bessie's pioneering achievements were an inspiration for generations of African American men and women. Many years later, I had the privilege of expressing my deep admiration and gratitude to Bessie's grandniece who was in a wheelchair at a Tuskegee Airmen convention. As I knelt beside her, she reached out, smiled, and gave me a tender pat on my face. That was a powerful, poignant moment for me; it seemed I had at last made a spiritual connection with "Queen Bess!" Perhaps, the late William James Powell, an American engineer, soldier, civil aviator, and author who promoted aviation among the African American community, said it best:

> *"Because of Bessie Coleman, we have overcome that which was worse than racial barriers. We have overcome the barriers within ourselves and dared to dream."*

Jacqueline Cochran

When I began my Air Force career in 1963, Jacqueline "Jackie" Cochran was still a very active, living pioneer in American aviation. Although there were no women pilots in the Air Force at that time, Jackie was considered one of the most gifted racing pilots of her generation. Jacqueline Cochran was born in 1906 as Bessie Lee Pittman in the Florida Panhandle. She was the youngest of the five children born to Ira and Mary Pittman. Although her father's work caused the family to move frequently, Bessie's childhood was similar to other families that lived in small southern towns. Her life was uneventful, and at an early age, she married Robert Cochran, a young aircraft mechanic at the nearby naval base in Pensacola.

The young Cochran family later moved to Miami, Florida for four years. While there, a son was born; however, the marriage subsequently failed, and Bessie moved back to northwest Florida to be near her parents. Tragedy struck the family when Bessie's now five-year old son died accidently when his clothes caught fire while he played alone in the backyard. Jackie worked as a hairdresser in Pensacola and eventually moved to New York City where she was hired at a prestigious salon at *Saks Fifth Avenue*.

Jackie wanted to break from her troubled past and create a new image, so she changed her name from *"Mrs. Bessie Cochran"* to *"Miss Jackie Cochran."* Apparently it worked when "Jackie" met Floyd Bostwick Odlum, founder of *Atlas Corporation* and *CEO of RKO* in *Hollywood*. Odlum was fourteen years older than Jackie and was reputed to be one of the ten richest men in the world. Apparently he was overwhelmed by Jackie and helped her establish a cosmetics business. While still living in New York, Jackie was invited by a friend to take a ride in an aircraft and was smitten by the thrill of flying. She soon began taking flying lessons in the early 1930s and learned to fly an aircraft in just three weeks! Two years after she soloed, Jackie obtained her commercial pilot's license. She married Odlum in 1936, and took advantage of his astute finance and marketing abilities to publicize her cosmetic business now called *Wings.* Before long, Jackie was flying her own aircraft around the country promoting her products.

Backed by her husband, Odlum, Jackie was able to act out her new-found passion and began to make her mark in aviation. While still using her Cochran surname, she flew in the MacRobertson Air Race in 1934. Three years later, Jackie worked with Amelia Earhart to open the air races to women where Jackie became the only woman to compete in the Bendix race. That same year, she set a new woman's national speed record, and by 1938, she was considered the best female pilot in the United States.

Before the United States joined World War II, Jackie Cochran was part of "Wings for Britain", an organization that ferried American-built aircraft to Britain. While there, she volunteered her services to the Royal Air Force and worked for the British Air Transport Auxiliary (ATA). She also recruited qualified women pilots in the United States who came to England and joined the ATA. In 1943, Jackie Cochran had a key role in the formation of the wartime Women's Auxiliary Army Corps (WAAC) and Women Airforce Service Pilots (WASP). As director of the WASP, Jackie supervised the training of hundreds of women pilots at the former Avenger Field in Sweetwater, Texas. She was also the first woman to fly a bomber across the Atlantic Ocean. Later she received the Distinguished Service Medal and the Distinguished Flying Cross for her superior performance and out-standing contributions to the war efforts of WW II.

Often called the "Speed Queen," Jackie won five *Harmon Trophies* and was considered the most outstanding woman pilot in the world. Until her death in 1980, no other female pilot held more speed, distance or altitude records in aviation history than she did. Today, every military woman aviator in America owes a profound debt of gratitude to this great patriot that God intentionally created for a very noble purpose. As a retired military and civilian pilot, I am proud to have flown in the same sky where Jackie left contrails for me to follow!

Nurses—Angels of Mercy

The most poignant memories in my life occurred during times when our nation was involved in World War II, the Korean War, and the Vietnam Conflict. This is a reflection of my youthful mind that was impressionable and inquisitive; and it "captured" colorful, photographic images that have lasted a lifetime. Many of these significant events in my life were etched on a mental canvas like photographic images that could be recalled in living color at any time. Such was my first experience with nurses. When I was about twelve, I was hospitalized with a severe throat ailment. Despite the racial barriers at that time, I fell in love with the sincere compassion, kindness, and the sweet disposition of one of our night-shift nurses. She was a beautiful, neatly kept nurse who looked great in her sparkling white uniform from head to toe. The vision of that angelic face faded, but the memory of her gift of care and kindness lasted a lifetime. Fifteen years after that event, the memory of it suddenly merged with me while I served as a combat pilot in Southeast Asia.

Nightingales in Vietnam

My next close encounter with nurses was really not close at all, due to racial prejudice that still existed in 1966. Nevertheless, the dedication, commitment, and sacrifice of nurses that I witnessed from a distance deserve mentioning in this book. This experience occurred in the crucible of survival during my first combat tour in Vietnam. In July 1966, the pending arrival of the first nurses assigned to Cam Ranh Bay, Vietnam caused an unbridled uproar. The flight surgeon that lived in our compound received a lot of attention and was elevated to a place of high importance among all the pilots. Allegedly, he had the *real* word on the nurses' arrival date, and he promised to put in a good word for those he thought worthy enough to get to "first base." Consequently, the bachelors did everything possible to win the flight surgeon's favor and sought to secure a place at the head of the planned receiving line. The married pilots were relegated to the position of spectators on the day the nurses finally arrived, so it didn't matter to me that I was flying when the great event occurred.

The first six nurses assigned to Cam Ranh Bay apparently had been hand-picked for their commitment, fortitude, and willingness to step into a raw war zone. With all due respect, none of them would have successfully competed in a beauty contest based upon age, size, shape, or hairstyle. Furthermore, the Lieutenant Colonel was said to have deliberately chosen the least attractive nurses in the Air Force. Her intent was to mitigate the expected challenges they would face in the den of ravenous wolves under the duress of war.

First of all, the Lieutenant Colonel underestimated the attitudes and state of lonely men. Secondly, it only took about a week for the nurses to be transformed into the most beautiful females ever to hit the beach! However, due to the great credit of the nurses, they managed to hold the most voracious suitors at bay. As a result, they gave unstintingly of their time to those in real need of their medical services. Ordinarily, my observations of the nurses over the next several months would not be noteworthy, except for the racist attitudes and actions of some pilots and officers with whom I served. More than once, their not so subtle comments and actions indicated the nurses were "off limits" to me, the only black fighter pilot on the base. As a happily married man, I had no intention of trying to enter into the "dog fights" that were now in full season. Nevertheless, I highly resented those who were intent on making sure I kept a safe distance from the nurses.

One day, one of the nurses decided to sit down at the table where I was having lunch alone. Immediately, we were surrounded by some unintelligent individuals who made demeaning and scurrilous remarks. My immediate rage erupted from the anger and disgust of my entire life, and I wanted to respond with unspeakable violence. To this day, I am grateful that the Lord's divine intervention prevented me from doing so. Despite this incident, the greatness of these patriotic women shone through on a daily basis.

When Cam Ranh Bay became the medical processing center for war casualties, those nurses demonstrated the greatest personal commitments I have ever seen. Many of the wounded troops were broken, blind, maimed, or suffering from a plethora of critical injuries. Most had to be stabilized before being air-evacuated to the states. At other times, it was apparent that the nurses worked feverishly alongside the doctors to save the critically wounded. Many times their efforts went for naught.

These "Nightingales" spent twelve to eighteen hours per shift providing medical attention under the most difficult circumstances. Sometimes I witnessed their tears after a futile attempt to save a young life, or felt their grief and frustration after holding the hands of a soldier who died. I observed the impact of this in their faces and their drooped shoulders as they walked to their quarters. At other times, I overheard the comments or boasting of a pilot who allegedly had shared some intimate time with a nurse. On another occasion, I saw the scratched face and black eye of a would-be suitor who did not understand the word, NO!

As I reflect on the times long ago, my memory is clear of the dedication and sacrifices these nurses made. Some gave beyond the call of duty and in ways that cannot be described or understood apart from the crucible of men and women at war. Not enough can ever be said for those ladies who came to Cam Ranh Bay in 1966. I believe they embodied the character, essence, and soul of all nurses who serve our nation in peace-time or in war. Their many personal sacrifices were profound, selfless, and too often, unheralded. My perspective was confirmed many times by nurses I knew at other times and places throughout my career. Thus in my humble opinion, no monuments will ever be sufficient enough, no words can truly tell their stories, nor can the gratitude they so richly deserve ever be adequately expressed. I call these "Nightingales" a very select group of God's special angels.

Nancy Leftenant Colon—A Tuskegee Airmen Nurse

I had the great pleasure of meeting Nancy Leftenant Colon over thirty years ago at an annual Tuskegee Airmen convention in Denver, Colorado. She was a beautiful, effervescent, outgoing, lady whose smile made all who came into her presence feel uniquely special. I was even more impressed when I found out she had been a nurse with the Tuskegee Airmen during World War II. The years had been kind to Nancy as her appearance was that of a much younger woman. A long-term, wonderful friendship resulted from that initial meeting, and my admiration of this great lady has not diminished over time. Nancy continues to be active in medical related issues in her state as well as nationwide. She has a well-spring of energy and shows no signs at slowing down. I am extremely pleased to share a bit of what makes Nancy so special.

Nancy was one of twelve children born of the marriage between James Leftenant, Sr. and Eunice Middleton of the village of Goose Creek near Charleston, South Carolina. The name "Leftenant" is pronounced like the British and other nations use it, but no one knows how a black family ended up with it at the beginning of the 20th century. Regardless, James and Eunice had six boys and six girls. Nancy was born September 29, 1920 and will be ninety-three years old on her next birthday. Her family moved to Amityville, New York when she was three years old. The Leftenant home was a friendly and happy place that often attracted many of the neighborhood children because of her mother's charity, compassion, and kindness for others. Despite twelve children of her own, Eunice always found room for another who needed a place to play or to find refuge.

Despite the era of the Great Depression, getting an education was a high priority in the Leftenant household. At the outbreak of WW II, one of her brothers was drafted into the Army. Nancy and the rest of her siblings completed high school. Nancy graduated from Amityville High School in 1939 and worked a year to earn the $100 registration fee for the Lincoln School for Nurses in Bronx, New York. She was accepted and graduated three years later. Following her nursing training in January 1945, she volunteered for military service and was commissioned a Second Lieutenant into the U.S. Army Nurse Corps. Later that year, one of her brothers, Samuel Gordon Leftenant, a Tuskegee Airman was killed in action over Austria while escorting bombers to Berlin. He was one of the pilots from the famed 99th Fighter Group, which was commanded then by Colonel Benjamin O. Davis, Jr.

After completing her first assignment at Lowell General Hospital, Fort Devens, Massachusetts, Nancy was assigned to the 332nd Medical Group with the Tuskegee Airmen at Lockbourne Army Air base in Columbus, Ohio. While at Lockbourne in 1948, she made history by becoming the first African American nurse to be accepted into the Regular Army Nurse's Corps. Later, she elected to transfer to the new Air Force Nurse's Corps. Nancy wanted to become a flight nurse; but because of her race, she met considerable resistance for nearly five years. Numerous physicals were taken and applications were repeatedly denied. Fortunately, she gained an advocate in Dr. Vance H. Marchbanks, Jr., the hospital commander, and an original Tuskegee Airman and pioneer Flight Surgeon in the military. With his help, Nancy was finally accepted and successfully completed the flight nurse's training in 1952 Gunter AFB, Alabama.

Nancy served as a flight nurse at Tachikawa, Japan between 1953-1955 where she supervised the evacuation of patients from Okinawa, Taiwan, and Korea. During the siege of Dien Bien Phu, Vietnam in 1954, she was one of the flight nurses assigned to evacuate the wounded soldiers of the French Expeditionary Force. Her next assignment was at USAF Hospital in Wiesbaden Germany from 1958-1960 where she was charge nurse. In 1960, Nancy took time out of her busy professional life to return to the United States to get married to Bayard Colon whom she had met earlier in New York. Bayard, from Manhattan, Virginia, was also a Tuskegee Airman who served during WW II. They were married September 3, 1960. The Colons had a happy, wonderful life together until a sudden massive heart attack ended Bayard's life.

After twenty years of dedicated service in the Air Force, Nancy retired in 1965 with the rank of Major in the Air Force at McGuire

AFB, New Jersey. She returned home to Amityville, New York and continued as a high school nurse until retiring for a second time. In 1978, the Amityville School District commemorated the thirtieth anniversary of Nancy's appointment as a nurse in the Army Nurse Corps. A proclamation declared the month of April as "Nancy Leftenant Colon" month. The district was also directed to hold classroom discussions on the historical significance of the accomplishments of this "Native Daughter."

Nancy continues her commitment and dedication in perpetuating the legacy of African-Americans who participated as aircrews, ground crews, and operational support training in the Army Air Corps during WWII. She became a key member of the national organization, Tuskegee Airmen Inc. (TAI) in 1974 and served as Executive Secretary for eight years. She was the first female elected to serve as TAI's national president from 1989 -1991. Along with several hundred original Tuskegee Airmen, Nancy was a recipient of the Congressional Gold Medal awarded by President George W. Bush in March 2007. Today, she is still an active members of Tuskegee Airmen, Incorporated.

Mid-20th Century Forward

The outstanding contributions and performance of minorities and women during World War II, at home and overseas, could no longer be ignored. The blood, sweat, and tears of sacrifice were clearly mixed in the mortar that held America together during its darkest of times. These heretofore unrecognized great patriots were more than ready to help move our country and the world forward from the ravages of war. Fortunately, America had a courageous president who was able and willing to follow his moral conscience.

In 1948, the US military became the vanguard of equal treatment and opportunity for minorities and women when President Truman issued Executive Order 9981. The president's directive ordered desegregation of all the armed services. His historical decision was the result of the superior performance of the famed Tuskegee Airmen and other African American, minority, and women units during World War II.

Against the advice of senior civilian and military leaders, President Truman insisted:

"the highest standards of democracy were essential in the armed services and that there shall be equality of treatment and opportunity for all persons, without regard to race, color, religion or national origin."

Concurrently in 1948, the Women's Armed Services Integration Act allowed women to serve as permanent and regular members in the Army, Navy, Marine Corps, and Air Force. Although women had soundly proven themselves during the war, the act precluded women serving on aircraft and vessels of the Air Force and Navy that might be engaged in combat. In time, such barriers would eventually fall.

Over the past fifty years, women have made considerable strides in moving up the professional ladder in promotions and responsibilities. The capabilities, commitment, dedication, and perseverance of women caused barrier after barrier to fall. By the end of the 20th century, women had been admitted and succeeded in the service academies. Scores of others had become flag officers and top non-commissioned officers. Still others blazed the trails in the skies and space, and opened new frontiers in every segment of our society. Many others established numerous "firsts" for women, and have become household names, such as Sally Ride, Christa McAuliffe, and Mae Jemison.

In 2013, women continue to break new records in every branch of the U.S. military. Much of this change is due to necessity. In an all-volunteer military during the last third of the 20th century, less than one percent of America's population serves across all branches of the military. The percentage of women volunteers generally exceeds those of men. Also, technological advancements have dramatically impacted the way wars have been fought over the last century. Women, however, have stepped up boldly and met the challenge in remarkable ways. In just the last thirty years, the complexity and compositions have changed in fighter squadrons, platoons, squadrons, aboard ships, and in other combat units.

Today, women serve as wing commanders, ship captains, and regiment leaders. Female pilots are flying the frontline jet fighters and have served in the elite aerial demonstration teams, such as the USAF Thunderbirds. When researching the marvelous history of women over the past five decades, it was difficult to single out any one, rather than another. Nevertheless, the names that follow reflect the *collective* accomplishments of countless others in their respective fields.

The late **Major General Jeanne M. Holm** was the first female one-star general of the United States Air Force and the first female two-star general in any service branch of the United States. General Holm served in the *Women's Army Auxiliary Corps* during World War II and later was credited with being the driving force behind the expansion of women's roles in the Air Force. She held several key positions related to personnel and women prior to retiring in 1975. After retiring, General Holm worked as a consultant for the Defense Manpower Commission. In March 1976, she was named special assistant to President Gerald Ford for the Office of Women's Programs.

In November, 2008, **General Ann E. Dunwoody** became the first female officer in U.S. military history to earn four stars. She currently serves as commander, U.S. Army Materiel Command. In March, 2012, **General Janet Wolfenbarger** became the first female four-star general in Air Force history. In 1980, General Wolfenbarger graduated in the first class with female cadets at the Air Force Academy. Today she serves as Commander, Air Force Materiel Command, Wright-Patterson Air Force Base, Ohio. General Wolfenbarger commands 83,000 people who manage $60 billion annually in research, development, test and evaluation.

In July 2013, **Lieutenant General Michelle D. Johnson** became the nineteenth Superintendent of the U.S. Force Academy. She is also a 1981 distinguished graduate of the Air Force Academy, a Rhodes Scholar, and a command pilot with more than 3,600 flying hours in multiple aircraft.

Today, fifty-seven active-duty women serve as generals or admirals, five of whom are lieutenant generals or vice admirals, the Navy's three-star rank. Women make up nine percent of the Air Force's general officer ranks. These include four lieutenant generals, twelve major generals, and eleven brigadier generals. As an Air Force veteran, I am very proud of my years of association with professional women officers and enlisted personnel. Major General Irene Trowell-Harris is one of several who became a flag officer.

Major General Irene Trowell-Harris (Retired) is a 38-year veteran of the US Air Force and Air National Guard (ANG). She was commissioned in the New York Air National Guard in 1963 and held the positions of chief nurse, nurse administrator, flight nurse instructor, and flight nurse examiner. In 1986, General Trowell-Harris became the first nurse in ANG history to command a medical clinic. She completed her storied career as assistant to the Director, Medical Readiness, and Nursing Services, Office of the Surgeon General, Headquarters USAF, Washington, D.C. In August 1998, she became the first female in history to have a Tuskegee Airmen, Inc. Chapter named in her honor, the Major General Trowell-Harris Chapter, Newburgh, New York.

Enlisted Women

The legacy of enlisted women in the service to our nation dates back to the American Revolution. Allegedly, a woman named Deborah Sampson, disguised as a man, enlisted in the Continental Army, and served for seventeen months in combat before being wounded and honorably discharged. Hundreds of women followed the example of Sampson and served disguised as men in the Confederate and Union Armies during the Civil War. By the turn of the 20th century, the armed forces eliminated this practice by thorough physical examinations of all potential recruits. Prior to World War I, women were officially allowed to serve as nurses and orderlies. Since then, the commitment, dedication, performance, and sacrifice of enlisted women in the military have been unequalled in any other profession.

Today, top enlisted women leaders in army, marines, navy, air force, and coast guard reflect the outstanding service of over 163,000 women. The following are a few examples of their superior performance and personal achievements:

Chief Master Sergeant Brenda K. Kirby is the Command Chief Master Sergeant for the 192nd Fighter Wing of the Virginia Air National Guard at Langley AFB, VA. She works directly for the Wing Commander and advises him on matters impacting the enlisted force, utilization, quality of enlisted leadership, management/supervisor training, and quality of life concerns. In addition, she is responsible for ensuring the commanders' policies are known and understood by the enlisted force, and she monitors compliance with Air Force standards. Chief Kirby is a twenty-eight year veteran with multiple stateside and overseas assignments, including assignments to Italy and Germany, and a deployment in support of humanitarian missions and *Operations Southern Watch, Northern Watch and Enduring Freedom.*

Master Chief Evelyn P. Banks is the Command Master Chief for Naval Sea Systems Command located in Washington, DC. This Mississippi native has served for twenty-nine years in numerous assignments on land and at sea on ships such as *USS SAMUEL GOMPERS, USS ACADIA, USS GERMANTOWN,* and the *USS ABRAHAM LINCOLN.* While on the Lincoln, she completed a historic ten-month deployment in support of Iraqi Freedom. Chief Banks has also served several tours as a recruiter, senior enlisted advisor, and most recently as Command Master Chief at the United States Naval Academy.

Master Sergeant Latisha Turner, from Eighth Army's 2501st Support Detachment, Yongsan Garrison, South Korea was the U. S. Army's selection for the 2013 Federally Employed Women Meritorious Service Award. This prestigious award honors leaders who have made significant contributions to diversity, equality and the advancement of women in their organizations. It is given to six military members, one from each of the services. Master Sergeant Turner is a nineteen-year veteran who serves as the chief of the logistics section for the 2501st Support Detachment. The detachment serves as Eighth Army's liaison with the First Republic of Korea Army and Third Republic of Korea Army. She has also been vice president for Sisterhood Ministries, a non-profit organization that has helped countless female Soldiers within the local Fort Campbell, Kentucky and the nearby community.

Additional examples of the outstanding achievements of women are included in the Air Force Association's 2013 selection of twelve outstanding airmen. These are **Master Sergeant Tessa Fontaine**, Counterintelligence and Cyber Counterintelligence Superintendent, National Reconnaissance Office, Chantilly, Virginia; **Master Sergeant Celeste C. Okokon**, Dental Hygienist, 7th Bomb Wing, Dyess Air Force Base, Texas; **Staff Sergeant Lauren A. Everett,** Aerospace Medical Service Journeyman, 48th Inpatient Squadron, RAF Lakenheath, England; and **Senior Airman Casey L. Anderson,** Mental Health Technician, 59th Mental Health Squadron, Joint Base San Antonio-Lackland, Texas.

It has been my distinct honor to serve with many other female officers and non-commissioned officers who achieved senior ranks before retirement. I am especially proud to have been the retiring official for two daughters who served in the Air Force, one of which was graduated from the Air Force Academy. Our youngest daughter came up through the enlisted ranks and is scheduled to retire as an officer in 2014. America can be grateful and proud of the dedication and patriotism of all the American women who serve or have served our nation throughout history all over the world.

High Risk of Uncharted Territory

The advancement of women in the U. S. military is deserved and laudable on many accounts. The impact, however, of the latest inclusion of women in the most dangerous and hostile war environments is unchartered territory fraught with uncertain consequences. The ultimate sacrifices of women in past wars and conflicts can serve as a sobering reality of the consequences of women in harm's way. Since WW I, approximately 1,100 women have been killed in action. One hundred and forty-two of these are the result of the War on Terror.

Hundreds of women have received medals for serious injuries and for personal valor under fire. Military hospitals nationwide have cared for many female heroes who have lost legs and arms.

As a Vietnam combat veteran, I have personally suffered or witnessed the ravages of war on countless men and a few women of a generation ago. The emotional, physical, and psychological scars of World War II, the Korean War, and Vietnam War are still visible and are being felt in ways not readily seen. To this day, I have a clear and painful memory of the 58,000 young lives that were lost in the debacle of Vietnam. The many years of suffering that the prisoners of war in North Vietnam endured were especially egregious to the men and their families. The mere thought of hundreds of American female prisoners suffering years of confinement pales by comparison. The emotional, physical, and sexual abuse numbs the mind, and the exploitation of our female comrades in arms is incomprehensible.

I believe those assigning women to the highest risks areas in war should use extreme caution. Apparently they lack the experience, knowledge, or wisdom to consider the total impact of war on the lives of women, their families, marriages, and their futures. Despite what the present-day Pentagon officials persistently stress, I do not believe there can be "gender-neutral standards" for combat assignments. There are simply some demands that require a certain physical capability normally not found in women. For example, women who serve in Army tanks must be able to repeatedly load fifty-five-pound tank shells. A female infantry soldier must routinely carry backpacks of gear that weigh sixty to seventy pounds. In addition, if needed, she would need to be able to carry a wounded 200-pound male comrade. Nevertheless, there are a few exceptional women who can meet the toughest emotional, mental, and physical requirements. When necessary, such females should be employed on a case-by-case basis.

Those women who elect to pursue service in all areas and categories need to carefully consider their aspirations and goals regarding marriage, family, and their God-given ability to give birth to a child. A hardened, combat female veteran is not likely able or willing to return home and resume the role of a caring, nurturing mother. The stay-at-home dad who remains behind while his wife goes off to war will face many unprecedented challenges as a husband and father. Thus, those involved in assigning women to *all* combat roles need to recognize that the long-term emotional, moral, and social consequences of such decisions have yet to be determined. Therefore, the question arises: is such a policy worth the unknown risks. Already, over two million men and women have served during the wars in Iraq and Afghanistan. Approximately 44,000 have been wounded, and nearly 6,100 have been killed. There are vivid examples to consider from the women who suffered horrendous physical and mental consequences from the wars of Iraq and Afghanistan. Only time will tell what the ultimate impact will be. In the final analysis, the decision of where they want to serve in the military should still be left up to the women who volunteer.

WOMEN IN AVIATION AND THE MILITARY

Katherine Wright Haskell

Bessie Coleman

Jacqueline Cochran

Harriet Quimby

WOMEN IN AVIATION AND THE MILITARY

Nurse Nancy Leftenant Colon

Major General Jean Holm

Major General Irene Trowell-Harris

General Ann E. Dinwoody

WOMEN IN AVIATION AND THE MILITARY

Gen. Janet C. Wolfenbarger

Lt. General Michele Johnson

Master Chief Evelyn P. Banks

Chief Master Sergeant Brenda K. Kirby

CHAPTER FIVE

Victory Over Adversity

Power That Overcomes Adversity

*"There is nothing—no circumstance, no trouble, no testing—
that can ever touch us until, first of all, it has gone past God
and Christ, right through to us. If it has come that far, it has
come with a great purpose, which we may not understand at
the moment. But as we refuse to become panicky, as we lift our
eyes up to Him and accept it as coming from the throne of God
for some great purpose of blessing to our hearts, no sorrow will
ever disarm us; no circumstance will ever cause us to fret, for
we shall rest in the joy of what our Lord is. That is the rest of
the victory."* Alan Redpath

Indeed, adversity is a part of life, and no one escapes the occurrences that will come, often unexpectedly or when it is most incon-
venient. Crippling illnesses, divorce, and/or death are three of the
most difficult challenges that women face. In the world today, many
women suffer or feel crippled from a plethora of events that may
have occurred earlier in their childhood or during their young adult
lives. Still, older women sometimes suffer because of neglect by their
spouses or families in their later years when support is needed the
most. The anguish and pain during these circumstances cause them
to give up in despair. Nevertheless, God is faithful and will not leave
those alone who believe and trust Him. He has said:

"Never will I leave you; never will I forsake you." Heb. 13:5

Before I continue, let me make a resounding declaration that often is not proclaimed loudly enough: Nothing, no one, nor any circumstance can diminish the creative greatness that God put in women at the moment of their conception! He infused them with these attributes at the beginning of the creation of the earth. Neither death, nor the most heinous, despicable act perpetrated by male, female, or society can take this greatness away. Even in the winter season of a woman's life, her essence and worth are still valued by God and by all who take the time to see, hear, and appreciate her. Thus, when a woman truly embraces her inherent, God-given greatness, she has the power to overcome any adversity or challenge in her life.

The Bible says:

"The grass withers, the flower fades, but the word of our God stands forever." Isaiah 40:8.

Likewise, the greatness of a woman is as eternal as the Word of the Lord. This message needs to be preached more often in the church pulpits; from every rooftop; in every village, town, and city; and from the highest mountain. I say let the word go forth: girls, young ladies, and older women embrace your God-given greatness and shake off the shackles and shrouds that would keep you a victim!

There are trained professionals and established organizations designed to facilitate the care and healing of abused girls and women and their dedication and efforts are to be applauded. However, they would do well to emphasize the Biblical message of victory over adversity, no matter how ugly the experience has been.

The stories that follow highlight women who have suffered adversity but overcame it by faith, fortitude, and perseverance. Hopefully these exemplary characters will encourage all who may be going through their own trials and tribulations. In some cases, the names have been changed to protect the privacy of the individuals; nevertheless, the events are real-life experiences.

Coping with Death

Thirty-seven years ago, my wife and I had our first close-up experience with helping a next-door neighbor cope with the sudden and tragic death of her husband. My wife, Peggy, was immediately able to rely upon her Christian faith to minister to the young widow. As a recent "reborn" Christian, I was less spiritually prepared to deal with the deep despair and pain our neighbor suffered following the loss of her husband; however, we both recognized the raw, emotional vulnerabilities with which this thirty-five year old widow struggled. To our amazement, she soon began a relationship with a co-worker and got married within six months of her husband's death. That second tragedy ended less than four months later when she got divorced!

As previously stated, the death of a spouse or loved one is the greatest adversity that anyone can face. Usually death is a devastating experience that leaves in its wake broken hearts, emotional disasters, shattered dreams, and long-lasting clouds of despair. In such cases, women often fall prey to ever-present wolves that seek out victims who have been weakened by some adversity in life. Women coping with death are often ready and visible targets. Such was the case with our grieving widow who entered into another relationship with a man before her heart had healed and while her mind was still clouded by sorrow.

So what advice do I give to grieving widows today? Whether you are a Christian or not, if ever there was time to believe in and trust God, it is now. I have seen people struggle throughout my life to cope with death or other adversities in many wrong ways. When a woman loses a loving husband, child, or other family member, she needs to realize that another man or person cannot possibly fix her brokenness. When a heart has been shattered and a spirit mortally wounded, we need to go to Him who created us for refuge and restoration. Others can come along to offer condolences, compassion, and solace, but only God can give lasting consolation and peace. He is always ready to reach into our cages of despair and give a helping hand, but those imprisoned must realize that the handle is on the *inside* of that cage! The person inside must reach for it to open the door and allow the

Lord to come in. I have not experienced the loss of my wife, but I have suffered the loss of many other loved ones —mother, father, sister, brothers, and a multitude of friends. Thus, I am totally confident in pointing women, or anyone else coping with death, to God who removes its sting. In Him we can be victorious and continue the life we are blessed to have on the road ahead.

Melodie Homer—Victorious in Adversity

Melodie Homer is the president and founder of *The LeRoy W. Homer Jr. Foundation.* The foundation was founded in 2002 in memory of the First Officer of United Airlines #93 when it crashed in Shanksville, PA September 11, 2001. Its mission is to encourage and support young adults who wish to pursue careers as professional pilots, and it promotes awareness about aviation careers to disadvantaged youth. Melodie is also currently employed as a clinical nurse instructor at a local community college. She has over fifteen years of experience in oncology, both in patient care, and the pharmaceutical industry; and she holds advanced certification in this specialty. Melodie has authored two health-related children's books and has co-authored a chapter in a nursing textbook. She recently published her memoir *"From Where I Stand: Flight # 93 Pilot's Wife Sets the Record Straight.*

When the tragedy of September 11, 2001 rocked our nation and the world, Melodie was a young working wife and mother of a ten-month old daughter. She and LeRoy had been very happily married for three and one-half years, and they were settled into a life that promised to be a great future. Like millions all across American and around the world, the terrorist attacks in New York, Pennsylvania, and Washington, DC tragically changed Melodie's life forever. The loss of her precious husband and father of her baby shattered their beautiful world and was near unbearable in the days and months that followed. With a deep faith, close-knit family, caring friends, and the amazing grace of God, Melodie has forged ahead with courage, fortitude, and perseverance. I am honored to include a short story about her in this book, for she is truly a *Godly Creation.*

Melodie is the oldest of three children of Jamaican parents, Waldron and Ena Thorpe who immigrated to Ontario, Canada. She is a Canadian citizen and was born in 1966. Her mother was a nurse until retirement and her father was an entrepreneur. The Thorpes were people of deep faith, and they raised their children to appreciate the value of education, be independent, and to care for others. Melodie's brother is a manager with the Lowes Corporation and her sister is an attorney in Atlanta, Georgia. Since Melodie was about four years old, she wanted to emulate the great example of her mother and become a nurse. She was educated from grade school through college in Canada and earned a nursing diploma at Mohawk College in 1987. After a trip to Europe, Melodie returned to Canada and began work as a registered nurse for two years. In 1989, she moved to California and worked as a registered nurse while earning a bachelor's degree at Loma Linda University and a Master's Degree in nursing at Azusa Pacific University in California.

While Melodie was growing up in Canada, young LeRoy Homer grew up on Long Island, New York as one of nine children, seven of them girls. Young LeRoy had dreamed of flying since he was a boy; and he began flying lessons at fifteen. He completed his first solo flight at sixteen and already had his private pilot license when he entered the US Air Force Academy. By then, this self-assured, soft-spoken man had an ever-present smile, and his friends described him as having a heart of gold.

LeRoy graduated from the US Air Force Academy in 1987 and received a pilot training slot to Del Rio, Texas. He graduated in 1988 and began his military career flying C-141s. He served in Desert Shield and Desert Storm and later received a commendation for flying humanitarian operations in Somalia. After completing his commitment to the Air Force, LeRoy joined the US Air Force Reserves and attained the rank of major. He joined United Airlines in 1995 and that same year met Melodie Thorpe, his future wife. Two years later they were engaged and got married in 1998. On that horrendous morning of 9/11, the heroic actions of several passengers and the flight crew of Flight #93 saved Washington, DC from a second attack. Thus, Melodie's husband, LeRoy died as an American patriot.

Only those who have walked in the shoes of the 3,000 families who lost loved ones that day can ever know the pain and suffering they bear, even now. Each has dealt with and endured this indescribable adversity in many different ways. By the grace and mercy of God, most are overcoming it and moving on with their lives. Instead of succumbing to her profound grief, Melodie demonstrated her faith by reaching out and helping others. While coping with her tremendous loss, she created the *The LeRoy W. Homer Jr. Foundation* in 2002 just one year after 9/11! Her courageous commitment and dedication to help others is clearly evident over the past eleven years.

Since The Foundation began in 2002, fifteen scholarships have been granted, and fourteen recipients have received their private pilot license. Nine of these individuals have graduated from four-year programs with degrees in aeronautical engineering, aeronautical science, aviation, flight technology, and aviation business. The Foundation's first scholarship recipient recently completed his flight training for the US Navy. Another has completed the ROTC program and has just been accepted into the Navy pilot program. One recipient is currently serving in the US Marine Corp, and two female recipients have been selected for pilot slots in the US Air Force. Five students are pursuing their undergraduate degrees, as well as adding additional ratings—instrument, complex, commercial, and single engine qualification. Another recipient recently became a certified flight instructor.

Melodie's incredible gift of helping others was also demonstrated by the adoption of a two-day old baby boy nine years ago. Today she is the mother of two—her thirteen-year old daughter and nine-year-old son. In addition, she has been a past volunteer of the *Starlight Foundation* and the *Make A Wish Foundation*. Melodie's recent book, *From Where I Stand*, tells the rest of her great story and I highly recommend it as the next book you read. She chronicles the events of that September 11 day and the "new normal" that ensued. She is raising her two children and celebrating their milestones while dealing with the persistent post-traumatic stress disorder. Melodie Homer readily admits that the last eleven years have been a daily struggle, yet she firmly holds on in faith that *"there is a better future ahead."*

Crippling Illnesses—Sylvia "Sparks" Byrnes

Life's adversities sometimes come in the form of debilitating or life-threatening illnesses. Those who suffer such maladies often struggle to fight the temptation to seek patented answers or to blame God for being mean and uncaring. At other times, those afflicted fight the notion that they are being punished for a past failure or unconfessed sin. Conversely, people of faith believe that God can and will use the suffering of others to reach unbelievers or to encourage some who may be confronting similar calamities. "Sparks" Byrnes is a marvelous example of the latter. When I decided to write this book, I knew that it should include Sparks, who has long demonstrated the greatness of women during adversity. She has been a tremendous inspiration to many for over twenty-five years.

Sylvia Haugh was the third of three children born to Hubert and Blanche Haugh in Philipsburg, Pennsylvania. Despite a limited education, her father was a great provider, and Sylvia grew up in a modest, loving home with her mother, and an older brother and sister. She loved animals and had numerous dogs, cats, and a horse. She learned to ride at an early age and would eventually own horses in her adult life. Sylvia's father was her personal hero, but she experienced her first great challenge in life at thirteen-years-old when he passed away. Her loss was devastating and affected her deeply; nevertheless, she grew up surrounded by family, friends, and teachers who helped her discover a love for art.

After graduating from high school, Sylvia enrolled in Penn State University where she met her first husband. She got married in her junior year and followed her husband into the Air Force. Within a few years they had two daughters and a son. The latter was born mentally challenged, but was raised along with the other two children. Over the years, the family was stationed in Turkey, New Hampshire, and Ohio. Sylvia's husband was next sent to Vietnam for a year. During this time, Sylvia returned to college and received a degree in Art Education.

The second great adversity in Sylvia's life occurred when her husband returned from Vietnam and no longer wanted to be married to her. He had found someone else and they were soon divorced. The children went to live with their father to maintain a modicum of stability. At age thirty-two, she began a new life as a teacher in Dayton, Ohio. For the next nine years she worked near Wright-Patterson Air Force Base, and many of her friends and associates were people from the base.

While living and teaching school in Dayton, Sylvia met a tall, good-looking Air Force major who seemed very interested in her. His name was Donn A. Byrnes who had grown up in the Air Force and had been a fighter pilot. He later earned a degree in Electrical Engineering and worked on several major aircraft development projects at Wright-Patterson. A cautious relationship ensued because Donn was also divorced and had the responsibility for four girls. The two became closer as Sylvia discovered that she could trust Donn, and that he kept his promises. Furthermore, Donn discovered that Sylvia's personality had very interesting "corners" that ignited a "spark" in him. He wanted to keep those corners as they were, and he soon proposed marriage to her. That did it for Sylvia and she became "Sparks" for Donn in 1971. Henceforth, Sylvia would be known as "Sparks." He was forty and she was thirty-six. The uniqueness of their relationship and tone for the rest of their lives together was established when Donn's four daughters accompanied Donn and Sparks on their honeymoon!

The Byrnes remained at Wright-Patterson AFB, Ohio until 1975. Donn was reassigned for his final assignment to Kirtland AFB, New Mexico. When he retired from the Air Force in 1978, Donn and Sparks bought a few acres on a desert mesa south of Albuquerque in Los Lunas, New Mexico. They began to build a house that took about twenty years to complete. They enjoyed "projects" immensely and shared a love for making crafts, ceramic pottery, and metal works. Sparks also began a small animal farm and allowed local children to come pet her animals that included horses, goats, chickens, dogs, cats, and an assortment of others. In addition, Sparks grew a garden and did considerable canning from the produce, most of which wound up as gifts to friends. For several years life was beautiful, and their collection of admirers and friends grew in great proportions. Their association with Kirtland AFB Chapel programs was particularly rewarding when Sparks got very involved with the Protestant Women of the Chapel. Her daughters grew into young women and Sparks' son was now fifteen years old.

In 1987, at the age of fifty-seven, adversity struck again. Sparks began to limp when walking and was subsequently diagnosed with multiple sclerosis (MS). This was a tremendous emotional challenge, but Donn stuck by her at every turn. Sparks refused to say, "Why me Lord?" Instead, she took this great setback in stride and sought spiritual strength from her friends at the Kirtland AFB chapel. Her personal faith was greatly magnified in 1988 when she woke up at 2:00 a.m. and had a "Come to Jesus" meeting with God. After reading the Bible and praying fervently, she concluded that "things just happen!" Sparks recognized that her life was tremendously blessed, and she gained the strength to face life with MS and not be hampered by its effects. To underscore this tremendous resolve in 1989, she decided to ride to the bottom of the Grand Canyon on a mule!

About this time, Peggy and I returned to Albuquerque after retiring from the Air Force. We soon resumed our friendship with the Byrnes that was established nine years earlier. By now their children were grown, married, or working in the area. Sparks was still walking upright with the aid of forearm crutches. She was as beautiful as ever and that special smile was ever in place. All who met or knew her marveled at such an indomitable spirit and independence.

Over the next few years, Sparks' condition deteriorated moderately and she had to rely on a wheel chair and a specially equipped van to get around. By now, she had a well-trained German Shepard that never left her side and readily protected her from danger while traveling alone. Very sadly, she had to give up her beloved animals and gardening. Instead of going into a deep depression that is normally associated with MS, Sparks chose to focus on what she *could* do and maintained an incredibly active life. The women of the base chapel became her close personal friends and she considered them great assets.

During my interview with Sparks, I asked what she wanted to say to others who might be facing adversity such as hers. She said,

"One should strengthen his or her relationship with Jesus and rely on God for all things. Pick your friends carefully and surround yourself with great people that you can rely upon when needed. Meditate and pray; ask God for strength to persevere when things get tough."

I flew into Albuquerque for the second time within a year for the funeral services of one of my dearest friends, and former Air Force officer, Donn A. Byrnes. Donn, an author of three books, had graciously helped me get started on my first published book, *An Uncaged Eagle*. But his wife, Sparks, was an amazing woman renowned in her own right as an artist, poet, and stellar craftswoman. Many throughout New Mexico and the United States have been blessed with gifts of her handiwork.

It was hard to believe only three months had passed since I sat in the Byrnes' living room interviewing Sparks. It was a special visit as we reflected over the many wonderful experiences and difficulties shared through the years. Over the thirty years of deteriorating mobility, Sparks was now confined to a motorized wheel chair. Ever present was that smile of peace that she displayed, no matter how difficult her plight. But now she faced the greatest challenge of her life—the loss of her beloved Donn! Donn passed away after a brief bout with cancer. He was diagnosed with Stage IV colon cancer in November 2011 and died January 23, 2012. His death was so sudden that he missed his first appointment with an oncologist.

I arrived at the funeral chapel where Donn's service was being held and was greeted by many mutual associates and friends from our fifteen years of residency in Albuquerque. Equally poignant were those missing who had also passed away during the eight years since Peggy and I relocated to Phoenix, Arizona in 2003. While we waited for the service to begin, my mind reflected back over the thirty-one years we had known the Byrnes family. Donn, Sparks, and their seven children were a blended family from their previous marriages. It was bittersweet joy to recall the beautiful relationship we shared, especially between Sparks and Peggy. As the service began, the family entered the chapel from the side. Sparks wheeled herself to the front of the pews and took a position before Donn's casket. Amazingly, she had a demeanor of peace and serenity, and she smiled at those present as if to assuage *their* grief for the loss of Donn. Throughout the service, Sparks' composure was incredible as different ones testified to the outstanding person Donn had been. Many testified about the uniqueness of Donn and Sparks and how they inspired others as a beautiful, loving couple.

Sparks maintained her composure and poise throughout the graveside service for Donn at the Santa Fe National Cemetery. Afterwards, friends hugged and expressed condolences to her and Donn's family. When I leaned over to embrace Sparks, my tear-filled eyes met hers. No words were necessary. She knew instantly that the love and admiration I had for Donn now passed to her for as long as I live. As I drove away from the cemetery, I thought, "What an incredible great lady!" Not even death could diminish her greatness, and death certainly was not the victor that day. Sparks' greatness is a brilliant light that will keep the dark cloud of the loss of Donn away. She and Donn were blessed with a special kind of love, and true love never dies. My prayer was that God would continue to shed His grace and mercy upon her until that final day. I look forward to the time when all of those who love the Lord will be with Him eternally in the *"new heaven and the new earth."*

Unrequited Love—A Nurse's Personal Sacrifice

Sometimes life can be a strange and inexplicable journey with cloudy outcomes or conclusions. Often, it's a winding road, steep mountains, dark valleys, or a tumultuous sea full of storms and crashing waves. Despite these uncertainties, there can be a once-in-a-lifetime love affair. This may happen in the most unlikely places, such as during war in a strange and faraway land. In the latter case, life for some is cut too short, and hearts are left forever empty, shattered, and unfulfilled. Yet, the broken-hearted must pick up the pieces and go on because life demands nothing less. Such was the fate of Mary Ruth Clark, a U. S. Army nurse in World War II. Today, at ninety-seven years old, Ruth, as she is called, waits for her lost love to walk through the door where she lives. Sixty-eight years have not dimmed the image or the love she had for her fiancé who was killed in action in the Pacific in 1945.

I first heard Ruth's incredible story early in 2011 at the funeral of her nephew-in-law, George Locke of Albuquerque, New Mexico. George was my dear friend and former boss on a project in the 1990s. He was the husband of Betty Clark Locke, the niece that Ruth raised. So who is Ruth Clark and what made her such a great human being?

Ruth was born September 15, 1915 on a small farm in Crofton, Kentucky. She was the fourth of five children, four girls and a boy, born to Ollie and John Clark. The family lived through World War I, the "Roaring Twenties," the Great Depression, and Prohibition of the early 1930s. Ruth worked on the farm, while attending school. Early on, she showed special qualities of caring for others rather than being concerned for her own needs. Ruth excelled in school and graduated at the age of fourteen. She first heard about nursing at an early age and said, *"From the first time I knew about nursing, I decided that was what I wanted to be."* However, she had to continue working on the farm until the late 1930s before being accepted into nursing school at the Deaconess Hospital in Louisville, Kentucky. World War II started in 1941, the day Ruth graduated and she volunteered to join the Army "to help save lives."

In 1942, Ruth joined a group of thirty other nurses from across the country. On May 5, 1943, the unit departed on a troop train for San Francisco, California to prepare for deployment to the Pacific Theater. Ten days later, the unit boarded the U.S.S. West Point for a two-week journey to Melbourne, Australia. After an overnight stay, they traveled by train to Brisbane for their first military training. Since the nurses had no previous military experience, this training included military customs and courtesies; field sanitation; defense against air, chemical, and mechanized attack; personnel administration; military requisitions and property responsibility. They were also issued jungle clothing and personal medical kits.

The final stop for the nurses was Charleville or "Bush country" for a six-month stay. The load and condition of patients was not critical but still required considerable care. The nurses next traveled to Warwick Farm about twenty miles from Sydney to take care of troops from the 32nd Infantry Division. This front-line unit suffered heavy casualties and numerous malaria cases. The nurses worked twelve-hour days, seven days a week, since many patients had sustained multiple wounds, were in severe shock, or required immediate amputations. Ruth worked as a surgical nurse and was involved in some of the most traumatic cases.

In November 1943, Ruth's group arrived in Milne Bay, New Guinea. The tropical climate caused malaria, scrub typhus, dengue fever, and tropical dysentery, which together resulted in four times as many casualties as did battle-wounds. The nurses also were susceptible to these diseases and had to take Atabrine to guard against malaria. As the war progressed, the group left New Guinea and arrived in Morotai, Netherlands East Indies. Here they were actually in the line of fire, and the post was bombed every night for two months. Ruth and her cohorts treated the wounded by day and slept in foxholes at night. Later, the unit moved on to Luzon, Philippines and served until the end of the war.

Despite the rigors of war, Ruth, like scores of other nurses and women, managed to snatch a few cherished moments of escape from time to time. Some experienced the love of a soldier who crossed their path. Although fraught with great uncertainty, these relationships were deep and intense. The lovers knew that war would likely deny them a chance for a permanent love affair, yet they desperately seized the precious moments that fate allowed. Those who have not served during combat cannot understand the dynamics of the heart in the crucible of survival, day-by-day or moment-by-moment. Those who have experienced an intimate relationship during war and later lost a lover, suffer a choking agony beyond expression. Their long-held memories defy description, logic, and time. The love between a man and woman that is experienced during war is eternal, and such love never dies.

During the four years that Ruth served in the Pacific, she allowed her heart to embrace the love of a soldier twice. After a brief affair, the first soldier was killed in action. Although Ruth's first experience ended abruptly and painfully, she ventured again into the dark unknown. Despite being filled with trepidation, she allowed her heart to love another soldier. This time the relationship lasted long enough for the soldier to give her an engagement ring. They took the risk and dared make plans to be married on his next break from combat. Once again, Ruth's destiny and hopes came to a tragic end. Her fiancé was killed in battle! After twice suffering such painful wounds of the heart, Ruth vowed to never love again and decided that she would never marry. She kept secret the ring given to her and the story of her broken heart for over sixty years!

August 14, 1945 was just another day in the routine of Ruth when the news came that Japan had surrendered. The war was over! The news ignited a spontaneous and wild celebration, and the hospital staff and patients joined in the revelry. For those who had a lost a sweetheart, the end of the war was a hollow victory. Thus, Ruth sought to be alone with her thoughts of the man she would never see or hold in her arms again. The overwhelming emptiness gnawed at the pit of her inner being and the ache and sorrow were relentless. Only God knows the pain Ruth bore that night, and only He could give her the resolve and strength to go forward in the days and weeks that followed.

When World War II ended in 1945, Ruth came home to a society that readily accepted nurses as professional members of the nation's health care system. The war had changed the perception of nurses forever. Ruth also faced the death of a sister who left a seven year-old girl to be raised. Since she had experienced the loss of her own mother when she was four years old, she did not hesitate to take little Betty Clark, her niece, as her own to raise. Ruth's experience during the war enabled her to grow personally and professionally. This enabled her to quickly gain employment in the Veteran's Administration Hospital in Louisville, Kentucky.

Over the next thirty-five years, Ruth lived her childhood dream of providing care and comfort to others as a nurse. She worked in several hospitals in Kentucky and Arkansas, and held positions as a surgical nurse supervisor, head nurse, and provider of youth training programs. Throughout her professional career, she always put the welfare of others ahead of her personal desires. After retirement, Ruth continued to help others as a Pink Lady, Sunday school teacher, and tour guide. She did a beautiful job raising her niece, Betty, through high school and college. Today, Betty and other relatives tell stories of this remarkable, kind, and compassionate woman who lived her life making others comfortable and happy.

Ruth's family got the surprise of their lives when she gave the ring from her sweetheart to her grandniece for a wedding gift. Betty had seen the ring while growing up, but she was never told about Ruth's love and heartbreaks during WW II. Ruth finally told the story behind the ring.

When I heard Ruth's incredible story of love and sacrifice, it brought back memories of my childhood during WW II, and I was anxious meet this great creation of God. In October 2011, I took a trip to Albuquerque, New Mexico to interview Betty and Ruth. In particular, I asked Betty about possible suitors or male relationships in Ruth's life and found out there were no significant men in her life. Ruth told Betty that she didn't ever want her to feel neglected. Simply, Betty's happiness and well-being always came first, and there was no time to get seriously involved with a man.

Today, Ruth lives in an assisted care facility a few minutes from Betty's home. She had been told about my visit and seemed to be waiting for another visitor when we arrived. While being introduced to her, she looked me over carefully as if trying to discern a familiar face. Soon, she wanted to know if I was comfortable and if my coffee was okay. Although Ruth is ninety-seven years old, she is still able to move about, though slowly. Her blue-grey eyes are still keen and observant, yet somehow I felt that she was a bit disappointed in my visit.

After the visit with Ruth, Betty told me a stunning vignette to this story. Recently, Ruth had told Betty that she sometimes imagines her long-lost sweetheart will walk through the door while she's sitting in the lobby. Thus, sixty-eight years later the memory of his face is still vivid in her mind! I was saddened that I was not the face for which she had been waiting. Nevertheless, Ruth confirmed that true love between a man and woman is indeed very rare. Such love is only possible when the Lord allows two hearts to be united in Him. Since her youth, Ruth's life is a testimony that she is a gift from God; and only He could have possibly fulfilled her life after her painful losses during the war. Although ever so brief, I believe Ruth did experience the love of a lifetime. I sincerely pray she'll meet her sweetheart again in the realm of life after death and though interrupted by war and many decades, they will rekindle a love that is eternal.

From Disaster to Victory—Mia

The story of "Mia" is an incredible true story of victory over adversity. As a young girl, Mia became pregnant with her first child at thirteen; and gave birth to a second child at fifteen. At seventeen, she married the father of the children who proved to be an abusive drug dealer. Mia hit rock bottom at twenty; and narrowly escaped a jail sentence at twenty-one. Life could have ended there for Mia and her two children; but through a revived faith in God and an extraordinary personal effort, she achieved victory over adversity. After a life-changing turnaround, Mia completed high school, earned both a bachelor's and master's degree. Today she is an office director of a major corporation! The following is her story:

Mia was born in East St. Louis, Missouri in 1981 and was the sixth of eight children, five brothers and two sisters. Her mother had been married twice and had five boys when she met Mia's father who had an older daughter. They lived together without formally marrying, but the man treated the five boys as if they were his own. Mia and a younger sister were born of this union. She remembers having a decent life growing up because both parents worked hard to provide excellent care for their children. Her parents got along well, and Mia initially had excellent relationships with her mother, father, and her other her siblings. Mia considered herself a very happy kid at that point in her life.

Early on, Mia was considered to be a very special child. She started kindergarten at age four and learned to read and write early. She was inspired by the apparent love between her parents and wrote her first song at age seven. By then, she knew that "girls were different than boys," and she wanted to have a love like her mom and dad when she grew up. In the meantime, she also discovered a talent for singing. Her aunt owned a tavern, and Mia was frequently allowed to polish her young singing skills for the customers. She was also considered a "tom boy," ran track, and made top grades in school.

Mia's second grade teacher, Mrs. Jones, had a significant impact on her young life. Mrs. Jones had a granddaughter the same age as Mia. The two were friends, a lot alike, and were considered "gifted" children. Mia was about eight years old when her little friend was tragically killed by a runaway truck. Shortly after this accident, Mrs. Jones became critically ill and died a few weeks later. Mia was doubly saddened by these losses when death struck again in her immediate family. Her older sister from her father's earlier marriage was killed by a deranged husband. At such an early age, these tragic deaths had a profound impact of Mia for years to come as she struggled to understand God. Her mother was a Jehovah Witness and her father dabbled in Islam. Since Mia could not understand either, she began to rebel against religion and an uncertainty about God resulted.

The family continued to live in East St. Louis where her mother worked at General Motors. When the job required a move to Indiana, Mia and her younger sister came with her while their father remained in Missouri. The move resulted in a break-up between Mia's parents, and it resulted in a growing estrangement between Mia and her mother when another man entered their lives. Neither Mia nor her young sister got along with this man, and they suffered in the relationship with their mother. Often, they were left to fend for themselves and sought solace wherever they could. Disaster was imminent in Mia's life.

Mia began her menstrual cycle at eleven years old and knew she was developing early into womanhood. By thirteen, she had an eighteen-year-old boyfriend. Wanting to be impressive, Mia lied about her age and told the boy she was sixteen. The boy became a frequent visitor when Mia's mother was at work. It didn't take long before Mia and the boy became intimate, and she lost her virginity at age thirteen. She became pregnant after the second sexual encounter. Her mother became suspicious of the signs of pregnancy and took Mia to a clinic where her condition was confirmed. With the help of the clinic nurse, Mia refused her mother's request to have an abortion. Despite her mother's lack of close supervision, she still had high hopes that Mia would finish school and go on to college. Since Mia had demonstrated a high aptitude and earned excellent grades, a school administrator insisted that Mia be kept in the regular school system. This benefactor believed that Mia could still have a bright future. As a result, Mia was allowed to complete middle school in May and became the mother of a baby girl the end of the eighth grade.

Mia and her boyfriend continued their relationship after the baby was born. They were supported by their respective parents and lived at home. The relationship between Mia and her mother went downhill for a while, but soon improved after Mia made it clear that she intended to resume school the following semester. Fortunately, Mia had considerable support from other family and relatives.

Remarkably, Mia's academic performance continued in the ninth grade and she soon earned the respect of her high school counselors and teachers. She began taking birth control pills after the birth of her daughter and continued to have intimate relations with her boyfriend. Despite her precautions, she became pregnant with a second child at fifteen when the first child was just ten months old. This reality did frighten her and caused her to consider the history of both her mother and grandmother who began having children as teenagers. Although very young, Mia resolved at this point to break the mold of such a disheartening cycle. She was more determined than ever to finish high school without becoming pregnant again. Since many girls in the bi-racial school Mia attended suffered similar circumstances, continuing in school did not pose an insurmountable obstacle. Thus, she gave birth to a son and eventually graduated from high school at seventeen. Incredibly, Mia graduated with a 3.8 grade point average and had earned a few college credits!

When the second child was six months old, Mia moved into an apartment with the children's father. Although a high school drop-out, he had a considerable source of income. Mia suspected that her boyfriend was involved in illegal activities, but was happy not to look into the mouth of the "gift-horse." Thus they got legally married and began what Mia called "a nice family life."

While still seventeen, Mia lost her father. Earlier, he spoke at length on the telephone with Mia and her younger sister and asked if either of them had anything to tell him before saying goodbye. The conversation ended with him expressing his deep love for them. He died forty-five minutes later! The sudden death of her father caused Mia to think very seriously about her relationship with God. Her father died while still practicing Islam, which she never trusted, so she worried about his salvation. She reconsidered her earlier experiences of regularly attending church with her grandmother and realized that she had drifted far away from God. The immediate good that came from the death of Mia's father was her becoming more spiritual, and she decided to have a closer walk with God.

Mia was still determined to attend college, so at the age of eighteen she enrolled in college to pursue her childhood ambition. Somehow she knew that education was the key to long-term success, and that it was crucial to ensuring a real future for her children. As time passed, Mia's husband viewed her success in college as a threat to his control over her, financially and intellectually. By the time she was nineteen, the marriage began to fall apart when her husband became emotionally and physically abusive. Mia, however, had become addicted to an extremely comfortable lifestyle that included a beautiful tri-level home with a swimming pool, expensive cars, diamond rings, and expensive clothing for her and the children. She allowed the repeated hollow apologies from a non-repentant husband to keep her in an increasingly dangerous relationship. When she did call the police for help, her husband did not suffer any negative consequences because of his friendly relationship with some of the cops.

The final blow-up in the marriage happened when Mia was about twenty-two years old. Both she and her husband were arrested when the police were summoned to a particularly violent domestic disturbance. Both were later released from jail, but that fateful night Mia resolved to change her life once and for all. She prayed fervently to God: *"God if you free me from this present situation, I'll serve you for the rest of my life!"* Early the next morning, her husband was rearrested by federal officers and held on numerous drug charges. During the ensuing trial, the Feds also tried unsuccessfully to implicate her, but they did not have sufficient evidence to do so. The trial ended with her husband being sentenced to thirty years-to-life in the federal penitentiary.

Fortunately, Mia's home, cars, and other possessions had been paid for and were in her and the children's names. Consequently, she was able to stay put for a while. Always adept at being creative, Mia started a day care center and earned enough money to take care of her family as a single parent. Later, her husband's brother successfully evicted her and the children from the home and confiscated most of the personal property. Mia decided not to fight this turn of events and moved back in with her mother for a year. She worked in factories and other places to earn money to care for her family. In addition to this Herculean effort, she reenrolled in college and majored in psychology. When a job opportunity came along, Mia moved to Phoenix, AZ and continued to work hard to save a few dollars per month.

Despite the turbulence in Mia's life, her daughter and son weathered the storm because of her fierce devotion to them, and because she was completely focused on making their lives better. Her marriage was legally terminated in 2003 while her husband was still in prison. While working full time, Mia earned an associate degree in 2005. With the help of financial aid, Mia continued to work full time and earned a BS degree in 2006 and a MBA in 2007. When asked what motivated her to achieve these incredible accomplishments, she readily stated: *"God and my children! I was determined to overcome the earlier mistakes in my life and prove to my children that they do not have to be victims of their circumstances. I wanted to show them that they could be successful and lead God-fearing lives."*

Today, at thirty-one years old, Mia is an office manager of a major corporation and has purchased a home. She was able to make the down payment using her savings of $15,000; however, with tears in her eyes, she stated that her greatest achievements in life are her two children. She's tried to be a good example and confirm that no matter what difficulties they may face, how horrible the circumstances, they can still rise above it and make something of their lives. She taught them that they can overcome any tribulation by keeping God first in all they do. Of particular importance to Mia is the close, candid relationship she has with both her daughter and son. The nineteen-year-old daughter is a sophomore in college and is committed to living a life of abstinence until marriage. Mia's teenage son stumbled in this area but had the courage to confide in her and recommit to a similar personal challenge.

Thus far, Mia has kept her promise to God that she made nearly ten years ago. Because of her faith in God, her children, and work, she has avoided any long-term relationship with another man. She believes strongly that her faith in God and a commitment to Him has kept her from getting involved intimately with men. Moreover, she has a ready message for any man who shows an interest in her:

"Look, I am celibate, and I will not sleep with you. The next person I sleep with will be my husband!"

Mia's advice to other women who are contemplating marriage is this:

"Put God first, believe in Him. Have faith; nurture the seeds of that faith. Be careful of how much of yourself you give to someone else. Believe that your gift of self is 'sacred.' Keep that until God brings that special man into your life." She goes on to say, *"Make sure you are attracted to that person and that he has a personal relationship with Christ."*

Today, Mia has an optimistic outlook for her future. She would like to get married again after her children are out of the home and on their way toward successful careers. She admits that maintaining sexual abstinence is one of the greatest challenges for a single Christian woman. But she believes that men respect women when they respect themselves in that regard. Because she has rededicated her life to Christ, Mia believes that she restored her "spiritual virginity." She is confident that there is still something deep within her that has never been touched! Now she is content to let God lead her; if marriage is to be, it will be in His will.

When conducting the interview for this story, I often became emotional, as Mia would begin to cry, while remembering some of the more excruciating details of her life. I excused myself a few times just to regain my composure. What you have read is only a small part of what I was told, but I trust you will be inspired as much as I was. I am convinced that God created this young woman to be an inspiration to many. He used her trials and tribulations to demonstrate His love, compassion, and faithfulness to anyone who dares to trust Him. To God be the glory!

Dignity Instead of Submission

I was seventeen when I met Dee. She interviewed me for a job at the new restaurant where she had recently been hired as the manager. By now she was in her early thirties and had become astute in running a business. In addition, she was a stunningly attractive brunette with beautiful hazel eyes that were covered with tinted glasses. She dressed stylishly and had an "all business" demeanor but was courteous and respectful. The thing that struck me most about Dee was her absence of prejudice, aloofness, and discomfiture, normally exhibited by a white woman when personally speaking to a black man, young or old. This was especially so in the privacy of her office.

The new, western-styled restaurant featured a bevy of young carhops attired in cowgirl outfits with hats and boots to match. I was hired as a dishwasher with a promise to move up depending upon my performance. Everybody who worked there thought the world of Dee, our kind and caring boss. It didn't take Dee long to appreciate my work ethic and quick grasp of knowing what was needed regarding materials and supplies necessary to keep the kitchen going.

The high school kids quickly flocked to the place, and business was booming during the summer of 1955. By September, I had successfully worked through the kitchen and subsequently moved out to the front counter. There I filled the trays for the carhops and mixed malts and milkshakes, and made volumes of root beer floats. By the end of six months, I had also become Dee's trusted employee who kept a record of the inventory of supplies and equipment for the restaurant. Fate soon revealed Dee's fine inbred character that came under attack.

The married owner of the restaurant was a big, tall Texan who began to come by almost daily to "check on the business." His arrogance and swagger let most of us working there know he had a big crush on Dee. It was obvious that he wanted much more than Dee's talent as a smart, successful manager of his business. Often she was obliged to interrupt her duties and meet privately in her office with him. Just as often, Dee would emerge flushed and clearly irritated by the visit.

On one occasion after the owner's visit, Dee called me to the office, ostensibly to work on an inventory of supplies. As I entered the office, her body language and expression cried out for help. My earlier experience with my mother's personal suffering had sensitized me to a woman in emotional distress. Dee sensed that I understood her predicament and that I wanted to help her, but this was truly a bridge much too far for the both of us. Although I was man enough to feel compassion for this beautiful young woman, the circumstances of race, society, and status made it impossible for me to act upon it. Despite these incredible barriers, I still wanted to reach out and embrace her as a friend and console her. Unable to do so, I simply stood silently as she vented her emotion to the point of tears. The expression on her face told me how much she appreciated my unspoken compassion and friendship. Incredibly, the barriers imposed on us by society and circumstance did not preclude our effective silent communication. After Dee collected herself, I quietly excused myself and resumed my duties out front.

A short time later, I arrived at the restaurant to find that Dee had quit suddenly and no one knew where she had gone. We all were saddened by her departure and very angry with the owner because we felt he was the cause of Dee's quitting. For a long time, I pondered the events that had occurred. Years later, I realized that this aspiring young woman was put upon by a boss who was dead set on taking advantage of her position as an employee. Instead of giving in to keep her job, she quit to maintain the character and dignity instilled in her by humble, righteous parents from the backwoods of Arkansas. Dee would be in her eighties today if she is still alive. Whenever I thought of her over the years, I prayed that the Lord granted her a long, full, happy, and prosperous life. Surely she deserved that. Dee left an impact on me. I am grateful for the lesson of character, compassion, and respect I took from that experience over fifty-eight years ago!

VICTORIOUS WOMEN

Melodie Homer, Widow,
9/11 Airline Pilot

Mary Ruth Clark, WW II Nurse

Sylvia "Sparks" Byrnes

CHAPTER SIX

Four Women In My Life

Overview

"Charm is deceitful and beauty is vain, but the woman who fears the Lord, she shall be praised." Proverbs 31:30

Unequivocally, I can truly say that Daisy, Zella, Peggy, and Elsie—my mother, older sister, wife, and mother-in-law, are four of the most extraordinary women I have ever known. I am also tremendously fortunate to be the father of six adult daughters, two by birth, and four either by adoption or through mutual acceptance and love. God has blessed me immensely through these women, and they have had the utmost influence in my life. All that I am today can be attributed to their collective love, compassion, long-suffering, and ceaseless intercession before God on my behalf. I confess that I haven't always deserved such goodness; even now I may fall short of the glory of God. By witnessing how God worked in the lives of these women, I eventually came to love Him with all my heart, soul, and strength. In doing so, He opened my eyes and mind to understand that *all things are possible* through Him; *without* Him nothing is possible. Thus, the love I received from these incredible women has come **through** God, and the human imperfections and shortcomings of us all have been transformed into His perfect love **between** us. That is the real miracle in my life, and I truly praise God for it. I invite you to take a journey with me along memory lane as I highlight the virtues of the four most important women in my life.

Daisy Anderson Toliver (Feb 12, 1912–Jan 15, 1961)

Daisy was the second of nine children born on Abraham Lincoln's birthday to Bob and Zella Cole Anderson in the small village of Deberry in East Texas. She was the granddaughter of former slave, Shade Anderson, and Easter, a Native American. Bob was a tough taskmaster as the children grew up, but the family was close-knit and took pride in their honesty and strong work ethic. Early on, Daisy exhibited attributes of dependability, maturity, and a unique love for her parents and siblings. At eighteen years of age, she met Booker Taliaferro Toliver at a church social. Daisy was particularly impressed by the quiet, independent nature of young Booker, and he was taken by her outgoing spirit and aspirations for a better future.

Booker was born to David and Minnie Davis Toliver, October 4, 1911. He was also the grandson of a former slave, William Henry Davis who migrated from Alabama and settled in the small town of Bellevue in northwest Louisiana. Henry was a successful landowner and farmer, and he fathered twenty-six children with four wives during his lifetime. The marriage between Booker's parents failed early, so he struck out on his own at fourteen years of age. He found work about sixty miles away at a sawmill in Deberry, Texas.

Although "courting" in those days was under the watchful eyes of a girl's parents, Booker soon won favor with Bob, Zella, and Daisy. With Bob's permission, Daisy and Booker were married on May 24, 1930. Bob and the rest of the family built a small house for the young couple, and they started their lives together near the Anderson clan. That same year, the Andersons suffered the loss of Zella after the birth of her last child. Daisy and Lonnie, her older sister, were called upon to care for and nurture the baby boy during the early years of his life.

Over the next three years, a son Wilbert and daughter, Zella Faye, were born to Booker and Daisy. The country was in the midst of the "Great Depression," and it became increasingly difficult for Booker to support his family on the meager wages from the sawmill. Though deeply attached to her family, Daisy agreed to move with Booker back to Bellevue where the Davis clan was successfully subsisting on the farm. By then, Henry's descendants had grown to nearly one hundred, and most lived on tracts of land bequeathed by the great patriarch. Again, with the help of relatives, Booker built a small home and settled comfortably among the Davis Clan. The proximity of his homestead to a small farm owned by a white man, Frank Vickers, proved to be troublesome. Apart from the persistent problem between Booker and Vickers, life was uneventful for most of the Davis descendants. Booker and Daisy added another son and daughter to the family, William and Arneater, but William died when he was only a few months old. I and a younger brother, David, were born in the next few years.

My first recollection of my mother was when I was about two years old. In a quiet, peaceful world, I experienced the care and warmth of a loving family whose center was *"Ma Deah,"* the colloquialism for *Mother, Dear.* From my earliest memory, Ma Deah was a compassionate caregiver, fastidious homemaker, and loving wife and mother. She was a young, industrious woman who also catered to the community with a store of homemade cakes, cookies, and candies while serving as the local hairdresser. As such, our small home always had visitors who relished my mother's treats or services.

The tranquility in our black community came to a sudden and traumatic end in 1942. The feud over land boundaries between my father's land and Vickers finally erupted into a physical altercation. Vickers got the worst of it, and my dad had to make a rapid escape to save his life. The fact that a black man struck a white man was intolerable in the white community, and an example had to be made to "keep the blacks in their places". The "appropriate" response to an "uppity n-----" was simple—lynch him!

My mother endured daily harassment from the local sheriff, Vickers, and known Ku Klux Klan members that came looking for my father. This was a horrific experience for my mother and her five young children, ages eleven to ten months, respectively. Despite the grave danger, my father returned late one night to check on the family, but his visit did not go undetected. We were awakened early the next morning by barking dogs and menacing voices outside our house. Frank Vickers, the sheriff, and the Klan had gathered outside our home intent on doing bodily harm to my father. My mother was barely able to restrain my father while dispatching my older brother to rouse the Davis clan for help. With help of armed relatives, a standoff resulted, and my dad escaped for the second time.

Vickers and his henchmen continued to harass our family without warning, and they issued menacing and profane threats when having to leave empty handed. My father returned late one night to get us out of Bellevue. We were hidden beneath bedding, clothing, and a few other household goods in the back end of a large panel truck. Our escape could have ended tragically, but the hand of Providence was clearly upon us. We arrived safely in Shreveport thirty miles away to begin the next saga of our lives.

As World War II progressed, several Davis descendants migrated to California to take advantage of the prosperity brought on by the mobilization of our nation. My father joined the relatives in Oxnard, California and soon found a job and home for our family, which now included my younger brother, William Ray. Once again, Daisy was obliged to uproot and move farther away from her family in east Texas. When money became available, she loaded us six children on a train and headed to California to join our father. But she harbored a dream of returning to Shreveport to build a home near her folks in east Texas.

We arrived at the Los Angeles Union Station the summer of 1944 filled with the excitement for a new life. The cavernous station was filled with scores of uniformed men and families in a beehive of humanity. My father was finally spotted, and my mother and we children descended upon him with outstretched arms. He had purchased a 1941 Buick four-door sedan that comfortably accommodated our family of eight. We gathered our baggage and were soon on our way to our new home in Oxnard. The apartment was small and meager, but my mother was more pleased to have her family together again. Within a short time, we adjusted to a completely integrated society and soon forgot the terrible experiences of the South. After enrolling four Toliver kids in school, our mother quickly found a job and started earning money for her dream home. With both parents working, we moved into a larger apartment near Oxnard Naval Training Base.

Life during WW II in Oxnard was idyllic in the beautiful paradise of California. It was a great time to be growing up where the energy of patriotism and togetherness filled the air. Everyone was committed and focused on doing his or her part to winning the war and to bringing our boys home safely. The war finally ended when Japan surrendered unconditionally on August 14, 1945. Shortly thereafter, the country began to demobilize; and many families were hard hit because of the loss of well-paying jobs. My father was reluctant to leave California, but Ma Deah insisted on returning to use her wartime savings to build a house in Shreveport. She got her wish, and the family joined a caravan of relatives headed back to Louisiana. We arrived in Shreveport, Louisiana on a cold night in November 1946. The return was a portent of many sad things to come.

The first major hurdle that faced the Tolivers was readjusting to a totally segregated culture and world. The stark contrast between California and Louisiana was reflected in the hostile attitudes of white people in every segment of society. Also, the lack of jobs in the post-war era posed an additional challenge in finding meaningful work, especially in the south. These factors added extra pressure on the marriage between my parents, and my father decided to return to California while the family remained in Shreveport.

My mother's determination, hard work, and persistence paid off. In early 1947, she used her savings earned in California to begin building a new home. By mid-summer the house was partially completed, and we moved in despite the work that needed to be completed before winter. Money from my father was minimal, so my mother started a drop-off laundry service for nearby white folks in the area. The four older children participated in this enterprise, and we earned enough money to complete the inner walls and room partitions of the house just before Christmas. Despite our meager existence, Wilbert and Zella helped my mother ensure a bit of cheer in our home.

After a very tough year, my father returned to Shreveport the summer of 1948. His absence had been a major factor in the deteriorating relationship between him and our mother. Time and distance had been the enemy; and the love, and the trust they once knew was irreparably broken. Sadly, neither of them seemed capable of bridging the gap. One night, an argument became extremely caustic, and we older four children immediately sided with our mother to protect her from physical abuse. Angered and perplexed, my father gathered his belongings and left the house in a rage. This tragic estrangement lasted for thirty-three years!

My mother's suffering after my father's departure was overwhelming. I had never witnessed such complete despair. Nor could I comprehend the heart-rending impact of a failed marriage after eighteen years and six children, ages four to sixteen. For many weeks afterwards, I awakened to my mother's early morning prayers and weeping. I often knelt beside her, cried with her, and tried to understand the God from whom she sought help. Sometimes my two younger brothers woke up and joined us. We did our best to console Ma Deah, but the task was just too daunting for our young minds. Nevertheless, her profound faith in God during the excruciating emotional pain gave us a small measure of hope.

Despite the challenge to feed, clothe, and care for six children, Ma Deah's fierce determination and trust in God eventually provided the basis of my faith and trust in prayers. The seeds of my faith were planted in the soil of our adversity, and my mother's tears sustained them until they took root! Ma Deah also insisted that each of her children attend a church revival to get "saved"; there were no options. Eventually, we complied to avoid her "earthly retribution" or the "hellish wrath" she was still capable of dispensing to disobedient children!

In the early 1950s, thirty-eight year old Ma Deah struggled with chronic fatigue, loneliness, and other emotions not readily discernible. She eventually succumbed to the attentions of a "male friend" who helped out the family from time to time. This relationship became intimate and eventually resulted in a brother being born into an already difficult situation. The man supported his son, but he was not willing to be a father to six additional children. The criticism endured by my mother from some of the neighbors, church members, and peers was very painful, and I had my first bitter taste of hypocrisy from those who lived in "glass houses." I also made hasty youthful judgments against my mother and her friend. Years later, the mistakes in my own life caused me to realize the folly of holding others to a higher standard than I could achieve myself.

Notwithstanding her human frailties, Ma Deah never ceased to urge us forward and kept us focused on getting an education. Having reached only the eighth grade, she held education in great esteem, and graduation from high school was a "must" for each of us. Wilbert graduated in 1951 and was accepted for a work-scholarship program at Tuskegee Institute, Alabama. That same year, Zella married her childhood sweetheart, Anthony "A. W." Rye, and started a family of her own. With the two older siblings gone, I became the "man of the house" and was immediately put to the test. Ma Deah became critically ill and was hospitalized for over a month during the summer of 1951. It was especially difficult that year due to the scourge of polio that hit the entire nation. Miraculously, Ma Deah was not stricken with polio, but she nearly died from rheumatic fever and a terribly weakened heart. She fought back like a broken-winged bird, but it took many weeks to recover. That year, Ma Deah and I developed a very strong bond of mutual appreciation, respect, and a dogged determination to face the future regardless of the difficulties encountered.

The next several years continued to be a challenge, but Ma Deah's determined efforts to resist defeat compelled all of us to persevere. She encouraged us forward with the following exhortations:

"Can't is dead; and couldn't was whipped until he died."

"Nothing beats a failure but a try.

"Keep your face toward the sun and the shadows will fall behind you."

"The Lord will make a way out of no way!"

In additions to these frequent admonitions, my mother strongly encouraged us to aim high in setting our goals:

"Aim for the sun; if you miss it, you'll hit the moon. If you miss the moon, hitch your dream to one of those millions of stars; then always have faith in God!"

I embraced these profound words of my mother to forge ahead throughout my life. Not only were they comforting during difficulties, but I could still hear her voice in each of them.

With such encouragement, my younger sister, Arneater, finished high school and got married in 1955. Wilbert graduated from Tuskegee Institute in 1956. This was a great day for Ma Deah as she saw her first born achieve an enormous goal. The rest of us were also filled with admiration and pride in our older brother. The next year, my sister, Zella, started college at Grambling State in Louisiana, and I followed Wilbert's example and enrolled at Tuskegee Institute. Two years later, David finished high school and joined me at Tuskegee.

In 1958, Ma Deah fell ill again and became progressively worse over the next three years. She had a recurrence of rheumatic fever, severe arthritis, and symptoms of lupus. By the end of 1960, Ma Deah was practically bedridden. Zella, David, and I came home for Christmas, but our visit was overshadowed by our mother's deteriorated condition. We did our best to make her as comfortable as possible, and even though her plight seemed dismal, we prayed for a miracle.

On Sunday morning, January 15, 1961 (Dr. Martin Luther King's birthday), I received the dreadful news that Ma Deah had passed away. Wilbert, David, Ray, and I returned home for the saddest time of our lives. It was a dark, overcast sky with a bone-chilling freezing rain on the day of our mother's funeral. In spite of the horrible weather, scores of people gathered to pay their respects. The gathering included a multitude of relatives, friends, neighbors, school mates and teachers, and many that we didn't know had known our mother. Every space in the church was occupied, and some had to leave because there simply was no space for them to stand. The testimonials, confessions, and praises, confirmed an "Angel Unawares" had been in our midst. While Ma Deah left a host of grieving loved ones behind, she had forged a legacy of love, compassion, hard work, and selfless service to her family, friends, and neighbors.

The family gathered after the funeral to say our good-byes. Grandpa Bob, my mother's father, admonished all of us to follow the great example of Ma Deah. She truly had been a loving mother, daughter, sister, and friend to so many. We vowed to continue our pursuits for a better life through education, faith, and hard work. The immediate path ahead was bleak and uncertain, but all of us knew that we had a charge to keep: Daisy Lee Anderson Toliver deserved a *living legacy!* With God's help, each of us committed to living the rest of our lives to make that a reality. Of her seven children, four graduated from college and earned Master's degrees; two became educators for over thirty years; four served the country in the military, one retired as a Colonel after twenty-six years, another retired as a Master Sergeant after twenty-four years. All were/are Christians.

Zella Faye Toliver Rye (April 28, 1933–)

Zella was the second child born to Daisy and Booker Toliver in Deberry, Texas. She was five-and-a-half years older than me, and demonstrated the "instinct of motherhood" at an early age. Along with my older brother, Wilbert, she had the responsibility of seeing after four younger siblings. My first recollection of her was similar to that of my mother, Daisy. Zella was very attentive, caring, and protective of her charges. I can never remember a time when she was not hovering over us younger children, making sure our needs were met before hers, or standing before us in the presence of danger.

After the family's escape from Bellevue, she was primarily our babysitter as our parents and brother sought work in the cotton fields and on farms near Shreveport. After migrating to Oxnard, California, she continued to be the big sister in charge. When the family returned to Shreveport, Zella was entrusted with even greater responsibility in caring for the younger children of the family. She was only fourteen when our father left the family. By then, Ma Deah relied heavily upon her to help keep the family laundry business going, and when necessary, discipline the sometimes precocious younger brothers. Zella was our tutor for schoolwork, teacher in home chores, and comforter in times of despair. She was also a fierce protector against those who dared threaten any of the family. At eighteen, Zella married her childhood sweetheart A. W. Rye, Jr.; however her strong commitment to the family did not diminish. By then, I had developed a close, mature relationship with Zella. Like her, I now had a very protective attitude for everyone in the family.

A. W. truly adored and loved Zella, and it wasn't long before her mother-in-law discovered the precious jewel she had inherited as a daughter. By the time the second and third children were born— her first grandson and second granddaughter- "Big Mama" was one proud mother-in-law and grandmother! It became a virtual fight for the opportunity for us to keep the grandchildren from time to time.

After six years of marriage, Zella and A. W. decided they needed more education to provide a better life for their family. Our brother paved the way by working his way through college and graduating the year before. Zella was inspired to follow his example. To achieve this goal, A. W. worked two to three jobs at a time so that Zella could pursue a college education. With the help of her in-laws, our family, and my younger brother, David, as baby sitter, Zella enrolled at Grambling State University in the spring of 1957. With sheer determination and hard work, she earned a B.A. degree, with honors, in just three years. She achieved this major feat while shouldering the burden of our chronically ill mother who was now largely bedridden.

Over the years, Zella and A.W. proved to be a Godsend to the Toliver family. They were persistent beacons of hope that kept us younger siblings encouraged and focused on our goals in life. Like our mother, Zella relied on a deep faith in God and prayers; and she made sure that we regularly attended Sunday school and church. When times became exceedingly difficult, Zella kept us from giving in to despair caused by the woeful circumstances in our lives. With the kindness and generosity of A. W., she always found a way to bring joy into our lives. They never let Easter or Christmas pass without providing gifts, clothing, food, or some other much needed support. When our mother fell ill and was confined to bed for nearly three years, Zella and A. W. were the primary caregivers. The rest of us were either away in college or unable to assist. When our mother died shortly after Zella graduated from college, she and A. W. took full responsibility for funeral and burial expenses. Through their love and support, the rest of her siblings were able to move forward after such a painful loss.

Zella's career in education spanned over thirty years as a classroom teacher, supervisor, and school administrator in the Shreveport School District. In 1968, their first child, Linda, finished high school and enrolled at Southern University in Baton Rouge, Louisiana. A. W. fulfilled his deferred dream and enrolled at Wiley College in Marshall, Texas. Both father and daughter graduated four years later, and A. W. taught school for the next twenty years. Anthony III, the son of Zella and A. W., joined the U.S. Army; and their third child, Debra followed in her mother's footsteps and graduated from Grambling State University a few years later.

In the years that followed, Zella was the unshakable, immoveable "rock" in the family. When our sister died at age thirty-two, Zella took Arneater's four-year old daughter and raised her to adulthood. Years later, she took in her mother-in-law and a granddaughter. As we progressed through life, Zella's home was always the place to which we returned. During my twenty-six years in the Air Force, her address was my home of record. Her prayers for my family and me were ever present before the Lord, and when I served two combat tours in Southeast Asia, Zella prayed me through the perils and rigors of war.

Zella has been a faithful servant in Goodwill Missionary Baptist Church for over sixty-five years. The Toliver children were baptized in this church and moved away in time. Zella, however, has been a mainstay, and is one of the longest continuous members. She has served as a choir member, Sunday school teacher, program director, fund raiser, and whatever else needed to be done. She has also worked diligently in the community through numerous organizations to help the less fortunate. Countless hours have been spent taking care of unwed mothers, the poor, and the homeless. When other relatives needed a home or required special care, Zella answered the call. The ceaseless compassion, generosity, love, and patience of Zella and her husband, rescued scores of people and kept them from falling into an abyss of hopelessness.

Five years ago, Zella suffered a massive stroke during back surgery, and she is now confined to a wheelchair. Her mind, however, is still as sharp as ever, and she can be found directing the care for others who may need her help. Recently, her children, grandchildren, family, and friends gathered in Shreveport to celebrate Zella's eightieth birthday. It was a wonderful celebration of her life, but a very special person was missing. A. W. had passed away two years earlier. They had had been married fifty-nine years. Along with scores of others, I have been mightily blessed by these two precious people. I am very proud to say they have been my first role models and dearest friends.

Margaret Ann "Peggy" Hairston Toliver (June 6, 1938 -)

I began this section of the chapter on June 6, 2013, the seventy-fifth birthday of Peggy, the love of my life! Her youthful looks, good health, and sharp intellect belie that fact, for she is truly a miracle lady who is highly favored by the Lord. The love that our children, family, and friends have for Peggy was evident by the telephone calls, dozens of birthday cards, and beautiful gifts received from across the country. I don't know of a single person who does not appreciate and admire my wife of fifty-one years. What makes this woman so unique?

On June 6, 1938, the third of four children was born to Harvey Wally and Elsie Caulk Hairston in Baltimore, Maryland. She was named Margaret Ann, after her maternal grandmother, but was soon nicknamed "Peggy." The remarkable fact about her parents is they were married for seventeen years before their first child, son Harvey, was born. Elsie was thirty-seven years old! Thus, the subsequent births of daughters Elsie and Peggy, and son, Jimmy, were considered miracles from God. The Hairstons and Caulks were very close-knit families, and the rejoicing and celebrations for each birth continued for years. Since most of the relatives were more like grandparents, a bit of spoiling of each child was inevitable.

The Hairston children had a great life growing up during WWII in a warm, loving family, community, and church. On D-Day, June 6, 1944, Peggy was certain everybody was celebrating her sixth birthday! She grew up under the very strong Christian influence of her mother, grandmothers, aunts, and church members. While attending a church youth conference at sixteen years of age, Peggy answered the altar call and made a resounding profession of faith to follow Jesus Christ. Many years later, Peggy's mother told me her spirit-filled commitment was strong and unwavering, and that it set the entire course of Peggy's life. Her father, Harvey, didn't attend church often, but he was a faithful financial contributor. Moreover, he was an outstanding provider for his immediate and extended families. The Hairston children had a fun-filled life growing up and participated in activities such as the school band, thespian group, and academic clubs. Thanks to their mother, all of them were avid readers as far back as they could remember.

Peggy graduated from high school and attended Morgan State University in Baltimore, earning a Bachelor of Arts degree in English in 1960. A year later, her father funded her continued education and encouraged her to attend the renowned Tuskegee Institute. He had read about the great educator, Booker T. Washington, and scientist, George Washington Carver, and thought it would be great for her to go learn about these great men. She planned to earn her Master's Degree in Education at Tuskegee Institute by mid-summer of 1962. Given her adventurous spirit and thirst for knowledge, her father promised to send her to study in France after she finished at Tuskegee. Unknowingly at the time, Peggy's father initiated the final convergence of the paths of destiny for Peggy's and my life!

On a warm September afternoon, nine months after my mother passed away, I met Peggy at Tuskegee Institute. As the new Air Force ROTC Cadet Corps Commander, I stood on the campus gazebo addressing potential freshmen recruits for the program. A young lady standing near the back of the crowd caught my attention, and I observed her for the duration of the presentation. Somehow, she looked familiar, so I made my way to her after the completion of the program. The allure of this young woman was even more startling up close. She was quite attractive, articulate, and surprisingly at ease in responding to my greeting. Her easy smile accentuated the soft radiance of a face with sparkling brown eyes. I was especially impressed by her calmness and poise, and I thought, "This freshman really has her act together." Over the next few weeks, I duly acted like an "upper classman" whenever I encountered Peggy on campus; but shortly thereafter my self-inflated ego was unceremoniously deflated when I discovered that Peggy was not a freshman but a graduate student!

Several weeks passed before I gathered enough courage to pay Peggy a visit. I had failed miserably in making a good first impression, but I was determined to recover and somehow earn her affections. Surprisingly, the strong feelings I had developed for her were unlike any I had ever felt before for a young woman. One evening, I abruptly cut to the chase and asked Peggy to marry me! The seriousness of my "unromantic" proposal caused Peggy to sit back for a few moments as she looked at me in disbelief. With a total loss of self-control, I blurted out what had been building in my heart for weeks. Despite the absence of even a kiss or an intimate embrace, I had fallen in love with Peggy and wanted her to be a part of my future. Peggy laughed nervously and spoke haltingly, *"Dick, you can't possibly mean that. You hardly know me; you have so much planned for your life and so do I."* Without hesitating, I said emphatically, *"Then let's do it together!"* Peggy did her best to brush me off, but her response lacked sufficient conviction to deter my bold pursuit. We continued seeing each other over the next several weeks, but she kept me at arm's length.

I replayed my initial "proposal" to Peggy over and over in my mind, and each time reached the same conclusion. I was definitely in love with Peggy, but realized getting her to reciprocate would be a steep hill to climb. In my attempt to showcase *my* attributes, I failed to fully appreciate the source of Peggy's character and strength. At twenty-three years old, she was a chaste, committed, and devout Christian who took very seriously the Biblical caution against being "unequally yoked." Conversely, my commitment to a Christian life was weak at best, and some of my personality faults apparently caused Peggy to back away.

I continued to pursue Peggy with fervor and made at least two more "proposals." While the intensity increased with each effort, my determination and perseverance could not match Peggy's resolute walk with the Lord. Each time, she rejected my offers as kindly as possible and finally made her "escape" during the Christmas break. While at home, she made a valiant attempt to put a safe distance between us with a "Dear John" letter. The rejection almost worked because I fully intended to squash my feelings for Peggy, and I didn't visit her when she returned. But who can control two hearts that are destined to be joined together? Swallowing my pride, I finally showed up at Peggy's dormitory one evening in late January 1962. It proved to be the turning point of our lives.

Peggy had another surprise for me; she bounded into the lounge smiling and acting like I was a long-lost friend! Her joy at seeing me was real, and I strained to maintain my self-control. Peggy grabbed my hands and smiled at me with a fire in her eyes I hadn't seen before. She suddenly embraced me and planted a soft, warm kiss on my lips as I stuttered in mid-sentence. After all these years, I still cannot find words to fully describe the assurance and sweetness of Peggy's love expressed in that first embrace and tender kiss. Nor can I describe the emotional explosion and powerful awakening of all my senses that night.

We sat looking at each other for a long time trying to fully grasp what had just happened. Our hearts had been inextricably united by a power not yet realized by either of us. Slowly, I realized why Peggy seemed so familiar to me the first day I met her. She was the girl that often escaped in my dreams! We both decided that our destiny had been providentially ordained; when God made each of us, He had the other in mind. Given that truth, we began the most extraordinary, improbable, and intense year of our young lives. I recalled my Mother's teaching: *"Where there is a will, there is a way!"* With that in mind, I unleashed my ingenuity and skills, revised my academic schedule, found a place to live, and negotiated work with Tuskegee Institute for the coming summer. My adrenalin and motivation were running on all cylinders. In the short expanse of the next twelve months, Peggy and I were married, earned our respective degrees, I received my Air Force Commission, and we had Gail, our first child!

We began our lives in the Air Force at Eglin AFB, Florida on a very high note. Although the nation was in the throes of the civil rights struggle, we were provided a house on base and welcomed by warm and friendly white neighbors. My career got off to a great start and during the next eighteen months, our second daughter, Renea, was born. I was subsequently assigned to Craig AFB, Alabama to begin pilot training—my life-long dream. Despite intense racial strife during the next thirteen months, our son, Michael, was born; I earned my pilots wings; and received a jet fighter for my follow-on assignment to Davis Monthan, AFB Arizona. The future promised to be exciting for me as an Air Force fighter pilot, but the calm before the first real storm in our lives was about to be broken!

Following my initial checkout in an F-4 Phantom jet, I was given a three-week notification before being shipped out to Vietnam. There was no easy way to tell Peggy she was about to be left alone with three young children while I went off to war. Worse yet, I had to leave before getting the family adequately settled in an apartment. Peggy and I were not the least bit prepared for a long separation, let alone my going to war. The practical and emotional requirements for such an event were overwhelming but had to be dealt with in an incredibly short time. The reality of my pending deployment slowly sank in, and I deeply regretted the unexpected, awesome load about to be placed on Peggy's shoulders. The only consolation was that Peggy and the children would be with family and friends in Baltimore while I was gone.

I deployed to Vietnam the day after Christmas, 1965. It would be an incredible year that changed our lives forever. The separation, loneliness, perils, and uncertainties wreaked havoc on our family and marriage. I still cringe when remembering that Peggy had to endure each day without knowing whether I was alive or dead. Through it all, Peggy kept her faith in God and prayed without easing for my safe return. Moreover, she wrote me a letter every day that I was gone. Even though the mail would sometimes be delayed several days, her love letters gave me strength and cause for hope. God blessed us mightily by allowing me to return safely eleven months later. There were no visible scars, but the emotional stripes were another matter to be dealt with in the months ahead.

On the evening of December 5, 1966, over 200 men, women, and children boarded a huge four-engine jet for the flight to Frankfurt, Germany. Final destinations included U.S. bases in England, Germany, Italy, and other locations in Europe. My family and I were headed to Hahn AB in the Eiffel Mountains in Central West Germany. Apart from the noise of babies and small children, the eight-hour flight across the Atlantic was relatively quiet. Many of us were still lost in our thoughts about those missing or killed in Vietnam. Yet, we were very grateful to have survived and to be back with our families.

After a few weeks, my family was settled in a small village near the base, and another stage of my career got underway. However, Peggy and I struggled to reestablish the great relationship we had prior to my departure for Vietnam. We were not alone in this predicament as many other young couples experienced the same frustrations. Unknowingly or unwittingly, most of us guys came home expecting our wives to be the sweet, dependent, devoted young wives we left behind. We still expected to be "lord and master" of our households. Conversely, most of us failed to appreciate the profound effects our wives and families suffered from the prolonged stress, uncertainties, and loneliness during our absence. Nor did we understand that war had ripped the precious innocence of our youth from our lives and destroyed it forever. While the men were away, out of necessity, the wives became independent. They cared for the families, managed the finances, kept the car in good order, and performed all the daily chores. These courageous women were no longer the helpless, sub-missive young spouses that our inflated egos expected.

As pilots, we escaped to our cockpits and to the many Happy Hours at the Officer's Club. Meanwhile, the wives were left alone to care for the children and home front, often while trying to assimilate in foreign communities. These unrealistic demands and expectations often left our wives in tears, and more than a few gave up and returned to the States. Thankfully, I was one of the fortunate few. While on a temporary assignment, I discussed my problem with a friend and his girlfriend. During the discourse, she helped me understand the tribulations Peggy endured during my year in Vietnam, and helped me see the situation through the eyes of a woman. The light came on for me that day and I began to "find my way home." After many months, I felt the desire to truly embrace my wife and children. I sent word ahead to Peggy, and when I returned, she excitedly met me on the steps of our apartment. Finally, it was great to be home after more than fifteen months! The real heroine in this near disaster was Peggy. Our marriage was saved by her deep, abiding faith in God, gentle spirit, and willingness to endure my callous attitude and behavior during these trying times. I was truly blessed to have "An Angel Unaware' in my own home!

My career continued to progress during the next several years; however, they were filled with a number of challenges. Peggy's father passed away just before Christmas in December 1967, and my young sister died in January 1969, leaving five children in need of care. Peggy and I adopted the older child, twelve year-old Glenette. A year later, we returned to the States and were obliged to take in Peggy's mother, Elsie, now in failing health. With a family of seven, we headed west to our new assignment in California. Two years later, I received my second assignment to Southeast Asia. Once again, we had to prepare for the clarion call of "Duty, Honor, and Country!" On the day of departure, Peggy and the family accompanied me to the airport. When it was time to go, I looked into Peggy's eyes and saw the mirror of my own soul. I could see the agony of our second separation for war, but she kept silent the gnawing concern for the uncertainty of our future. I still heard the quiet cry of her heart, and we both felt the pain of letting go, as lovers and soul mates. When walking away, I didn't look back for fear I didn't have the strength to continue the onerous journey. Only God heard my mournful, silent prayer for another safe return.

The combat over the skies of Southeast Asia was very intense when I arrived in June, 1972. When added to my first combat tour, I had flown 446 missions over South Vietnam, North Vietnam, Laos, and Cambodia. Unquestionably, Peggy, my mother-in-law, children, and a host of others prayed me through to the successful end of the most stressful year of our lives. The final accounting of the prisoners of war, those missing in action, and the loss of 58,000 young Americans were especially difficult and disturbing realities of the Vietnam War. The wives, children, and families of these astounding casualties would suffer for many years to come. Those of us who had been deeply involved over the years were left with a sense of futility and guilt for having survived. Many suffered in silence and hoped these anxieties and frustrations would pass in time.

I tried desperately to reconnect emotionally with Peggy and my family upon my return, but the year-long suppressed feelings for them left me detached and numb. The person I became in order to perform effectively in combat had to be left behind in Southeast Asia. It was a struggle to mentally separate from him and resume the role of a loving husband and father. There were just too many faces of the missing and dead flooding my mind. The feelings of guilt and remorse for being allowed to come home to a wife and family were too overwhelming. Once again, Peggy's compassion, love, and understanding were my saving grace. She and her mother had been a great tag-team in caring, nurturing, and teaching our children while I was away; and it showed in their positive attitude and behavior. Both of these ladies were "naturals," and I realized how fortunate the children and I were for having them in our lives.

The scourge of war haunted me for several years, and it was Peggy who helped me continue with my career to reach even greater professional heights. In 1974, I was assigned as an operational test pilot for the F-15 air superiority fighter, the greatest in the world. Despite one of the most exciting and successful assignments in my career, I still carried some emotional baggage of unresolved issues in my life. Peggy and many others continued to pray faithfully for my deliverance, and one day God decided to answer their prayers. I encountered a lightning strike while piloting an F-15 jet at twenty thousand feet. That proved to be the Lord's "creative two-by-four" that finally got my attention! As I wrote earlier in this book, that dramatic event resulted in my spiritual rebirth and a changed my life forever. With God's help, I finally became the husband and father that Peggy and my family deserved.

My career continued for another thirteen years, and my appreciation of Peggy grew with each passing year. The life I have been blessed to have for the past fifty-two years has been an incredible and rich journey. Peggy has been the greatest earthly gift in my life, and I have had the incredible blessing of her pure, unconditional love throughout our marriage. I could write an entire book and still fail to truly describe the greatness of this woman that I have witnessed up close and personal. I'll simply conclude by adding the following postscript:

> *Peggy Toliver is the epitome of the military wife. She met a myriad of challenges head-on with courage and fortitude during her husband's Air Force career. She is an exemplary model of fidelity, integrity, and motherhood as evidenced by three biological children and five additional ones taken into our family by love. Her life-long faith in God is unwavering and has sustained her through severe bouts of colon and liver cancer. Today, she is deeply involved with many family activities, church and community, and is chief editor of her husband's speeches, publications, and books. She continues a full life, cancer free for over twenty-five years. Peggy has traveled extensively and has touched lives throughout the United States and overseas. Family and friends alike proudly call her an "Uncaged Eagle" who is truly the "wind beneath their wings!"*

Elsie Caulk Hairston   (March 31, 1899–February 18, 1997)

Elsie Frances Roberta Caulk was born at the close of the 19th century in Baltimore, Maryland. Many of her ancestors had been "free Negroes" who lived along Maryland's eastern shore. Consequently, Elsie and her siblings completed high school in the early 20th century and resided in prosperous communities of the African Americans of that day. In 1919, she met and soon married Harvey Ellis Hairston from Richmond, Virginia. Early on in her life, Elsie became a devout Christian and was deeply committed to her family and church. As stated earlier, one of the most significant circumstances of her life was the inability to conceive children for seventeen years. In her own words, she always believed that God would one day honor her ceaseless prayers for children. Peggy was one of the four blessings that eventually arrived.

I met Elsie at Tuskegee Institute when Peggy and I got married. She totally accepted me at first sight; she hugged me affectionately and called me "son." At that moment, she became my "Mom," and a beautiful relationship began that lasted until her death thirty-five years later. Moreover, she immediately filled a void left by my mother's death a little over a year earlier. Eight years later, Mom became part of our household for the next twenty-seven years and traveled with the family during several stateside and overseas moves. During this time, she became known as "Grandma" to the scores who met and loved her at home and abroad.

Grandma was truly a Godsend in our family as a model of faith, hope, and love. She was the calm in the midst of the storms of life that we encountered. Grandma was there for Peggy and the children during my second combat tour in Vietnam. She was there when I came home a year later—tired, disillusioned, bitter, and angry over the futility of that war. Her prayers sustained me through my struggles, and she never gave up even when I strayed from my Christian teachings. When I stumbled as a husband and father, Grandma still covered me with her love and prayers, and the Lord allowed her to witness His "intervention" in my wayward life. I am certain her intercession with Him saved me from the wrath I deserved.

Grandma didn't just love me, she loved everybody. I can't remember a single person she didn't love. She dearly loved her children, her sisters and brothers, good people and bad people, sinners and Christians alike. In thirty-five years, I never heard her say one disparaging word about anybody. She just loved people like Jesus called us to do. Grandma was my close personal friend, confidant, and tremendous prayer partner, but she did most of the praying. My success in the Air Force and in life was due largely to the ready access to God through Grandma's direct, open line to Heaven.

After a brief illness, Elsie Frances Roberta Hairston passed away in our home on February 18, 1997, shortly before reaching ninety-eight years of age. For a long time I sat quietly holding her soft, gentle hands and reflected on her life. It was as if I could almost "see" her ascending to Heaven's gate with outstretched arms. Not surprising, she never looked back! We had been blessed to have a saint in our lives and our home, and it was comforting to know that the love she had for all of us would never die. Grandma was truly a virtuous woman.

"Many women do noble things, but [she surpassed] them all. Charm is deceptive, and beauty is fleeting; but a woman who fears the Lord is to be praised." Proverbs 31:29-30.

FOUR GREAT WOMEN IN MY LIFE

Mother, Daisy Anderson Toliver

Sister, Zella Faye Rye

Wife, Peggy

Mother-in-Law, Elsie Caulk Hairston

CHAPTER SEVEN

A Message for Men

Living in Ignorance

Men, let me begin by being brutally honest with you, and please allow me to speak to you in the first person. At the outset, please know that much of what I am sharing comes from lessons learned BY just living and from making and recovering from mistakes. I sincerely trust you'll take the words that follow as opportunities to learn from my missteps. Although I was intellectually smart when I began as a husband and father, I really didn't know what my *godly role* was supposed to be. I thought just being a reasonable, thinking, *"good guy"* was enough, and I relied upon my limited ability to do the right thing. I had been taught well by those I've already identified, but I was woefully short in Biblical knowledge and understanding. I believed in God and frequently prayed, especially during difficult times. I also had a great appreciation for the obvious things that God had created; however, I still thought of Him as an abstract being well beyond my grasp.

Seeing the Light

I am almost ashamed to admit that I once had a very hard head and a rebellious, hardened heart. This awful attitude was allowed to develop because of unresolved issues in my life and the preoccupation with my Air Force career. Both almost cost me my family and my life. Despite the expansive and magnificent evidence of God's creation, it took three dramatic events before I finally "saw" the Lord's greatness. The first awakening resulted from two combat tours in Vietnam seven years apart. The next was encountering a lightning strike while I was piloting an F-15 jet at twenty thousand feet. The last event occurred four years later when I ejected approximately six seconds before my crippled jet made a seventy-foot fiery crater in the ground.

The cumulative impact of combat resulted in a prolonged struggle to overcome the adverse emotional consequences of Post-Traumatic Stress Disorder. I believe the lightning strike was the Lord's "creative two-by-four" wake-up call. The near-death ejection incident caused me to realize that my "skill and cunning" account was woefully overdrawn! That day, God finally got my attention once and for all; it was decision time. I had strayed very far from my earlier Christian teachings and had failed in my personal and professional relationships. I tried to cover my shortcomings with good deeds and a false outward image; however, my best behavior fell well short of God's expectations and my responsibilities as a husband and father. Also, my "grace account" was woefully over-drawn, and my "green stamps" were no longer redeemable! There was no more wiggle room. I needed a major overhaul in my attitude, commitment, and dedication or I was doomed to suffer the dire consequences of open rebellion against God. I don't mind telling you, it was one of the most frightening places in my life. But by the grace and mercy of God, I was given a second chance to get on the right path and live according to His plan for me.

What God Requires

I began my "new walk" by attending Bible studies and by establishing new relationships with committed Christians. As my spiritual growth increased, my actions and performance as a husband and father also improved. I definitely felt a new accountability for my attitude, actions, and behavior. The clarity in the scriptures was especially convicting and the messages seemed to speak to me personally:

"For the wrath of God is revealed from heaven against all ungodliness and unrighteousness of men, who suppress the truth in unrighteousness, because that which is known about God is evident within them; for God made it evident to them. For since the creation of the world His invisible attributes, His eternal power and divine nature, have been clearly seen, being

understood through what has been made, so they are without excuse." Romans 1:18-20.

When I meditated over these words, I was inspired to be a better man, husband, father, and Christian. Clearly most men are without excuse to *"see"* and *"know"* God. The entire earth provides visible evidence each day we are blessed to wake up and experience the greatness of God's creation. These blessings include a new born baby, healthy children, man's incredible intellect, nature's marvelous beauty, medical research and breakthroughs, technology, endless inventions, and much more. Given such powerful evidence, man cannot escape the purpose for which God made him.

Getting to *know* God also gave me a greater appreciation for the different roles for men and women. When He created women, He imbued them with the *"motherhood"* instinct. Likewise, man was created with the *"fatherhood"* instinct for a godly purpose. God made and strengthened the man to love, protect, and safeguard his wife, family, and home. This basic instinct is apparent in every species of the creation. Accordingly, men cannot nor should not attempt to escape this God-given responsibility. Instead, we should be humble and thankful for being entrusted with an awesome opportunity to enable women and children to be what God intended them to be. By doing so, we are blessed to be an instrument through which God works His purpose for all of humanity. Whether a man believes in God or not, he is going to be held accountable for how he lives and treats women and children on earth. Thus, the urgency today to be Godly men, husbands, and fathers is greater than any other time that I have witnessed in my life.

Biblical Imperatives

Some men may go through their entire lives and appear to be successful in all they do; however, there are biblical imperatives by which we all will ultimately be judged. When a man chooses to be a godly husband and father, the biblical imperatives provide the applicable instructions. The first one is to have the right relationship with God. God commands us to love Him *"with all our heart and with all our soul and with all our strength."* Deuteronomy 6:5-6. This is a two-way love relationship. Just as God loves us, we are to love Him in return. Until such a relationship is established, nurtured, and preserved, no one can truly love another the way God intended. This is absolutely imperative between a husband and wife, but it is also true for any serious relationship—other family members, neighbors, friends, and professional associates. If you want genuine, lasting personal and professional relationships, let God be at the center. In doing so, we submit to His universal reign and accept His divine grace and mercy in all matters of our everyday life.

Another crucial biblical imperative is recognizing that *"all have sinned and fallen short of the glory of God"* (Romans 3:23). Thus, we need to confess our sins and ask the Lord to *"forgive our sins and cleanse us from all unrighteousness"* (1 John 1:9). If we are to be the man that the Lord requires, we must understand and believe that the *door of forgiveness* leads toward making peace with God and man. So don't allow failure or mistakes of the past to burden you unnecessarily. Know that the sins of your father do not have to be your albatross if you decide to make peace with God yourself! You do not have to fail as a father because your father before you failed. If you decide to make a covenant with God, the sins of your father *will not* be a stumbling block for you. If you have deep, unresolved issues in your life, the Lord is a forgiving God. He alone is able to remove the stain of guilt and set you free.

The next biblical imperative addresses God's plan for families. The first and second chapters of Genesis in the Bible explain the origin of the creation, including God's model for family that is anchored on the husband and wife. Amazingly and inexplicably, God created both male and female in His image, then *"God blessed them and commanded them to… Be fruitful and increase in number."* Genesis 1:28. He equipped them to do this by giving the seed of life to man. Next, He gave woman the unique *anatomical, biological, emotional,* and *physiological* attributes to nurture the seed of man on its nine-month journey until receiving the breath of life. Furthermore, God established the "oneness" between a husband and wife by proclaiming *"For this reason a man will leave his father and mother and be united to his wife, and they will become one flesh." Genesis* 2:23-24. I firmly believe these scriptures clearly establish the model for a godly family as the marriage between a man and a woman, and children born of them.

Perhaps the most difficult biblical imperative for men to accept pertains to their responsibility to wives as follows:

"Husbands, love your wives, just as Christ loved the church and gave himself up for her." Ephesians 5:25

Admittedly, this is a powerful command because husbands are charged to love their wives so much that they would readily give their lives for them. On their wedding day, most husbands would probably say *"yes,"* but the real test requires the husband to *live* this commitment every day of the marriage. A true-life example of this commitment was vividly demonstrated in a tragedy in Tucson, Arizona on January 8, 2011. A deranged man killed six people, including a nine-year old girl and wounded Congresswoman Gabrielle Gifford and seventeen others. When the hail of bullets began to fly, Mr. Dorwan Stoddard, 76, told his 75 year-old wife to dive for cover then dove on top of her. Mr. Dorwan was one of six people killed that day! His instant heroic demonstration of love for his wife should be an inspiration for every husband who is blessed to still have a wife to love.

When God blesses a man with a good woman who loves and cherishes him and has his children, he should do everything possible to reciprocate that love. He should strive to nurture and preserve that commitment and trust. Although a woman is capable of the most profound love, passion, and desire, she has a fragile heart that is always at risk of being broken beyond repair. When a man carelessly lets that happen, there may never be a second chance to mend such a broken heart and destroyed trust. The result is a profound tragedy for both that may never be overcome.

The Bible goes on to say that a wife should respect her husband. But these biblical standards require that both the husband and wife be totally committed and submissive to God in order for them to be met.

God also meant for the marriage between a man and a woman to be a permanent and holy union, and multiple scriptures confirm this expectation:

"Therefore what God has joined together, let not man separate… Anyone who divorces his wife, except for marital unfaithfulness, and marries commits adultery." Matthew 19: 1-8

"Marriage should be honored by all, and the marriage bed kept pure, for God will judge the adulterer and the sexually immoral." Hebrews 13:4

Despite the preponderance of divorces in our society today, even in Christian circles, God's Word still stands. However, permanency will not likely be achieved unless both parties in the marriage are committed to God and to each other. No one should be deluded about the hard work required by both the husband and wife in keeping their marriage together. To be successful, each has to be determined and willing to work each day to protect their investment in the lives of each other. Conflict resolution in a marriage is a "give and take" proposition. Simple math equations do not apply in such cases, and score keeping is a terrible idea!

The final biblical imperative I want to stress has to do with our children. I can tell you from personal experience that it is critically important that fathers get this one right. They rarely get a "second chance" to make a "good first impression" in the lives of their children. Missed school plays, graduations, and special events cannot be easily overcome. Careful and intentional investing early in the lives of your children will be one of the most important things you do in life. It will also give the most gratifying "returns" when you get older or approach the end of your life. The *earned* love and respect of your adult children is priceless and unequalled by any other personal accomplishment in life.

God expects a father to be the spiritual head of the family and commands them to impress godly lessons upon their children:

"Talk about them when you sit at home and when you walk along the road, when you lie down and when you get up. Tie them as symbols on your hands and bind them on your foreheads. Write them on the doorframes of your house and on your gates." Deuteronomy 6:6-9

Fathers are also specifically admonished thusly:

"Fathers, do not provoke your children to anger, but bring them up in the discipline and instruction of the Lord." (Ephesians 6:4).

These biblical imperatives are reliable and trustworthy guidelines. God is still loving, faithful, and merciful to those who obey Him in our age and time. He is unchanging, but as husbands we are still held accountable for teaching our children about God and for allowing Him to dwell in our homes and lives. When teaching and training your children, strive to be God-like: love unconditionally, be patient and long-suffering, always be ready to forgive, and always conduct discipline in love. It is especially important to remember this:

"Do not withhold discipline from a child; if you punish him with the rod, he will not die. Punish him with the rod and save his soul from death." (Proverbs 23:13-14)

Fathers, pay very careful attention when loving, teaching, and imparting wisdom to your daughters. To the extent possible, always let this be a joint husband-wife undertaking. One should reinforce the other. Recognize that little girls are fragile, impressionable, and trusting. Fathers are the first examples of what men should be and how young ladies should be cherished, handled, and treated. This is the crucial area in a girl's life where self-esteem is developed or lost! Pay very special attention to what you do here; the impact will be reflected throughout your daughter's life! Also recognize that each child is different and unique. One or the other may require handling with "kid gloves." If so, be alert to this and patiently do whatever it takes. When encountering things that only women can teach, step back and let the wife or another very trustworthy woman take over.

Common Sense Rules

A few common sense rules are highly encouraged at this point. Make a determined effort to learn the *"language of love"* of your spouse. Dr. Gary Chapman, a Christian counselor and author of *The 5 Love Languages: The Secrets to Love That Lasts* wrote about the importance of being able to express your love in a way that your spouse understands. These expressions are stated as: (1) Words of Affirmation, (2) Quality Time, (3) Gifts, (4) Acts of Service, and (5) Physical Touch. I believe the husband should take the lead in seeking to learn and apply the language of love to which his wife responds.

My wife and I were introduced to the languages of love over thirty years ago. We recently attended a marriage retreat and renewed our commitment to using the concepts of the language of love. I am thankful to say the concept is still working for us. The common sense application of the Five Languages of Love is this:

1. Affirm and help build up your wife's self-image by telling her that she looks good, the meal was great, and that her efforts around the home are noticed and appreciated.

2. If your wife responds positively to being together and doing things together, make a habit of such things. Watching sports on TV is a poor substitute for affection and love. A weekly "date" to the movies or a restaurant is a great place to start.

3. If your wife is not allergic to flowers, an occasional unexpected bouquet of roses just may be the "igniter" that day. Gifts don't have to be unduly expensive to get the desired effect. Whatever else you do, DON'T forget your anniversary and her birthday!

4. Try taking out the trash or doing the dishes after dinner without being asked to do so. If you know how, treat your wife to a home-made dinner with the room lit by candles. Try not to burn the house down, and please don't ask her to do the dishes afterwards!

5. If your wife comes home tired and slumps in a chair or sits down to take a break from house chores, it's a time to ACT! This is an excellent opportunity to stroke her back or rub her feet. Top it with affectionate words and a kiss. The "wow" factor in such cases can turn into exceptional results later.

Conclusion

I want to reiterate a significant truth: the Bible clearly teaches us that God intended the man to be the spiritual head of the family. But man, acting on his own, can never do the things I've delineated above. This is only possible if he is willing to submit to God and allow the Holy Spirit to be an indwelling presence in his everyday life. If we choose to live godly lives, we must regain an awesome respect for the Lord and *agree* with Him about righteousness and sin. We must follow His commands about marriage and family, about the sanctity of life, and fidelity in marriage. I cannot emphasize enough the value of a husband and wife who fervently pray together daily. My fifty-one years of marriage have been blessed in large measure by constant, committed prayers of my wife and me, especially during troubled and uncertain times.

We must also faithfully teach our children about God and how to love others as ourselves. This responsibility extends to grandchildren, great grandchildren, adopted children, and those who come seeking refuge in our homes through love. A godly husband and father ensures and promotes love as the binding force in his immediate and extended families. He takes this responsibility as a God-given opportunity to develop, nurture, and preserve effective inter-family communications. If our children are to have a viable future, husbands must provide a loving and nurturing family for them in which to grow and prosper. This is what God requires, and it's the parent's responsibility to make it happen. Above all, God must be the center of a family if any of these things are to be realized.

CHAPTER EIGHT

Accepting God's Plan

God's Plan for Humanity

As I conclude Section I of *Woman—A Godly Creation*, I sincerely trust that women everywhere and every age have been inspired and motivated to embrace or re-embrace the greatness that God has infused in you since the beginning of time. At the beginning of this book, I wrote about how God created man and woman and how He established the *"oneness"* between *them* and *Himself.* Accordingly, God gave a biblical command to man and woman to love Him with all their heart, all their soul, and all their strength. I truly believe that the commandment to love God is the crux of every other relationship between man and woman, parents and children, friends and neighbors, communities and churches, the nation, and even the world.

When relationships begin for all the wrong reasons, they will likely soon fail. When relationships break up, for whatever reason, man is not capable of fixing a broken body, heart, or spirit. If there are to be effective, fulfilling relationships, they must include the attributes of compassion, integrity, respect, trust, and above all, love! The Bible teaches that God is love, and if He is not at the center of both personal and professional relationships, I do not believe that these human interactions will ever have a lasting success. Regardless of all human aspirations, the plan for all of humanity evolves from the great Creator—God!

Unique Roles of Women

Giving birth to a child is still the most precious and unique God-given act of women everywhere. Those women who do not give physical birth still possess a God-given "instinct" of motherhood to use appropriately elsewhere. Many have adopted children, become guardians, or have been Big Sisters to countless children who lack motherly love. The latter concept embraces the sanctity of life and contradicts the notion that children born of another cannot be loved and cherished as one's own. I emphatically reiterate that *love* relationships trump *blood* relationships!

Another unique role for women is this: God often uses a mother, sister, wife, daughter, or other women to reach the hearts of men. He chose to give women that innate attribute that reflects His love and purpose for our lives. This truth is reflected in a myriad of stories about a "mother's love." Many of you who read this book can testify simply because you have been blessed to be recipients of such love. Moreover, the amazing power of a woman's love transcends circumstances, distance, and time. It is an everlasting manifestation of God's love for all of creation. Men are expected to love as God loves; but again, unless man loves God the right way, he will never be able to love others properly. This seems so simple, yet too many fail to this critical imperative of love.

We live in a world today where human behavior and practices contradict the biblical plan that God established for humanity. Young people, in particular, are ambivalent, confused, or outright rebellious. Sadly, they are the offspring of parents who failed to abide by biblical teachings and habitually avoided teaching their children about God and His expectations. Thus, there is an urgent need for believers to stand firm on godly principles. Historically, women have been at the forefront of the moral and spiritual advancement in our nation. I am confident that God will still use them to help regain and hold the moral high ground.

Just as I began with the *Creation Story*, I feel compelled to conclude this section of the book with words that a very wise king wrote centuries ago:

> *"Now all has been heard; here is the conclusion of the matter:*
> *Fear God and keep his commandments,*
> *For this is the whole duty of man.*
> *For God will bring every deed into judgment,*
> *Including every hidden thing, whether it is good or evil."*
> Ecclesiastes 12:13-14

PART II
THE HISTORICAL
GREATNESS OF WOMEN

Richard Toliver

CHAPTER NINE

Great Women of the Bible

"So God created man in his own image,
in the image of God he created him;
male and female, he created them." Genesis 1:27

Miracle of Birth

I have never ceased to be amazed and humbled by the fact that we, as human beings, are created in God's image. Though I do not understand all of it, I accept by faith this biblical truth. Furthermore, the miracle of birth that God works through a woman is still fascinating to me. Man is the necessary contributor of the seed of life; but God chose the woman to nurture that seed for nine months until He was ready to blow the breath of life into it. Anyone who has ever held a first child, or others that follow, has been blessed by such an incredible creation. Although God's mind is unfathomable, it is clear that He has intentionally used women for the purpose of furthering humanity since the beginning of time. I am very pleased to provide a few selected examples of my research to underscore that God worked a mighty work in the beginning through biblical women.

From Eve to Mary

Eve

According to the Bible, Eve was created to be the mother of all others born in the fullness of God's time. Despite the disobedience of Adam and Eve in the Garden of Eden, God still allowed Eve to be the mother of all humanity that followed. Eating fruit from the "forbidden tree" in the garden had eternal consequences, but Adam and Eve were allowed to continue to live and produce life beyond the garden. Their initial descendants included Cain and Abel, the first human beings to be born of a woman. As a result of the first biblical family, Eve is called the "Mother of all humanity." Thus began the eternal greatness of women!

The Women on Noah's Ark

The descendants of Adam and Eve continued to populate the earth, but they quickly forgot God, became self-serving, and were full of evil and wickedness. Only one man, Noah, and his family still worshipped God. The Lord eventually rained down His judgment, and the world was destroyed by the "great flood." Noah and his family were spared in an ark that God had directed him to build in the desert many decades before the flood.

Many may know the story of Noah's Ark and animals that were taken on board "two-by-two." Very little, however, is said about the *wives* of Noah and his three sons that also were on board. The women are not named in the Bible, but they were the critical "passengers" that ensured the future of mankind after the deluge of forty-days and forty nights. After the flood, the Lord blessed Noah, his sons, and their wives and said to them:

> *"Be fruitful and increase in number and fill the earth."…. "I now establish a covenant with you and with your descendants after you and every living creature that was with you…." "Never again will all life be cut off by the waters of a flood; never again will there be a flood to destroy the earth."…. "I have set my rainbow in the clouds, and it will be a sign of the covenant between me and the earth."* Genesis 9:1; 9; 11; 13

Noah's sons, Shem, Ham, and Japheth, and their wives established the families of the earth after the flood. Thus, all the people of the world are the descendants of Noah, his wife, their three sons, and their wives. Shem, Ham, and Japheth and their wives gave birth to the Semites, Hamites, and Japhethites, clans. Respectfully, these were the nations of the Jews, Arabs, Middle Easterners, the African nations, and Europeans.

Sarah and Hagar

According to the Bible, God called Abraham from his country, Ur of the Chaldeans, to go to a distant land in which the Lord promised to make him a great nation. At seventy-five years old, Abraham took with him his wife, Sarah, his nephew, Lot, their servants, and all of their possessions, and set out for the land of Canaan. Abraham and his family later traveled on to Egypt for a sojourn and eventually returned to Canaan.

Abraham and Sarah resided in Canaan for another ten years, but Sarah was still unable to have children. Given the custom of that time, Sarah suffered from despair and the shame of being barren. To compensate for this disappointment, Sarah gave Hagar, her Egyptian maidservant, to Abraham to bear children for her. Children born from such a union would still be considered Sarah's. So with Sarah's encouragement, Abraham discounted the covenant that God had established with him decades earlier. He slept with Hagar and she became pregnant, but things didn't turn out as Sarah had planned. Hagar began to despise Sarah, whose anger and mistreatment resulted in Hagar fleeing the tent of Abraham. An angel of the Lord found a despondent Hagar in the desert and encouraged her to return to Sarah and Abraham. Subsequently, Hagar bore Abraham a son, and they named him Ishmael.

Despite taking matters in their own hands, God kept His promise to Abraham. When he was ninety-nine and Sarah was eighty-nine, the Lord spoke these words:

> *"I am God almighty; Walk before me and be blameless. And I will establish My covenant between Me and you, And I will multiply you exceedingly…. and I will make nations of you, and kings will come forth from you…And I will establish My covenant between me and you and your descendants after you throughout their generations for an everlasting covenant, to be God to you and to your descendants after you. And I*

will give to you and to your descendants after you, the land of
your sojournings, all the land of Canaan, for an everlasting
possession; and I will be their God." Genesis 17:1-8

Abraham was still concerned about Ishmael and pleaded his case before God. His prayers were heard, and God promised Abraham that Ishmael would also be blessed. He would be exceedingly fruitful and become the father of a great nation of twelve princes. However, God reminded Abraham that His covenant would still be established through Isaac, whom Sarah would bear the following year.

Shortly after these divine pronouncements, Sarah conceived and gave birth to a son, Isaac, through whom the Lord extended the covenant with Abraham. Accordingly, Abraham and Sarah were the ancestors of the Israelites or Jews. Thus, the origins of both the Jewish and Arab nations can be traced back to Abraham, Sarah, and Hagar. The immutable fact is Hagar was a woman of color, and God used her to become the "mother" of the entire Arab nation. In spite of these biological and family connections, the conflict between the Jews, Arabs, and Egyptians has persisted for over 4,000 years!

Leah, Rachel, Bilhah, and Zilpah

God continued His covenant with Abraham through his son, Isaac, and twin grandsons, Jacob and Esau. Abraham's lineage was established further through Jacob, his two wives, Leah and Rachel, and their respective maidservants, Bilhah and Zilpah. Of note, the latter two likely were women of color, or dark-skinned women. From these unions, twelve sons and one daughter were born over a period of three and one-half decades. Leah was the mother of Reuben, Simeon, Levi, Judah, Issachar, Zebulun, and Dinah. Rachel, Jacob's true love, gave birth late in life and was the mother of Joseph and Benjamin. She died giving birth to Benjamin. Bilhah was the mother of Dan and Naphtali; and Zilpah was the mother of Gad and Asher.

As Jacob's family grew, he showed unbridled favoritism toward Joseph, and that caused a bitter rift between the ten older brothers and Joseph. In a treacherous act of jealousy, Joseph, was sold into slavery to a caravan of Ishmaelites on their way to trade with Egypt.

Ironically, these traders were the descendants of Ishmael, the son born to Abraham and Hagar, the Egyptian handmaiden, almost 200 years earlier! This treachery of Joseph's brothers would come back to haunt them many years later.

Joseph was just seventeen when he arrived in Egypt, but he soon found favor with Potiphar, his master. Later Potiphar's wife falsely accused Joseph of sexually assaulting her, and he was thrown into prison for thirteen years. Despite great trial and tribulation, God timely intervened. Joseph was later released from prison, gained favor with Pharaoh, and subsequently prospered in everything he did. He was eventually elevated by Pharaoh to a position second only to himself. Greatly pleased, Pharaoh gave Joseph, Asenath, the daughter of an Egyptian priest, to be his wife. **Asenath** was also a woman of color, and the two sons born of this union would later become part of the twelve tribes of Israel.

Jochebed, Miriam, Bithiah

After a generation, a severe famine fell upon Canaan. Jacob, who was now called Israel, sent ten of his sons to Egypt to buy grain. This event resulted in a second visit and ultimately led to an emotional reunion and reconciliation between Joseph and his brothers. Joseph forgave his brothers and invited his father and the entire seventy members of his family to move to Egypt. They did so and lived under the care and protection of Joseph for the rest of their lives. Thus began the 430 years of the Israelites' sojourn in Egypt.

After the death of Joseph and his immediate family, the remaining Israelites, now called Hebrews, were very fruitful and multiplied greatly in Egypt. A new king who didn't know about Joseph came to power, and he became alarmed over the multitude of Hebrews that now resided in Egypt. For the next 300 years, the Hebrew were forced into slavery and harshly treated by Pharaoh and the slave masters for many generations.

The more the Hebrews were oppressed, the more their women gave birth, and they spread throughout the land to the dread of the Egyptians. Fearing an eventual uprising, Pharaoh ordered the Hebrew midwives to kill all the babies if they were boys but allowed the girls to live. The Hebrew women feared God more than Pharaoh and refused to carry out this slaughter of innocent lives. The Hebrew population continued to grow, so Pharaoh finally gave an order to all of his people that every baby boy born must be thrown into the Nile River. This horrific edict caused great distress throughout Egypt because the new babies numbered into the thousands. Few dared to disobey the Pharaoh. One family did so.

Jochebed was a descendant of Levi and was married to Amram, also from the house of Levi. Despite Pharaoh's edict of death, they had a son, Aaron, and a daughter, Miriam. Jochebed gave birth to a second son, and they called him Moses. To save his life, Jochebed hid Moses for three months. When it was no longer possible to keep his birth a secret, she made a cradle of bulrushes, slime, and pitch so it could float on water. Jochebed had the incredible foresight to place Moses in the Nile River where Pharaoh's daughter, Bithiah, frequently bathed.

Miriam was dispatched to keep watch from a distance so as not to draw attention to the fact that the baby was Jewish. Apparently, Bithiah heard the baby, Moses, crying and sent her servants to rescue Moses from the Nile. When Miriam saw the Pharaoh's daughter gently holding Moses, she appeared and offered to find a nursing mother. Delighted, Bithiah agreed, and Miriam quickly fetched Jochebed who was appointed to nurse Moses for about two years until he was weaned. When Moses was returned to Bithiah, she adopted him and raised him as her son in the palace of Pharaoh. Thus, God allowed these three women to have crucial roles in Moses' life. If it were not for their collective courage, faith, obedience, and wisdom, the life of Moses may never have been spared. The historians, storytellers, and moviemakers omitted an incredible truth. God used a woman of color to be the foster mother of Moses!

The book of Exodus provides the great story of Moses' life and travails that caused him ultimately to flee Egypt and escape to the land of Midian for forty years. At the age of eighty, he was called by God to return to Egypt to eventually lead some 600,000 Hebrews out of slavery to Canaan, the Promised Land. Some historians suggest that Bithiah joined the Hebrews during the exodus from Egypt and later married one. Jochebed and Mariam continued to have significant roles and are highly revered in both Jewish and secular history. God worked a series of miracles through these three women to keep His covenant with Abraham that was established some 640 years earlier! Moreover, women from Sarah to Bithiah, Jochebed, and Miriam had a significant part in God's plan to establish the twelve Israelites tribes following their exodus from Egypt.

Ruth

The book of Ruth contains one of the greatest love stories of all time, but it is much more than that. It is the evidence of God's sovereignty and His divine plan for the salvation of humanity. The story began when a man, Elimelech, his wife, Naomi, and two sons, Mahlon and Chilion, fled from Bethlehem of Judea to the land of Moab to escape a famine. When Elimelech died, his two sons took Moabite women to be their wives. Later the sons died, and Naomi decided to return to Judah when the famine no longer existed. Her two daughters-in-law felt compelled to return with her, but Naomi urged them to stay in their homeland with their people and to find husbands to ensure their future. Despite Naomi's exhortations, Ruth dearly loved her mother-in-law and refused to stay behind. Ruth's words to Naomi are immortal:

> *"Don't urge me to leave you or turn back from you. Where you go, I will go, and where you stay, I will stay. Your people will be my people and your God my God. Where you die, I will die, and there I will be buried. May the Lord deal with me, be it ever so severely, if anything but death separates you and me."* Ruth 1:16-17

When Naomi heard these words, she said no more, and they returned to Bethlehem. The city was stirred by Naomi's return and astonished when they heard about the commitment of Ruth.

Ruth continued to show her love for Naomi by gleaning in the nearby fields to gather leftover grain for food. This field belonged to Boaz, a rich kinsman of Naomi's late husband. In the course of time, and with mentoring by Naomi, Ruth found favor with Boaz. Boaz worked through the customs of the day and purchased from Naomi all that belonged to her late husband, Elimelech, and deceased sons, Chilion and Mahlon. In doing so, he also earned the right to take Ruth for his wife.

Ruth became the wife of Boaz, and the Lord blessed them with a son and they named him Obed. Obed became the father of Jesse; Jesse became the father of David who later was anointed the King of Judah. The extraordinary lineage of David can be traced back fourteen generations to Abraham. This ancestry is connected twenty-eight generations to Joseph, the husband of Mary, who gave birth to Jesus Christ! Thus, Ruth's commitment, humility, and love placed her squarely in the lineage of Christ. More importantly, this lineage shows how the Lord can and does work through the frailties of men and women to carry out His perfect will for humanity.

Esther

The incredible story of Esther demonstrates how God used her to save His people from genocide. The rise of Esther from a young Jewish orphan to become the queen of Persia is a phenomenal story of God's faithfulness in the affairs of His people. During the 650 years after Ruth, the Israelites lived through the Period of Judges and under the Kings of Judah and Israel—Saul, David, and Solomon. The next 465 years saw the twelve tribes split into two nations, Israel, the northern tribes, and Judah, the southern tribes. The warring factions eventually resulted in the fall of Jerusalem and seventy years of the Israelite's captivity in Babylon. After the fall of Babylon, most of the Jews returned to Jerusalem, but some stayed in Media and Persia. The story of Esther takes place at this time.

King Xerxes, the king of Persia ruled an empire that extended from India to Ethiopia and consisted of 127 provinces. At the peak of his reign, Vashti, his queen, lost favor with him. He divorced her and banished her from his presence forever. To assuage his loneliness, King Xerxes was advised to search all the provinces for the most beautiful young virgins and select the most pleasing one to replace Queen Vashti. The king followed this advice, and thousands of virgins were collected throughout the vast empire. A Jew named Mordecai had adopted his beautiful young cousin, Esther, after her parents died. Esther was selected and taken to the king's palace, but Mordecai instructed her to keep their kinship a secret.

Esther quickly found favor with those in charge of the harem, and she was placed in the twelve-month preparation program prior to being presented to the king. She was given special provisions of cosmetics, food, and choice maids from the king's palace, and transferred to the best place in the harem. At the end of the preparation period, Esther was allowed the one-time scheduled appearance before the king. When King Xerxes saw Esther, he loved her more than all the virgins that had been presented to him. She immediately won his favor, and the king made her queen to replace Vashti. But the story didn't end there.

While Esther was in preparation, Mordecai discovered a plot to harm King Xerxes and told her. Esther told the king and gave credit to Mordecai for alerting her to the threat. The perpetrators were caught, found guilty, and hung. In accordance with the custom, these events were written in the Book of Chronicles in the king's presence. Later, King Xerxes promoted Haman, one of his officials, to the highest position and established him over all of the princes in the kingdom. Haman ordered all of the king's servants to bow down and pay him homage. Mordecai, the Jew, refused to do so. Haman became enraged and convinced the king that all the Jews were guilty of disrespect and violated his ordinances. As a result, Haman was allowed to plan and carry out the death of all Jewish men, women, and children throughout the land.

Mordecai sought Esther's help and reminded her that she was made queen for "*such a time as this*." The penalty of death faced anyone who entered the king's presence unless specifically requested by him. Esther broke this protocol and said, "*If I perish, I perish.*" She put on her royal robes, stood in the inner courts of the king's palace, and caught the approving eye of King Xerxes. Esther was called to the throne, and the king saw that she was troubled. Esther saw an opportunity to disclose the evil plot of Haman, and she skillfully arranged an event to expose him for who he was. Using Haman's own self-inflated ego, she arranged a private dinner for King Xerxes and Haman in her palace. There she exposed Haman for his deceit and treachery in the name of the king. Consequently, the very gallows Haman had built to hang Mordecai was used to hang him.

When King Xerxes reviewed the Book of Chronicles and found that Mordecai had never been rewarded for alerting him to the earlier death plot, Mordecai was then elevated to the place of authority previously held by Haman. Thus, the Jews throughout the empire were spared, and King Xerxes placed a tribute to Mordecai on the land and coastlands of the sea. The spectacular conclusion of this story reflects how God worked through a woman, Esther, to save His people from annihilation. Though young and beautiful, her greatness was demonstrated by her willingness to sacrifice her life to save her people.

Mary

The story of Mary, the mother of Jesus, is one of the most powerful and revered events in biblical history. God chose a young virgin to be the vessel through which the gift of salvation for man was given. Mary is highly esteemed in many religions and church denominations around the world. In particular, the Roman Catholic Church's veneration of the *"Blessed Virgin Mary"* is based on the Holy Bible. The incarnation of the *Son of God* through Mary established her place of honor as the *"Mother of God."* Thus, she has a central role in the Roman Catholic Church as well as in many other churches. This fact is reflected in art, music, poetry, prayer, and religious feasts and festivals.

I have always been touched by the biblical story of Mary, especially during the Christmas season. The many images of Mary and Joseph, the manger, the guiding star, the shepherds, and the wise men have been etched in my memory since I was child. I am still inspired by the story of Mary each year, and my family has celebrated the birth of Christ most of my life. But it was not until my wife, Peggy, daughter Gail, and I visited Israel in 2007 that the story of Mary, Joseph, Jesus and other biblical characters really came alive as never before.

We visited Nazareth, the home of Mary and Joseph, and where the Angel of the Lord appeared to Mary to announce the miraculous birth of Jesus. While standing at *Mary's Well,* we could almost hear the scriptures:

"Greetings, you who are highly favored! The Lord is with you... Do not be afraid, Mary; you have found favor with God... You will be with child and give birth to a son, and you are to give him the name, Jesus.

He will be great, and will be called the son of the Most High. The Lord will give him the throne of his father David, and he will reign over the house of Jacob forever; and his kingdom will have no end....

"The Holy Spirit will come upon you, and the power of the Most High will overshadow you. So the holy one to be born will be called the Son of God." Luke 1:28-35

Despite Mary's trepidation of the unbelievable presence and message of the Angel, Gabriel, this obedient and humble young maiden believed in God and accepted what was said. She didn't fully understand that Jesus would be the incarnate Son of God; nevertheless, she uttered the eternal message of obedience:

"I am the Lord's servant....May it be to me as you have said."
Luke 1:38

After Mary's well, we entered the Church of the Annunciation, which was erected centuries ago to commemorate the historic events said to have taken place there. We stood in amazement that God chose Mary, a child, to be the vessel through which He would enter the world in the flesh to save the world. We later visited Bethlehem, the birthplace of Jesus, some seventy miles south of Nazareth and five miles beyond Jerusalem. The Church of the Nativity has been erected over the alleged spot of the manger where Mary gave birth to Jesus. It is built over a cave that marks the traditional place of the manger, today marked by an in-ground star. These were some of the most spiritual moments that we had ever experienced. Mary, the young mother, was no longer just an improbable story of the past; she was real and we departed Bethlehem believing what happened there.

Not much is recorded about Mary and Jesus from His birth until He began His ministry at age thirty. The Bible tells of an event that took place when Jesus was twelve years old. After an annual pilgrimage to Jerusalem, Joseph and Mary were returning to Nazareth when they discovered Jesus was missing. After a frantic and futile search among relatives, they returned to Jerusalem and found Jesus in the temple, sitting in the midst of teachers, listening and asking questions. All those present were amazed with His understanding and answers. When His parents found Him, they too were astonished. When Mary asked Jesus why He had stayed behind, she did not understand His words:

> *"Why is it that you were looking for me? Did you not know that I had to be in My Father's house?"* Luke 2:49

Joseph, Mary, and Jesus returned to Nazareth, but Mary treasured these things in her heart. She was a direct witness as Jesus increased in wisdom, stature, and in favor with God and men. One can only imagine Mary's awe and pride in the one to whom she had given birth.

Before leaving Israel, we visited the Old City of Jerusalem and stood at what was said to be the courtyard of Pontius Pilate where Jesus was put on trial. Afterwards, we traversed the storied Via Dolorosa, the path that Jesus was forced to take on the way to His crucifixion. Murals and sculptures marked the fourteen points of suffering called the *"Way of the Cross."* There were specific depictions of Jesus stopping to console Mary and to warn the *"Women of Jerusalem"* of greater sorrows to come. This winding, uphill path led outside the city where Golgotha still can be seen in the distance.

We made our way along the path trying to imagine the agony that Mary suffered as she watched her son toiling and stumbling along, bleeding from the tortuous beating suffered earlier. The unspeakable tragedy of the suffering of Christ took place over 2,000 years ago, yet as we slowly retraced the steps, history became a movingly surreal experience. We could sense an overpowering identity with Mary and those who were Jesus' followers. By the time we reached the hill of Golgotha, we were overwhelmed by the reality of what happened there. I imagined what it must have been like when Jesus looked at His weeping mother, Mary, Mary Magdalene, and John, whom He commissioned to care for His mother.

I believe that Mary's suffering during the trial, condemnation, and crucifixion of Jesus Christ is the eternal model of suffering for mothers all over the world. From the moment she accepted the message of the enunciation, her heart was united with Jesus. She suffered excruciatingly with Him at the foot of cross. While Jesus died for all humanity, Mary bore the pain and suffering for all mothers in every generation that followed. The conclusion of our visit to Israel at Golgotha gave us a greater appreciation of how God used Mary, the mother of Jesus, in the His plan for the salvation of humankind. How and why God chose to do things this way is only known to Him. Nevertheless, I trust the preceding biblical stories give credence to the title of this book: *Woman—A Godly Creation*.

CHAPTER TEN

First Through the Nineteenth Centuries

The First Century

During and after Jesus spent time on earth, women began to have significant roles with His followers and the growth of the early churches. I have chosen to highlight a few historically noteworthy women in the following passages to confirm their greatness.

Lydia

Lydia is a New Testament character, who was a well-to-do businesswoman from Thyatira, approximately forty miles inland across the Aegean Sea from Athens. A biblical account of her is found in the book of Acts, chapter 16. Although most likely a Greek, she lived in the Roman settlement of Philippi where she met the great Apostle Paul and his companions. Lydia was called the "Woman of Purple" because of her thriving trading business of purple cloth and garments. She was a very righteous Gentile who worshiped God, the Creator, and she was one of a large group of sympathizers to Judaism. Lydia believed in the one God, but had not yet taken the final step of converting to Judaism. She listened intently to Paul when he first preached in Philippi and is regarded as the first Christian convert in Europe. After she and her entire household were baptized, she graciously opened her home to Paul, Silas, and their associates and helped the early church get its foothold in the area.

Given the customs regarding the inequality of women in Lydia's time, her boldness was particularly noteworthy. Her apparent social power was evident by her control and ownership of her household. Thus, she was allowed to invite a group of foreign men into her home without any reprisal from the community. Lydia is recognized as a saint by several Christian denominations including the Catholic, Orthodox Church, Episcopal, and Evangelical Lutheran churches. The Orthodox Church recognizes her as "Equal to the Apostles," which signifies her importance and level of holiness after her death.

Dorcas

Dorcas, the Greek translation for Tabitha, was a Christian disciple who lived in the biblical coastal town of Joppa. She was said to be a prominent widow who worked tirelessly with other women in providing charitable services throughout their community. The biblical story in Acts 9:36-42 relates the story that Dorcas became sick and died. Her body was prepared for burial and placed in an upper room. Because of her great reputation, the community members urgently sent for the Apostle Peter who was passing through the area. Peter came immediately and found all the widows weeping and showing all the tunics and garments that Dorcas had made while alive. The story continues with Peter sending the mourners from the room, and then he knelt and prayed over Dorcas until a miracle occurred. Dorcas was restored to life by the Apostle Peter and presented to all the saints and widows in Joppa. As this miraculous story spread throughout Joppa, many believed in the Lord.

Both Lydia of Thyatira and Dorcas are honored annually in January with a feast day on the liturgical calendar of the Episcopal Church in the United States of America.

The Middle Ages

Factors of Change

The traditional view of women changed considerably during the Middle Ages due to a number of influential factors of that period. A few of these are highlighted in the paragraphs that follow.

The Roman Catholic Church was perhaps the most influential and unifying factor on the culture, i.e., learning, preservation of the art of writing, and a centralized administration through its network of bishops. Historically, the roles of bishops and priests were restricted to men; however, with the establishment of Christian monasteries, other roles within the Catholic Church became available to women. From the 5th century onward, Christian convents provided opportunities for some women to escape the path of marriage and childbearing. Instead, they were allowed to acquire literacy and learning, and played a more active role in religion. Abbesses, or women who were the superiors of convents, became important figures in their own right. They often ruled over monasteries of both men and women, and they held significant power and land ownership. For example, Hilda of Whitby (614 –680) became an influential figure on a national and international scale. Others, such as Margery Kempe had a significant role in the development of theological ideas and discussions.

The arts, education, literature, midwifery, politics, and war were factors that changed the perception of women during the late Middle Ages (1200–1500). Ironically, the introduction of beer, largely made for men, gave women a foothold in business. Women in their homes mostly carried out the brewing of beer, so the tension over roles was minimized while the contribution to the welfare of the family was more significant. Furthermore, this assistance to the husband in the brewery business gave rise to the woman's role in other business ventures. The following two examples highlight the women of this era—Hilda of Whitby and Margery Kempe.

Hilda of Whitby

Hilda of Whitby (614–680) is revered as a Christian saint because of her exceptional degree of holiness, sanctity, and virtue. She had a significant role in the conversion of England to Christianity, and was recognized as a woman of great energy, a skilled administrator and teacher. Hilda had a reputation for having great wisdom, and kings and princes frequently sought her advice. Yet she was also known for her concern for just ordinary folk. Hilda was the founding Abbess (or mother superior) of a community of nuns of the monastery in Whitby. Today, the ruins of the Whitby Abby are located in a seaside town in the Borough of Scarborough in the English county of North Yorkshire, England. This seaside port and town emerged during the Middle Ages and was the place where Captain James Cook, the famous British explorer, navigator, and cartographer, learned his seamanship.

Saint Hilda is honored in the Roman Catholic Church, Anglican Communion, and Eastern Orthodox Church. She was canonized by The *Roman Curia,* or Congregation for the Causes of Saints, which oversees the complex process of the canonization of saints followed by approval of the Pope. Since the late nineteenth century, the interest in and devotion to St. Hilda has been revived. As the development of education for modern women progressed, Hilda became a patron saint. The schools and colleges named in her honor extend worldwide, as well as in America. St. Hilda's and St. Hugh's School on the upper west side of Manhattan, New York City opened its doors in 1950. These are independent Episcopal day schools that are coeducational and include toddlers through grade eight. Thus, more than thirteen centuries after her death, God is still using the life of St. Hilda to inspire and motivate both women and men to achieve His purpose in our time!

Margery Kempe

The amazing life of Margery Kempe (1373 -1438) was virtually unknown for over four hundred years because *The Book of Margery Kempe* lay hidden in a library until 1934. This tremendous discovery proved to be the first known autobiography in the English language, and it shed light on the very intriguing life of a woman in the Middle Ages. Margery Kemp was said to be a beautiful, intellectual, free-spirited woman who enjoyed the benefits of a very wealthy family. She was called by some the "original bourgeois princess" who frequently traveled around the known world and was the first to write about these trips in an intensely personal way. Moreover, she was a woman of substance and even ran a large brewery and grain mill for a while. After turning to religion, she traveled thousands of miles on pilgrimages to various holy sites in Europe and Asia. The thing that struck me the most was despite such a non-traditional life style, Margery was the mother of fourteen children!

The significance of Margery Kempe's autobiography is its great insight of a middle-class woman in the Middle Ages. Her book is a carefully constructed spiritual and social commentary with unprecedented intimate details. The book also expresses the conflict in late medieval England between institutional orthodoxy and increasingly public modes of religious dissent. Nevertheless, throughout Margery's spiritual life, she was challenged by both church and civil authorities on her adherence to the teachings of the institutional Church. Thus she can be an inspiration to women of today regarding the strength and adherence to their convictions. Margery Kempe is venerated annually in the Church of England and in the Episcopal Church of the United States.

Women Warriors

I wrote about the outstanding history of women in the military in Chapter Three. I am pleased to provide two sterling examples of women in the Middle Ages. They underscore the unprecedented greatness of women who answered the clarion call to serve their nation and their people on battlefields: Joan of Arc and Queen Nzingha a Mbande.

Joan of Arc

Joan of Arc was one of my first heroines in history. I was a young teenager in the early 1950s when I saw the movie titled by her name. In those days, Hollywood was more intentional in technical direction and selection of movie sites that gave authenticity to the story being told. Accordingly, the epic saga of Joan of Arc was presented in Technicolor and in panoramic scenes that allowed the viewers to be caught up in medieval history. I had already decided on being a military person, so Joan's exploits as a soldier and leader left a great impression on me. I had also developed a healthy respect for women, so it didn't seem strange to me that a young woman could lead an army. In retrospect, the tremendous cultural, gender, and religious biases of Joan's day made her existence and accomplishments even more astounding. She defied the convention of dress, servitude, and vocation in order to answer a divine call to serve her country. Since I was struggling with my own spirituality in the face of adversity, Joan's ultimate decision to die rather than disavow her faith had a particular impact upon me.

Joan of Arc was born about 1412 in eastern France near what was then the Holy Roman Empire. She was called the "Maid of Orléans," and was a national heroine of France and a Roman Catholic saint. While claiming divine guidance, she led the French army to several important victories during the Hundred Years' War and paved the way for the coronation of Charles VII. Her parents, Jacques d'Arc and Isabelle Romée, were considered peasants, but they were loyal to the French crown. Joan's father was also a minor village official and head of the local watch. When Joan was about twelve years old, she experienced the first spiritual vision while alone in a field near her home. She later recounted seeing visions of three saints who told her that she had been selected to help free France by driving out the English and bringing the lawful King Dauphin to power.

When Joan was sixteen, she persuaded a relative to take her to see the commander of a nearby garrison. She sought permission to visit the royal French court to get approval to become a soldier. Needless to say, Joan received a negative response; but she returned a year later. This time, she made a prediction about a possible military reversal and French victory near *Orleans*. Although skeptical, the uncrowned King Charles VII sent her as part of a relief mission to break the siege of Orléans. Dressed in a man's armor, Joan overcame the dismissive attitude of veteran commanders and gained prominence at the battle of *Orleans*. Miraculously, she led the troops to a victory over the English in just nine days!

Joan continued fighting the enemy in other locations along the Loire and led the French forces to several more swift victories. At seventeen-years-old, history records Joan as the youngest supreme military commander in history, male or female. Her incredible exploits eventually led to Charles VII's coronation at Reims, where she was given a place of honor next to the king.

Joan was eventually captured by the Burgundians and transferred to the English for money. She was subsequently put on trial and condemned for heresy by the pro-English Bishop of Beauvais. She was burned at the stake when she was just nineteen years old. Legend has it that as Joan was about to be put to death, she was heard praying for her executioners much like Jesus of Nazareth did! Over sixty years later, I am still saddened over the tragic ending of Joan's life. Nevertheless, she was an incredible example of how God raised up a young woman in the 16th century to unprecedented greatness for His purpose. In doing so, the entire nation of France was blessed through Joan at a time when the nation seemed hopelessly and permanently in the hands of the English.

Queen Nzingha a Mbande

Queen Nzingha a Mbande, (1583–1663), was also known as Ana de Sousa. She was a 17th century queen of the Matamba Kingdoms of the Mbundu people in southwestern Africa. Matamba was a kingdom traditionally led by women, and Queen Nzingha turned it into the most powerful state in the region. The queen was one of four children born to King Kiluanji and his wife Kangela. She was allowed to closely observe the administrative affairs of his kingdom and even accompany him to war. As a young adult, she served as an ambassador to Portugal during the period when the Atlantic slave trade and the consolidation of power by the Portuguese in the region were growing rapidly. Queen Nzingha was such a cunning and shrewd negotiator that the governor of Portugal agreed to her demands, and a treaty of equal terms was crafted. The Portuguese failed to honor the treaty, and a conflict existed between the Kingdom of Mbundu and Portugal for several decades.

After the death of her father, Nzingha became queen, and the struggle with Portugal continued. The conflict over land and slaves continued, and in 1641, Nzingha formed an alliance with the Dutch in an effort to recover lost lands. She defeated the Portuguese army in both 1644 and in 1647. Subsequently, she was unable to hold onto the land and therefore retreated to Matamba. There the warrior queen continued to resist the Portuguese until well into her sixties, often personally leading her troops into battle. She died a peaceful death at the age of eighty in December 1663. Today, the queen is memorialized in Angola for her political and diplomatic acumen, great wit, intelligence, and brilliant military tactics.

The Eighteenth Through Nineteenth Centuries

Many great women made outstanding contributions to the furtherance of our nation during the 200 years of a dynamic transformation in America. As earlier stated, it was about this time that their exploits began to be genuinely appreciated and appropriately documented. An appreciable list of achievers can be identified; however, I have chosen to highlight two great women of this era: Susan B. Anthony and Madam Marie Curie.

Susan B. Anthony

Susan Brownell Anthony (1820–1906) was the second oldest of seven children born to Daniel Anthony and Lucy Read of Adams, Massachusetts. Her father was a cotton manufacturer and abolitionist who embraced the Quaker religion. He was considered a stern, open-minded man, so Susan and her siblings grew up under the influence of hard work and a simple life. The children were not allowed to have toys or amusements in the house because their father thought such things distracted from the "inner light." Accordingly, the Anthony children were taught strict self-discipline, principled convictions, and belief in one's own self-worth. Susan grew up in a very close-knit family. One of her brothers became a publisher and was active in the anti-slavery movement in Kansas. A sister became a teacher and a women's-rights activist.

Susan showed unusual intelligence as a child and learned to read and write at the age of three. Her family moved to Battenville, New York when she was six years old. Susan was enrolled in a local school, but the teacher refused to teach her long division because she was a girl. Disappointed and upset, her father promptly moved her into a group home school where he taught the children. A female teacher in the school provided Susan with the early image of progressive womanhood that later shaped her belief in women's equality. Despite her exceptional attributes, Susan was very self-conscious of her appearance and speaking abilities, which she thought lacked sufficient eloquence. She eventually overcame her fears and went on to become a renowned public advocate for the women's movement.

In 1837, at seventeen, Susan was sent to Deborah Moulson's Female Seminary, a Quaker boarding school in Philadelphia. She was forced to end her formal studies a short time later because of the financial difficulties her family suffered from the *Panic of 1837*. The latter was a financial crisis in the United States that touched off a major recession that lasted several years. During this time, the Anthony family moved to Hardscrabble, New York. She left home to teach and pay off her father's debts. By 1846, Susan had advanced to headmistress of the Female Department of the Canajoharie Academy. The entire male faculty of the academy earned nearly four times more than women for the same duties, so Susan embarked on her first fight for wage equality.

In 1849, at age 29, Anthony quit teaching and moved to the family farm in Rochester, New York. She began to take part in conventions and gatherings related to the temperance movement. She attended the local Unitarian Church and began to separate from the Quaker religion because of the hypocritical drinking of alcohol amongst Quaker preachers. She became secretary for the *Daughters of Temperance*, an organization that gave her a forum to speak out against abuse, and this served as the beginning of Anthony's movement towards the public limelight.

In 1851, Susan met fellow feminist Elizabeth Cady Stanton with whom she joined in organizing the first women's state temperance society in America. They remained close friends and colleagues for the remainder of their lives. Together, they traveled across the United States speaking and attempting to persuade the government that society should treat men and women equally. In September 1852, Susan was invited to make her first public speech at the third annual National Women's Rights Convention held in Syracuse, New York. As a result, Susan gained notice as a powerful public advocate of women's rights and as a new and stirring voice for change. In 1856, Susan sought to unify the African-American and women's rights movements. She participated in every subsequent annual National Women's Rights Convention and served as convention president in 1858.

In early 1868, Anthony published, in New York City, the first women's rights weekly journal, *The Revolution*. Its motto was: *"The true republic—men, their rights and nothing more; women, their rights and nothing less."* The main thrust of *The Revolution* was to promote women's and African-Americans' right to suffrage. It also emphasized the issues of equal pay for equal work and more liberal church positions on women's issues and divorce laws. In 1869, she found herself on the opposing side of her long-time friend, Frederick Douglass. The American Equal Rights Association (AERA) had originally fought for suffrage rights for both blacks and women. Now the AERA voted to support the 15th Amendment to the Constitution, granting suffrage to black men, but not to women. In part, as a result of the decision by the AERA, Susan soon devoted herself almost exclusively to the advocacy for women's rights.

Susan continued her zealous quest for women's rights over the next thirty years. Major events of her life included an arrest, trial, and partial exoneration for voting in the 1872 presidential election; a tour of Europe in 1883; and joining with American social reformer, educator, and writer Helen Barrett Montgomery in forming a chapter of the Woman's Educational and Industrial Union in Rochester, New York. Before retiring, Susan was asked if all women in the United States would ever be given the right to vote. Allegedly, she stated,

> *"It will come, but I shall not see it...It is inevitable. We can no more deny forever the right of self-government to one-half our people than we could keep the Negro forever in bondage. It will not be wrought by the same disrupting forces that freed the slave, but come it will, and I believe within a generation."*

Susan B. Anthony, a great American lady, retired to Rochester, New York in 1900. She admonished her followers that *"Failure is impossible,"* and she encouraged them to be steadfast in the challenging long and difficult struggle ahead. Susan died on March 13, 1906 at the age of eighty and was buried at Mount Hope Cemetery. Fourteen years after her death, America's women gained the right to vote on

August 26, 1920 by passage of the Nineteenth Amendment to the U.S. Constitution!

Marie Curie

Maria Salomea Skłodowska Curie (1867–1934) was a Polish physicist and chemist who worked mainly in France and is famous for her pioneering research on radioactivity. She was the first woman to win a Nobel Prize and the only woman to win the prize in two scientific fields. She was also the only person to win in multiple sciences and the first female professor at the University of Paris (*La Sorbonne*). I first heard about "Madam Curie" while an engineering student at Tuskegee Institute. I stayed over for the summer to work and catch up on my favorite pastime of reading non-technical books. My landlady invited me to visit her trove of books and magazines, including *National Geographic* and *Reader's Digest.* I found the story of Marie Curie in the Reader's Digest and was totally fascinated by her life, marriage, and sacrifice. Several years later, I was even more impressed when I visited a museum that featured the work of the Curies. I believe the following highlights of her life are a fitting transition to great women of the 20th century.

Maria Skłodowska was born in the Russian Partition of Warsaw, Poland on November 7, 1867. She was the fifth and youngest child of two well-known and accomplished educators, Bronisława and Władysław Skłodowska. Her father taught mathematics and physics and was also the director of two Warsaw schools for boys. Maria's mother operated a prestigious Warsaw boarding school for girls until Maria was born. Maria's paternal grandfather Józef Skłodowski was also a respected teacher whose students later became leading figures in education, science, and literature. Thus, Maria and her siblings grew up among parents and grandparents who greatly influenced their choice of pursuits in mathematics and science.

Maria began attending boarding school when she was ten years old. That same year, her family suffered two back-to-back tragedies that would affect her for the rest of her life. Maria's oldest sister died from typhus. Two years later, her mother died from tuberculosis.

Despite these terrible losses, Maria completed high school for girls in June 1883 earning a gold medal. Her intense educational pursuits caused a near collapse, so she spent the next two years in the country-side with relatives, and the following year with her father in Warsaw. Maria and her sister, Bronisława, wanted to enroll in an institute of higher education institution but were denied because they were females. Undaunted, the sisters were accepted in the *Flying University*, an underground school that provided Polish youth with an education within the framework of traditional Polish academics and culture.

Bronisława graduated from the Flying University and moved to Paris, France to study medicine. Maria agreed to stay behind in Poland and work to provide her sister financial assistance for the next few years. During this time, she continued to educate herself, read books, exchanged letters, and began her practical scientific training in a chemical laboratory. In late 1891, at the age of twenty-four, Maria finally accepted the invitation to join Bronisława, who was now married to a physician who was a social and political activist. She began her studies in physics, chemistry, and mathematics at La Sorbonne. Maria lived briefly with her sister and brother-in-law until she was able to afford her own small apartment. Having survived very meager existence and cold winters, Maria earned a degree in physics in 1893 and began working in an industrial laboratory. With the aid of a fellowship, she continued studying at La Sorbonne and was awarded a second degree in 1894.

In 1894, Maria became "Marie," and she began her scientific career in Paris as an investigator of the magnetic properties of various steels. That same year, she met Pierre Curie, an instructor at the School of Physics and Chemistry in Paris. Their mutual passion for science soon resulted in a close relationship and Pierre's marriage proposal. Marie did not accept right away because she intended to return to Poland to teach; however, she was denied a position because of her gender. Maria returned to Paris in 1895, the year Pierre received his doctorate and was promoted to professor at the school. Marie and Pierre were married in a small civil ceremony on July 26, 1895. They had their first daughter, Irene, in 1897. Marie had found her true love with whom to share her life, mutual pastimes, family, and scientific research.

Marie continued her studies in Paris and was awarded her doctorate from the University of Paris in June 1903. Later that year, she shared the Nobel Prize in Physics with her husband, Pierre Curie, and with physicist Henri Becquerel. In December 1904, she gave birth to their second daughter, Ève. On April 19, 1906, Marie and her daughters suffered a devastating tragedy when Pierre Curie was struck and killed by a horse-drawn vehicle in Paris. In May of that year, La Sorbonne physics department retained the chair that had been created for Pierre and offered it to Marie. She accepted the offer in hopes of creating a world-class laboratory as a tribute to her husband, thus becoming the first woman to become a professor at La Sorbonne.

In 1911, Marie Curie was the sole winner of the Nobel Prize in Chemistry. Her achievements included a theory of *radioactivity*, techniques for isolating radioactive isotopes, and the discovery of two elements, polonium and radium. Later, Marie directed the world's first studies in the treatment of neoplasms using radioactive isotopes. She founded the Curie Institutes in Paris and in Warsaw; and during World War I, she established the first military field radiological centers. Although Marie became a French citizen, she never lost her Polish identity and used both surnames, Marie Skłodowska Curie.

Marie Curie's pioneering, innovative, and groundbreaking work as a scientist helped shape the world of the 20th and 21st centuries. Her research efforts helped overturn established ideas in physics and chemistry, but she also had an equally profound effect on the world's view of women. In achieving her success, Marie had to overcome insurmountable barriers, in both her native and adopted country, simply because she was a woman. After being accredited with extraordinary scientific achievements that significantly benefited the world, Marie succumbed to aplastic anemia brought on by her years of exposure to radiation. She died at the sanatorium of Sancellemoz (Haute-Savoie), France in 1934.

Marie Curie's legacy was manifested further by her two daughters. Irene, the older daughter, followed closely in her mother's footsteps as a scientist, specializing in radioactivity, and won her own Nobel Prize in 1935. Her younger daughter, Eve, was an artist, writer, and activist during WWII. In 1954, she married an American diplomat who later became head of The United Nations Children's Fund (UNICEF). Eve's husband received a Nobel Prize on behalf of the organization, and she subsequently traveled with him to over a hundred countries. Thus, Eve was part of a family that received five Nobel Prizes (Marie, two; Pierre, one; Irene, one; and Eve's husband one). Irene's early research into radiation resulted in her death from leukemia in 1955 at age fifty-eight. Eve's life spanned through the 20th century, and she died in 2007 at the age of 102.

Richard Toliver

GREAT ACHIEVERS OF THE 19TH CENTURY

Susan B. Anthony

Marie Curie

CHAPTER ELEVEN

Women of Color

Ancient civilization has its roots in Africa along the Nile River of Egypt, in the land of Canaan, and along the Red Sea. The topographical and climatological conditions in these regions give credence to the fact that women of these areas were darker hue, or *"Women of Color."* Conversely, historians, Hollywood, and contemporary media have persistently distorted this reality at the expense of truth. Even today, it is difficult to find an accurate portrayal of the role of minority women in our country. Although women of color historically have been ignored or have been portrayed in a negative manner, God purposely used them at crucial and pivotal times to advance humanity. Clearly, women of color are part of His master plan for the entire human race. The following discourse highlights a few of these great women.

Queens and Leaders

Queen Nefertiti (1370–1330 BC) was the "Great Royal Wife" of Egyptian Pharaoh Akhenaten. She and her husband were known for a religious revolution in which only one god, Aten, or sun disc, was worshiped. Some scholars believe that Nefertiti ruled briefly as Neferneferuaten after her husband's death and before the accession of Tutankhamen.

Nefertiti had many titles that reflected her beauty and influence during her husband's reign as Pharaoh. These titles included: Great of Praises, Lady of Grace, Sweet of Love, Lady of The Two Lands, Lady of all Women, and Mistress of Upper and Lower Egypt. Nefertiti was most famous for her exquisite beauty, as depicted in her bust, currently housed in Berlin Germany's Neues Museum. It was discovered in the workshop of the Egyptian sculptor, Thutmose, thought to have been the official court sculptor of the Pharaoh Akhenaten during the latter part of his reign. The sculpture exemplifies the unique appreciation ancient Egyptians had for capturing realistic facial features.

This sculpture is one of the most admired and copied works of ancient Egypt. I can personally attest that it is one of the most captivating and mesmerizing works of art that I have ever seen. Forty-four years ago, my wife and I visited the Berlin museum and viewed the glass-encased bust in a room with special lighting. It was the only piece in the center of the room, and it seemed to speak through the centuries of her beauty, color, and royalty. The dark hue of this ancient artwork was not lost on us, as we recalled the propensity of revisionists to depict history contrary to the truth of a woman's color or ethnicity.

The Kingdom of Kush (1070 BC–AD 350)

Archeological findings and research confirm that Kush was the ancient African kingdom of Nubia, also known as Ethiopia. Nubia is the homeland of Africa's earliest black culture. Nubian monuments and artifacts, as well as written records from Egypt and Rome, establish its origin as early as 3800 B.C. Situated along portions of the Nile River, it was a rich center of culture and military might in Africa. Their warriors were said to be known and feared by those who encountered them in battles. Much of ancient Nubia's development was connected to ancient Egypt, which ruled a large part of Nubia between 2000 and 1000 B.C. When Egypt collapsed into civil war, Nubian kings and queens ruled Egypt for about 100 years from 800 to 700 B.C. Today, ancient Nubia's lands are now part of modern Egypt and Sudan.

A close examination of the available history and the culture of Nubia, suggested that women were distinctly unique to the rest of the world at that time because of their significant roles as rulers and warriors. The emergence of queens as powerful participants in the politics of the day had its roots in the earliest Kushite religious tradition. In addition, Kushite rulers married and then often passed royal power into the hands of their queens. During the period called *"The Golden Age of the Meroitic Kingdom,"* ten sovereign ruling queens emerged and six other queens ruled with their husbands. Two notable examples include **Queen Amanirenas**, a warrior queen who reigned from about 40 B.C. to 10 B. C. She fought fiercely for the Nubian/Kushite kingdom and defeated the Roman armies at Aswan. In victory, she defaced a statue of Emperor Augustus Caesar, brought its head back to Nubia as a prize, and buried it in the doorway of an important building! The second was **Queen Daurama,** a ruler and founding "Queen Grandmother" of the Hausa Empire states in northern Niger and Nigeria.

The **Queen of Sheba** was a rich and powerful ruler during the reign of Israel's King Solomon about 950 B.C. Her kingdom was thought to be in what is called Yemen today. According to biblical history, she heard of the great wisdom of the king and decided to go meet and question him for herself. The queen took a trove of gifts including gold, precious stones, spices, and beautiful wood. Upon meeting each other, legend has it that they were immediately attracted to one another. It is said that Sheba was awed by Solomon's great wisdom and wealth, and she pronounced a blessing on Solomon's God. He reciprocated by bestowing upon her the "royal bounty" from his kingdom. The biblical passages that relate this story give no mention of love or intimate relations between Sheba and Solomon. Nevertheless, some scholars cite the single Bible book, "The Song of Songs" as Solomon's love song about the black woman, Sheba.

Another account of a woman of color in King Solomon's life is found in the Holy Bible:

"Then Solomon formed a marriage alliance with Pharaoh, king of Egypt, and took Pharaoh's daughter and brought her to the City of David, until he had finished building his own home and the house of the Lord and the wall around Jerusalem." I Kings 3:1

Kandake, Kentake, and Candace were the titles given to queens and queen mothers of the ancient Kingdom of Kush. One of these queens is documented biblically in the New Testament as follows: An angel of the Lord appeared to Phillip the Evangelist on the road between Jerusalem and Gaza. There he met an Ethiopian of great authority under Candace, the queen of Ethiopia. The man was also in charge of all the treasure of the queen and had come to Jerusalem to worship. He was reading from the prophet Isaiah when Philip approached him. After determining that the Ethiopian did not fully understand the Scriptures, Philip seized the opportunity to explain the Gospel. He did so with such clarity that when they came to some water, the man ordered the chariot to stop:

"And they both went down into the water, and (Philip) baptized him.… And the (man) went on his way rejoicing." Acts 8:38-39

Given the authority and trust conferred upon the Ethiopian by Queen Candace, some biblical scholars interpret this account as the spread of Christianity "to the ends of the earth." Once again, the role of a great woman was pivotal in this process.

Native American Women

In 1619, the first Europeans arrived in North America and settled in what is now Jamestown, Virginia. A year later, the Pilgrims arrived at what is now Plymouth, Massachusetts. These first settlers brought along their negative attitudes and biases regarding the roles of women and people who did not look like they did. Their perceptions were caused by the hypercritical sexism prevalent in the European political and social culture. European women were considered chaste, delicate, refined, and yet physically and intellectually inferior to men. Conversely, they were perfectly suited for the home and for serving as wives and mothers.

Despite the well-established order, systems of government, social customs, and traditions in Native American communities discovered by Europeans, they were still considered to be uncivilized savages. The superior attitude of the European men toward the Native American women was even greater than that of the European women who had come with them. Nevertheless, the Native American women, *women of color,* held key roles in their homes and communities. Despite living in tribes where polygamy was largely practiced, the roles and responsibilities of these women were completely different from those of white women of that era. Native American women did the farming, raised the children, and took care of the household and other responsibilities. They also held significant jobs such as prophets, midwives, medicine women, and even warriors. On the other hand, Native American men were responsible for hunting, protecting the village, and whatever was left to do. Although the prejudice and bias against the Native Americans persisted for centuries, it was the Native American women who displayed character, courage, intellect, and resiliency that belied the perceptions of the settlers. Later historical accounts, literature, and modern media presentations verify this fact. I have chosen one of these Native American women to emphasize these truths: Sacagawea.

Sacagawea

Sacagawea was the daughter of a Shoshone chief born about 1788 in Lemhi County, Idaho. When she was approximately twelve years old, Sacagawea and another young girl were captured by an enemy tribe and later sold to a French-Canadian trapper named Toussaint Charbonneau. Following the typical tribal custom, Charbonneau made Sacagawea one of his two wives. The Charbonneau family lived among the Hidatsa and Mandan Indians in the upper Missouri River area in North Dakota.

In late 1804, the *Corps of Discovery Expedition,* led by Captain Meriwether Lewis and Second Lieutenant William Clark, arrived in the Mandan area. The expedition had been commissioned by President Thomas Jefferson shortly after the Louisiana Purchase in 1803. A group of U.S. Army volunteers was selected for the perilous journey, which was expected to take from May 1804 to September 1806. Clark also brought along his personal slave, York, who had been with him for many years. The primary objective of the expedition was to explore and map the newly acquired territory and find a practical route across the Western half of the continent. They were also directed to establish an American presence in this new territory before European powers could claim it. As winter set in, Lewis and Clark decided to build a fort and stay until the next spring.

Lewis and Clark soon met Toussaint Charbonneau and subsequently hired him to serve as interpreter when they resumed their expedition. Charbonneau's wife, Sacagawea, was pregnant with her first child, but she was also hired to accompany them on their mission. Lewis and Clark believed that her knowledge of the Shoshone language and familiarity with the land would be valuable during their journey. This decision would prove to be a very wise choice as the journey unfolded.

In February 1805, Sacagawea gave birth to a son and called him Jean Baptiste Charbonneau. Two months later, the expedition left the fort and headed up the Missouri River in *pirogues,* small, flat-bottomed boats associated with the Cajuns of the Louisiana marshes. Using poles to steer against the river current was difficult, and in one instance, Sacagawea rescued items that had fallen out of a capsized boat. This was fortuitous as the retrieved items included the journals and records of Lewis and Clark. Sacagawea's quick action was highly praised and resulted in the Sacagawea River being named in her honor.

Despite traveling with a young child, Sacagawea proved to be invaluable in selecting campsites, food sources from the land, and the most navigable paths on the land and rivers. Furthermore, she served as a symbol of peace because a group traveling with a woman and a child were less suspicious than a group of men traveling alone. In August, 1805, the group located a Shoshone tribe and attempted a trade for horses to cross the Rocky Mountains. When Sacagawea was used as an interpreter, she discovered that the tribe's chief was actually her brother, *Cameahwait!* Through this miraculous good fortune, the explorers were able to buy the needed horses from the Shoshone to continue their westward journey. It was a joyful family reunion, but Sacagawea honored her commitment to remain with the expedition for the duration of the trip.

After a torturous and life-threatening 1,500-mile journey, the expedition finally reached the Pacific coast in November 1805. An incredible footnote is that Sacagawea carried her baby boy on her back most of the way! As key participants, she and the slave, York, were allowed to vote on where to build a fort to get them through the winter. Thus, a Native American woman and a black slave may have been the first recorded bi-racial voters in America! They built an outpost near what is present-day Astoria, Oregon and called it Fort Clatsop.

The expedition began its return trip east in March 1806. Once again, Sacagawea proved her worth by discovering and guiding the group through gaps in the Rocky Mountains. One such discovery was called the Bozeman Pass, which later became the route for the Northern Pacific Railway to cross the continental divide. Sacagawea, her husband, Toussaint, and young son, Jean Baptiste, stayed with Lewis and Clark until they reached Mandan Indian villages.

During the long, dangerous, and fatiguing journey, Sacagawea and her husband earned deep favor and respect from all the expedition members. William Clark, in particular, had grown very fond of Sacagawea's son, now called "Pomp." When the expedition continued downriver, Clark wrote Charbonneau a letter offering to take the boy and raise him as his own son. He invited Sacagawea and Charbonneau to come along to assist with the care of Pomp. After three years, Charbonneau and Sacagawea accepted Clark's invitation, traveled cross-country, and settled in St. Louis, Missouri in 1809. True to his word, Clark enrolled young Jean-Baptiste in the Saint Louis Academy boarding school.

Later, Sacagawea grew lonely for her homeland, so she and Charbonneau moved back to Fort Manuel Lisa Trading Post in North Dakota. Sometime after 1810, Sacagawea gave birth to a daughter, Lizette. Scant historical records, including Clark's later recorded notes, indicate that Sacagawea died in 1812 of an unknown cause at the age of twenty-four. Historical records also indicate that Toussaint Charbonneau signed formal custody of his son and daughter, Jean Baptiste and Lizette, to William Clark in 1813. It is believed that Lizette died later in childhood, and Charbonneau is thought to have lived until he was about eighty years old.

Sacagawea's son, Jean-Baptiste, grew up and lived an adventurous life. He enjoyed a lifelong celebrity status as the infant who traveled with the Lewis and Clark expedition to the Pacific Ocean and back. At eighteen, he was befriended by a German Prince who took him to Europe, where he lived in royalty for six years, fathered a son, and learned to speak four languages. The child later died and Jean moved back to America in 1829. He spent the rest of his life as a Western frontiersman, gold miner, hotel clerk, and a magistrate for the San Luis Rey Mission in California.

The foregoing story of Sacagawea is a remarkable example of God's greatness in women through the ages. Even when women were held in lesser esteem by men and cultures, the legacies of these two soared high. They are celebrated in many ways today, including special minted coins, days of tributes, monuments, statues, and sites bearing their names. Today, scores of Native American women continue to make outstanding contributions as advocates for their people.

African American Women

I believe that the contributions and significance of African American women in America warrant special attention because of their omission in much of documented history. Furthermore, the deep emotional scars caused by the brutality and pain of slavery stymied writing objectively about it. The incredible suffering of African American women was just too unbearable, and much of their history was endured in silence rather than recorded.

I struggled emotionally during my research and subsequent attempt to write a relevant story about black slave women. Nevertheless, I can state with conviction that no other culture of women has endured the incredible hardships and suffering as that which was forced upon black women. Recently, a number of books have documented African American history, so I chose only to highlight the greatness of a few African American women from the period of slavery to the 20th century.

From Africa to America

The first African slaves arrived in the present-day United States along with Spanish explorers as early as 1526. The first *documented* evidence is recorded in the history of the North American colony of Jamestown, Virginia in 1619. Slavery existed in America from the early years of the colonial period and was firmly established by the time the United States fought for independence from Great Britain in the 1770s. By 1804, all states north of the Mason-Dixon Line had either abolished slavery outright or passed laws for the gradual abolition of slavery. After Abraham Lincoln became president in 1861, eleven slave states broke away to form the Confederate States of America, resulting in the Civil War (1861-1865).

The abolition of slavery took place on January 1, 1863 when President Lincoln freed slaves in the Confederacy through the Emancipation Proclamation. While the Union victory freed the nation's four million slaves, the vestige of slavery continued to plague the relationships between whites and blacks in America. This divisiveness persisted from the turbulent Reconstruction era (1865-1877) to the civil rights movement that emerged in the 1960s, 100 years after the Emancipation Proclamation! So how does one characterize the greatness of African American women during the period of slavery? I believe a look at what they endured and had to overcome speaks to that.

The torturous journey of misery and oppression of African women and young girls began from the immediately upon capture in their homeland and subsequent forced enslavement. Despite their historical culture, royalty status, and personal worth, these African females were immediately subjected to dehumanizing treatment, physical abuse, rape, and torture. From the moment European men set foot on the African continent, African women did not meet their superficial image of "true womanhood." They were viewed as depraved, vulgar, subhuman, intellectually inferior, morally underdeveloped, and animal-like sexually. Given these horrific stereotypical attitudes, the treatment of African females knew no moral, physical, or sexual boundaries, particularly on the slave ships that crossed the Atlantic Ocean.

The journey of slaves across the Atlantic has been documented as one of the most wretched treatment of human beings in the annals of history. The emotional, mental, and physical deprivations forced upon the slaves defy description, even to this day. Male captives were usually chained together in pairs to save space, while women and children sometimes had more room. Men, women, and children were crammed into every available crevice and denied even space for breathing and biological relief. The plight of the African female was even more egregious. Women and young girls faced the additional violence of daily sexual exploitation by the European crews that was common practice, and a matter of ship policy. If the slave women resisted, they were whipped and mutilated.

From the moment they were snatched from their African homeland, through the dark valley of slavery in America and the Reconstruction era, and during the long night of racial oppression in the 20th century, they valiantly prevailed. These women overcame indescribable brutality, insurmountable obstacles, ravaging sexual exploitation, and unbearable denigration that defies human comprehension. Through it all, they embraced the power and strength derived from the Lord in their darkest hours of distress. God created in these women an unconquerable spirit and the *instinct* of motherhood to love, protect, and nurture every child that was given life and the fortitude to survive.

The brutality and sexual assaults were used to destroy the women's will to resist, while controlling or demoralizing the slave men. Ironically, this treatment of the slave women caused their resistance to be at least equal to or greater than that of the slave men. Many slaves committed suicide by self-starvation or jumping overboard. By the time the slave ships arrived in America, the dreadful treatment at sea had transitioned into a life of grief and woe as slaves became legal property of slave owners. Many of the women and girls were now pregnant by the abusing European ship crews. The inhuman treatment continued once the slaves reached America and consisted of brutal whippings, executions, and rapes. Such abuse was widespread, and the slave men were often powerless to help or protect their women. Nevertheless, many slaves fought back but were severely beaten or died resisting. Others carried deep, permanent emotional, psychological, and physical scars from the attacks.

Despite the hypocrisy of the racist Southern culture, by the late 18th century many mixed-race slaves and slave children clearly showed that white men often fathered children by slave women. In ironic contradiction, some master-slave relationships reflected a long-term emotional attachment. Others, mainly in the north, showed great benevolence toward their slaves. One of the most prominent long-term relationships existed between **Sarah Hemings** and **Thomas Jefferson,** an American Founding Father, the principal author of the Declaration of Independence, and the third President of the United States. Shortly after his election, Jefferson oversaw the purchase of the vast Louisiana Territory from France in 1803. He then commissioned the *Lewis and Clark Expedition* to explore the new west. Ironically, another woman of color, Native American Sacagawea, had a significant part in the success of one of Jefferson's storied achievements!

Sarah Hemings

Sarah "Sally" Hemings (1773-1835) was born a slave in Charles City County, Virginia. According to historical accounts, she was the youngest of six siblings born to a planter, John Wayles, and his slave, Betty Hemings. When Thomas Jefferson married Martha Wayles, his father-in-law gave the Hemings' offspring and other slaves as a wedding gift to the young Jeffersons. Thus, Sally Hemings was Martha's half-sister!

After eleven years of marriage, Martha died at the age of thirty-three and Jefferson never remarried. At age fourteen, Sally traveled with Jefferson's youngest daughter as a nursemaid and companion and joined Jefferson in Paris where he served as Minister to France. During the next two years, Sally and Jefferson apparently began an intimate relationship and she became pregnant for the first time. When she returned with Jefferson to Monticello, Sally continued to reside there until shortly after Jefferson's death on July 4, 1826. Of significance, Heming continued to be Jefferson's concubine throughout his political activities as Secretary of State, Vice President, and President for two terms (1790–1809).

Most biographers and historians have concluded that Thomas Jefferson had a long-term relationship with Sally Hemings and generally agree that her six children were fathered by him. Of note, Jefferson opposed slavery all his life in his speeches and writing, but he took little political action to emancipate slaves. He owned hundreds of slaves but freed only two slaves in his lifetime: Hemings' older brothers, Robert and James Hemings. He freed five other males related to Hemings in his will. No documentation was ever found freeing Sally; however, Jefferson's married daughter (Sally's niece), Martha Randolph interceded to prevent her from being auctioned off. In essence, this action freed Sally to live with her two youngest sons near Charlottesville, Virginia for the next nine years. In the 1833 census of Albemarle County, all three Hemings were recorded as "free white persons!" Sally continued thusly until her death at the age of sixty-two.

Harriet Tubman and Sojourner Truth

As grave and painful as slavery was for African American women, many found the courage and determination to resist total subjugation by their oppressors. It can be said that God gave them special courage to persevere, regardless of the magnitude of the burdens they carried; thus they became great heroines of all time. Others were given creativity, ingenuity, and intelligence not only to survive, but also ultimately to help advance the cause of freedom for African American people.

Just as the Lord heard the groanings of the Israelites in Egypt over 3,300 years earlier, the mournful cries of American slaves reached His ears. God called Moses to deliver His people from bondage; likewise, He empowered **Harriet Tubman** to lead hundreds of slaves to freedom. He gave **Sojourner Truth** incredible commitment and resolve to fight for the rights of slaves and the rights of women when the risks were high and the outcomes in grave doubt. Despite incredible hurdles, the courage, determination, and strength of these two women reflect greatness unsurpassed in women of any race, creed, or color. Their fortitude and tenacity were truly epic attributes. A brief highlight of the lives of Harriet and Sojourner confirms my discourse of woman as a *"Godly Creation!"*

Harriet Tubman

Harriet Tubman (1820 -1913) was born a slave named Araminta Harriet Ross about 1820 in Dorchester County, Maryland. While still a child, she suffered a severe head injury during a beating that caused life-long seizures, narcoleptic attacks, headaches, and visionary dream experiences. Harriet became a devout Christian and gave God the credit for her courage, dreams, and revelations. In 1849, she escaped to Philadelphia but almost immediately returned to Maryland to rescue many of her family members. Traveling at night and using the network of antislavery activists and safe houses known as the Underground Railroad, Harriet subsequently made more than nineteen trips to rescue more than 300 slaves. The Underground Railroad was a well-organized system composed of free and enslaved blacks, white abolitionists, and other activists.

Most prominent among these in Maryland were members of the Religious Society of Friends, often called Quakers. By now, the five-foot tall Harriet had earned the reputation of having never lost a "passenger" and was called the "Black Moses." Neither Tubman nor any of the fugitives she guided were ever captured. Later, she helped abolitionist John Brown recruit men for his raid on Harpers Ferry.

The Southern-dominated Congress passed the *Fugitive Slave Act of 1850* that required lawmen in Free states to assist in recapturing slaves. Large rewards were offered for the return of fugitive slaves, but Tubman used a variety of subterfuges to avoid detection and helped guide fugitives all the way to Canada where slavery was prohibited. At the outbreak of the Civil War, Tubman worked for the Union Army, first as a cook, then as a nurse, an armed scout, and a spy. She was the first woman to lead an armed expedition in the war. On one raid, more than 700 slaves were liberated in South Carolina! Harriet provided assistance in the form of Negro spirituals that she used as coded messages to warn fellow travelers of danger or to signal a clear path. She also carried a revolver for protection from the ever-present slave catchers and their dogs. It was recorded on one occasion that she threatened to shoot a slave if he insisted on turning back to the plantation from which they had escaped.

After the war, Harriet retired to the family home in Auburn, New York and devoted her life to caring for her aging parents and other relatives. In March 1869, she was married for the third time to a Civil War veteran named Nelson Davis, twenty-two years her junior. They spent the next twenty years together and in 1874 adopted a baby girl named Gertie. In her later years, Harriet worked along Susan B. Anthony to promote the cause of previously noted woman's suffrage. As she neared the end of her life, Harriet resided in a home that she had helped found years earlier for elderly African Americans. In 1913, surrounded by family and friends, Harriet Tubman died of pneumonia at the age of ninety-three. Allegedly, she told those gathered around her, *"I go to prepare a place for you."* She was buried with military honors at Fort Hill Cemetery in Auburn, New York. The city commemorated her life with a plaque on the courthouse. During this tribute, the great founder of Tuskegee Institute, Booker T. Washington, delivered a powerful keynote address.

Sojourner Truth

Sojourner Truth (1797-1883) was born a slave, Isabella Baumfree, in Swartekill, Ulster County, New York. She was one of about a dozen children born to James and Elizabeth Baumfree who were enslaved by a Dutchman, Colonel Hardenbergh. After the colonel's death, ownership of the family slaves passed to his son, Charles. Sojourner spoke only Dutch until she was about nine years old. In 1806, Charles Hardenbergh died, and for the next four years, Sojourner was bought and sold among several slave owners. In 1810, she was sold to John Dumont of West Park, New York. Dumont was generally kind to Truth, but his wife found ways to make her life very difficult. Nevertheless, about 1815, Sojourner met and fell in love with a slave named Robert from a neighboring farm. Since this relationship was forbidden, Robert's owner beat him to death and Sojourner never saw him again; however, she did give birth to his child. Two years later, she was forced to marry an older slave named Thomas with whom she had four additional children.

The state of New York began the legislative process in 1799 to abolish slavery, but it was not completed until July 4, 1827. Dumont reneged on an earlier promise to free Sojourner, so in late 1826, she escaped to freedom with her infant daughter. She had to leave her other children behind because they were not legally freed in the emancipation order until they had served as bond servants into their twenties. Sojourner and her baby made their way to the home of Isaac and Maria Van Wagener in New York, who took them. Van Wagener paid Dumont for Sojourner's service until the New York State Emancipation Act was approved.

During Sojourner's stay with the Van Wageners, she had a life-changing religious experience and became a devout Christian. Later, she learned that her five-year old son, Peter, had been sold illegally by Dumont to an owner in Alabama. With the help of the Van Wageners, she took the issue to court. After months of legal proceedings, Sojourner got back her son, thus becoming one of the first black women to go to court against a white man and win the case.

In 1843, Truth changed her name to *Sojourner Truth* and told her friends, *"The Spirit calls me, and I must go."* She became a Methodist and began traveling and preaching about the abolition of slavery. In 1844, she joined the Northampton Association of Education and Industry in Massachusetts. Founded by abolitionists, the organization supported women's rights, religious tolerance, and pacifism. While there, Sojourner met William Lloyd Garrison, Frederick Douglass, and David Ruggles. In 1850, she dictated her memoirs to her friend Olive Gilbert, and William Lloyd Garrison privately published her book, *The Narrative of Sojourner Truth: A Northern Slave*. That same year, she spoke at the first National Women's Rights Convention in Worcester, Massachusetts. In 1851, Sojourner left Northampton to join George Thompson, an abolitionist and speaker. She attended the Ohio Women's Rights Convention in Akron, Ohio and challenged the notion that equality was only for white, educated men and women. Capitalizing on her nearly six-foot frame, she rose and delivered her famous extemporaneous speech on women's rights, *"Ain't I a Woman."*

History suggests Sojourner "brought the house down," and was asked to speak to hundreds of others over the next decade.

During the Civil War, Sojourner helped recruit black troops for the Union Army and her grandson, James Caldwell, enlisted in the famed 54th Massachusetts Regiment. In 1864, she was employed by the National Freedman's Relief Association in Washington, D.C. In October of that year, she met President Abraham Lincoln while working diligently to improve conditions for African Americans and helping to end segregation. After the war, Sojourner tried unsuccessfully to secure land grants from the federal government for former slaves. She also continued to work for women's rights.

In May 1867, Sojourner was called to address the American Equal Rights Association. She had been advertised as one of the main convention speakers and spoke mainly about the rights of black women. Sojourner argued that the push for equal rights had led to black men winning new rights; therefore it was time to give black women the rights they too deserved. She stressed that *"we should keep things going while things are stirring"* because once the fight for Colored rights settled down, it would take a long time to warm people back up to the idea of Colored women having equal rights. This speech proved to be painfully prophetic!

Sojourner Truth died on November 26, 1883 at her home in Battle Creek, Michigan. Over 3,000 people crowded into the Battle Creek Tabernacle to pay their last respects to this renowned black heroine. The services were presided over by Uriah Smith, the Seventh-day Adventist author, editor, church leader, and founder of Battle Creek College. Sojourner was buried at Oak Hill Cemetery in Battle Creek beside other family members and many Seventh-day Adventist pioneers.

The Bridge to the 20th Century

In the introduction of this book, I wrote about the collective 500 years of direct female influence in my life (i.e., mother, sister, wife, daughters, and others). This experience was gained largely from growing up in an African American community. Rather than suffering a disadvantage, my being raised by black women proved to be fortuitous in my development and growth as a man. I have been blessed with the profound joy and privilege of experiencing African American women up close and personal. I know the "scent" of their essence, compassion, love, tenderness, and warmth. On a few occasions, I have also been the object of the ire and wrath of an angry black woman!

Explicit evidence of the greatness in African American women has been manifested in their descendants for many generations. Every African American woman and man of the 21st century owes a debt to our "ancestor mothers" that can never be paid. These women overcame devastating adversity so that we would have many freedoms they never realized. The opportunities and successes enjoyed by their offspring in the 21st century are reflected in a myriad of disciplines, including business, education, government, law, medicine, the military, and politics. Their "daughters" include Rosa Parks, Wilma Rudolph, Coretta Scott King, Myrlie Edwards-Williams, Betty Shabazz, Oprah Winfrey, Condoleezza Rice, Venus and Serena Williams, Michelle Obama and a host of just plain everyday people. I trust you now have a greater appreciation for the greatness that God imbued in African American women since the beginning of time.

WOMEN OF COLOR

Queen Nefertiti

Sacagawea

Harriet Tubman

Sojourner Truth

CHAPTER TWELVE

Women of the Twentieth Century

Major Breakthroughs

The global list of great women of the 20th century numbers into the hundreds and are duly documented in thousands of books and magazines. Furthermore, the Internet and social media tools provide ready access to history-making events as they occur. Hopefully, young people of today are being effectively informed through the medium to which they are accustomed and savvy. Therefore, I have chosen to highlight only a few of my favorite heroines who lived during my lifetime. These include Mary McLeod Bethune, Irena Sendler, Golda Meir, and Coretta Scott King.

Mary McLeod Bethune

I first learned about Mary McLeod Bethune when I was in the seventh grade during *"The Negro History Week"* in the early 1950s. In addition to the schools being rigidly segregated, the curriculum was also severely restricted. Accordingly, teachers were permitted only one week each February to teach Negro students about the historical accomplishments and contributions of black people in America. These dedicated teachers found creative ways to inspire us to thirst for more knowledge, often providing additional material for home assignments.

My favorite heroines then included Marian Anderson, Lena Horne, Billy Holiday, and Dr. Mary McLeod Bethune. Unlike the others, Dr. Bethune did not fit the image of an outwardly beautiful woman. She was a dark-skinned, unattractive woman but did not allow her physical appearance to diminish her tremendous character. Dr. Bethune refused to be the "wallflower of the dance;" nor did she allow the shackles of racial oppression to impede her determination, perseverance, and vision for educating young black children. As a young boy struggling with my "blackness," I was struck by the legacy of Dr. Bethune. To this day, I can truthfully say she inspired me to never think less of myself because of my outward appearance or race.

Mary Jane McLeod was born on a rice and cotton farm in a small log cabin July 10, 1875 near Mayesville, South Carolina. She was the fifteenth of seventeen children born to Samuel and Patsy McIntosh McLeod. Her parents and most of her siblings were former slaves, and the family continued to work for the former slave owner for a number of years. Everyone in the McLeod family labored in the cotton fields, and Mary Jane joined them when she was just five years old. She demonstrated an early desire to read and write and was the only McLeod child allowed to attend the one-room local school. It was run by the Presbyterian Board of Mission; and Emma Jane Wilson, the teacher, became a life-long mentor for Mary. Wilson attended what is now Barber-Scotia College (BSC) and later arranged for Mary to attend the same college from 1888-1894. BSC is a historically black college located in Concord, North Carolina. Built in 1867, it began as a female seminary to prepare the daughters of former slaves for careers as social workers and teachers.

Mary Jane had hoped to become a missionary to Africa, so she next attended Dwight L. Moody's Institute for Home and Foreign Missions in Chicago (now the Moody Bible Institute). Told that black missionaries were not needed, she decided to become a teacher. She taught briefly at her former elementary school in Sumter County. In 1896, she accepted a position at the Haines Normal and Industrial Institute, part of another Presbyterian mission in Augusta, Georgia.

The Haines Institute was founded by Lucy Craft Laney, a former slave who ran the school with the zeal of a Christian missionary. Mary spent only one year at Haines Institute, but she was deeply influenced by Laney. She adopted many of Laney's educational philosophies as she sought to improve the conditions of black people by educating primarily women. Focusing on that concept, Mary joined the National Association of Colored Women that was formed in 1896 to promote the needs of black women. She transferred back to Sumter, South Carolina to teach at the Kindell Institute where she met fellow teacher Albertus Bethune. They married in 1898 and had a son, Albert McLeod Bethune. Still on the move, Mary next traveled to Palatka, Florida to run a mission school and to provide an outreach to prisoners. Her husband apparently felt insecure and left the family in 1907 and died in 1918. Over the next twenty-five years, Mary demonstrated an incredibly high level of energy as she developed schools for girls, formed a co-educational college, and became a political activist and advisor to presidents and their first ladies. A brief summary of her extraordinary achievements follows.

In 1904, she started the Literary and Industrial Training School for Negro Girls in Daytona. Mary's parents and church members raised money by making sweet potato pies, ice cream, and fried fish to sell at nearby construction sites. The curriculum consisted of a rigorous Christian life and Bible study, home economics, and other industrial skills such as dressmaking, millinery, cooking, and other crafts that emphasized a life of self-sufficiency. Later, courses were added in science, business, math, English, and foreign languages.

In 1912, Booker T. Washington of the Tuskegee Institute visited Mary's school and provided counsel and encouragement. She had first gone to see Washington in 1896 and was impressed particularly by his ability to acquire generous donors. By 1920, the school had rapidly grown in resources, facilities, and student enrollment and Mary renamed it the *Daytona Normal and Industrial Institute.* In 1923, the school became Bethune-Cookman College after merging with the Cookman Institute for Men from Jacksonville, Florida. Despite the constant financial needs, the college survived the Great Depression and became known as a top college for Negroes in Florida. While being a major educator and administrator in Florida, Mary continued her activist role in the National Association of Colored Women (NACW). She was elected to serve as the Florida chapter president of the NACW in 1917. She became the national president in 1924. Notwithstanding the very limited funding, Mary's vision and hard work resulted in the establishment of a national headquarters with a professional executive secretary in Washington DC. NAWC also became the first black-controlled organization represented in Washington, DC.

In 1928, Mary McLeod Bethune was invited to attend the Child Welfare Conference called by President Calvin Coolidge. In 1930, President Herbert Hoover appointed her to the White House Conference on Child Health. In 1935, President Roosevelt selected Mary to serve as his special advisor for minority affairs. That same year, she founded the National Council of Negro Women (NCNW) in New York City. This unprecedented effort brought together twenty-eight different organizations to form a council to facilitate the improvement of quality of life for women and their respective communities. Bethune is said to have defined their purpose as follows:

> *"It is our pledge to make a lasting contribution to all that is finest and best in America, to cherish and enrich her heritage of freedom and progress by working for the integration of all her people regardless of race, creed, or national origin, into her spiritual, social, cultural, civic, and economic life, and thus aid her to achieve the glorious destiny of a true and unfettered democracy."*

During WW II, Mary McLeod Bethune played a significant role as a close and loyal friend to President Franklin and Eleanor Roosevelt. She had unprecedented access to the White House through her relationship with the First Lady who frequently said Mary was "her closest friend in her age group." In turn, Mary articulated the concerns of black people to the Roosevelts. Of particular note, many people associated with the Tuskegee Airmen program believe Mary influenced Mrs. Roosevelt to visit the fledgling program in Alabama to see for herself that black men could fly airplanes. The advent of Mrs. Roosevelt's flight with Charles A. "Chief" Anderson became the iconic evidence of black men's ability to serve our nation as aviators. Mrs. Roosevelt insisted that a picture be taken of her in an open cockpit of an aircraft with Chief Anderson, a black pilot. She presented that photo to a wide-range of media outlets all across the nation. It is believed that Eleanor and Mary Bethune used that evidence to convince President Roosevelt to finally permit the Tuskegee Airmen to enter the war in Europe. The rest is history!

Finally, yielding to time and health considerations, Mary McLeod Bethune resigned as president of Bethune-Cookman College in 1942. Nevertheless, she continued to work for the advancement of all people in America. On April 25, 1945, President Harry S. Truman selected Dr. Bethune to be a consultant at the organizing meeting of the United Nations

Dr. Bethune later became a staunch advocate for civil rights in the late 1940s and early 1950s. In 1954, the Chicago Defender published her opinion regarding the Supreme Court's repudiation of the "Separate but Equal" (Plessy versus Ferguson) doctrine that had denied African Americans equal rights for fifty-eight years.

> *"There can be no divided democracy, no class government, and no half-free country, under the constitution. Therefore, there can be no discrimination, no segregation, no separation of some citizens from the rights, which belong to all.... We are on our way. But these are frontiers, which we must conquer.... We must gain full equality in education ...in the franchise... in economic opportunity, and full equality in the abundance of life."*

Dr. Mary McLeod Bethune's body and heart finally gave out. She died of a heart attack on May 18, 1955 and is buried on the campus of Bethune-Cookman College in Daytona Beach, Florida. The scores of affiliations, awards, citations, honorary degrees, and memorials are too numerous to list here. Her son, Albert McLeod Bethune, sired five children and died at the age of ninety in 1989. Over a dozen, including five grandchildren, are still living. Dr. Bethune left an immeasurable legacy of sacrifice and service, not only for African Americans, to all humanity. The story that follows reflects another great woman, Irene Sendler. Like Dr. Bethume, she overcame incredible obstacles in the service to humanity.

Irena Sendler

During the mid-1940s, I was a young boy growing up in Oxnard, California. It was a beautiful, quaint, small town located near numerous military bases that were energized by the constant activities of World War II. It was also a great time to be growing up, as everyone lived and worked together to support our men and women at war. Children were taught to do their part by beginning each day in school with the Pledge of Allegiance, singing patriotic songs, reciting Bible verses, and praying for our country. The news reports in those days came over the radio, newspapers, and movie clips, and I soon learned about the atrocities of war suffered by people in the German-occupied countries in Europe. Those reports that reached America confirmed that many of the victims were young children like me, and I was especially saddened to hear that thousands suffered and perished under cruel Nazi persecution.

The news reports also told of many heroic people throughout Europe, who opposed the Hitler regime and risked their lives to save thousands of oppressed Jews. Although a student of history, I had not heard about the heart-warming, ingenious exploits of Irena Sendler until nearly sixty-five years after the war. Her story may still have been lost to the world except for four exceptional high school students and a visionary teacher from Uniontown, in rural eastern Kansas with a population of less than 300 people.

In the fall of 1999, Mr. Norm Konrad, a social studies teacher at Uniontown High School, encouraged some of his students to work on a year-long National History Day project. The objectives of the project were to extend the boundaries of the classroom, contribute to history, and to teach respect and tolerance of others regardless of creed, race, or religion. Initially, three ninth grade students, Elizabeth Cambers, Megan Stewart, and Jessica Shelton along with an eleventh grade student, Sabrina Coons, accepted Mr. Konrad's challenge. Later, additional boys and girls participated in the project. The amazing outcome of the *Irena Sendler Project* is the production of *Life in a Jar*, a student-produced drama that has been performed over 285 times all across the United States, in Canada and in Poland. Remembering my emotions as a young boy in the 1940s, the Irena Sendler story moved me very deeply, and I immediately considered her as one of *God's Great Creations*. I feel humbled and privileged to include a few words about her in this book.

Irena Sendler, also known as *Irena Sendlerowaw*, was born in Warsaw, Poland on February 15, 1910 to Dr. Stanisław Krzyżanowski, a physician, and his wife, Janina. When she was seven years old, her father died after contracting typhus while treating patients, whom his colleagues refused to treat, many of which were Jews. As a result, the grateful Jewish community helped pay for Irena's education. While studying Polish literature at Warsaw University, she joined the Socialist party and was later suspended for publicly protesting prewar Polish policies concerning Jews. At the age of twenty, she married a fellow Polish citizen, Mieczyslaw Sendler.

Irena lived in Warsaw and worked at the Urban Social Welfare Departments during the German occupation of Poland. When the Germans invaded Poland in 1939, she began aiding the Jews. Despite the high risk of death, she and her associates created more than 3,000 false documents to help Jewish families escape. In the summer of 1943, Irena was selected by the underground Polish Council to oversee its Jewish children's section. She used her official permit to enter the Warsaw Ghetto under the pretext of conducting inspections of sanitary conditions during a typhus outbreak. She was able to create an effective working relationship with others in the Warsaw Municipal Social Services Department that was allowed under the German occupation. This would soon become the path through which many Jewish children would be saved.

By World War II, Irena Sendler had become a Roman Catholic nurse and social worker who defied the Nazis and courageously served in the Polish Underground. She and two dozen compatriots smuggled Jewish children out of the Warsaw Ghetto in boxes, suitcases, sacks, and coffins. Sometimes they had to sedate the babies to keep them quiet. Some of the children were rushed away through a network of basements, secret passages, and even the sewers to reach safety. The children were then provided false identity documents and safe housing outside the ghetto. Despite the constant threat of death, Irena saved nearly 2,500 children during the Holocaust. The majority of the children saved by her group were taken into Roman Catholic convents, orphanages, homes, and given non-Jewish aliases. Their true names were written on thin rolls of paper in the hope they could be reunited with their families after the war. These priceless records were placed in jars and buried in a friend's garden!

In 1943, the Nazis finally captured and severely tortured Irena. At one point, they broke her legs and feet; yet she refused to divulge the names of her cohorts or where the lists of escaped children were buried. The hand of providence apparently intervened while Irena was passed because a Gestapo officer accepted a bribe from her comrades to help her escape. She went into hiding but continued the rescue of Jewish children for the remainder of the war.

After the war, Irena and her underground cohorts collected all the records of the names and locations of the hidden Jewish children and gave them to the Polish Council to Aid Jews. Sadly, nearly all the parents of the children had been killed at the Treblinka extermination camp or were missing. Sixty-eight years have passed since the end of WWII, and I simply cannot find adequate words to express the human sorrow of the Holocaust. Between 1942 and 1943, an estimated 1,000,000 men, women, and children were murdered at Treblinka. More than 800,000 of these were Jews. Incredibly, the heroism of Irena Sendler was suppressed by communist Poland and remained virtually unknown for sixty years. Miraculously, she lived to be ninety-eight years old!

Irena Sendler has been belatedly recognized and honored by the Polish government, the nation of Israel, Pope John Paul II, and the American Center of Polish Culture in Washington, D.C. She was posthumously awarded the *Audrey Hepburn Humanitarian Award,* named in honor of the late actress and UNICEF ambassador. The entire world owes an immeasurable debt of gratitude to those awesome students and their teacher from Uniontown, Kansas. Their noble efforts elevated Irena Sendler to the status of a global heroine, and they are *living memorials* to Irene Sendler. In a fitting tribute to herself, Irena Sendler left us these words:

"Every child saved with my help is the justification of my existence on this Earth, and not a title to glory."

Another great woman who lived during my generation also had an impact on the world. She is the late heroine from Israel, Golda Meir, a "chosen" daughter of God.

Golda Meir

My first recollection of Jewish people dates back to about the time Israel gained its independence from British rule and became a state in 1948. My education came from a most unlikely source, the African American pastor of the church my family attended. Reverend M. Stills led the congregation in praying for Israel each monthly Sunday night celebration of Holy Communion in Goodwill Missionary Baptist Church in Shreveport, Louisiana. After his sermon and just before passing out the communion elements, Reverend Stills would have us recite the scriptures below:

"I was glad when they said unto me,
Let us go to the house of the Lord.
Our feet are standing within your gates, O Jerusalem,
Jerusalem that is built as a city that is compact together;
To which the tribes go up, even the tribes of Lord....
To give thanks to the name of the Lord.....
Pray for the peace of Jerusalem: they shall prosper that love thee.
Peace be within thy walls, and prosperity within thy palaces.
For my brethren and companions' sakes, I will now say, peace be
within thee."
Psalm 122:1-8

For a man who had never been out of the country, he had a steadfast reverence for "God's chosen people." Since my family was struggling with poverty and daily racial oppression, I was baffled by our pastor's preoccupation with a country so very far away. In fact, I often muttered under my breath: *Reverend Stills, how about praying for some peace for the poor folk right here in Shreveport!"* Of course, I valued my life and didn't dare let my mother hear my inner thoughts.

Nearly twenty years later, the Six-Day War between Israel and its Arab neighbors caused me to have a dramatic appreciation for Israel. I realized that my pastor had been right all along in praying for the peace of Jerusalem. Over the next several years, I was motivated to become an avid student of Israel's history. I read about its *"Iron Lady,"* Golda Meir, years before the title was associated with British Prime Minister, Margaret Thatcher. Golda had an astounding strength of character, fortitude, and fierce resolve in fighting for Israel's survival, despite being surrounded by extremely hostile nations. After serving as the Minister of Labor and Foreign Minister, Golda was elected Prime Minister of Israel in March 1969. She was the first woman in Israel's history elevated to this office and only the third woman in the world to hold such an office. The late Prime Minister, David Ben-Gurion, is said to have called Golda *"the best man in the government."* Others called her the *"strong-willed, straight-talking, grey-bunned grandmother of the Jewish people."* Golda Meir had certainly become a heroine of mine.

Golda Mabovitch was born on May 3, 1898, in Kiev, the Russian Empire, now present-day Ukraine. Her father was Moshe Mabovitch, a carpenter, and her mother was Blume Neiditch. Seven other children were born to this couple, but five died in childhood. Two of Golda's sisters survived, Tzipke and Sheyna, who she was especially close to. In 1903, Moshe left to find work in New York City. In 1905, he moved to Milwaukee, Wisconsin, in search of a higher-paying job. He eventually found employment in the workshops of the local railroad yard and saved enough money to bring his family to the United States in 1906.

Golda grew up in Milwaukee and attended grade school while her mother, Blume, ran a grocery store. Golda showed unusual maturity early on by organizing a fundraiser and renting a hall for a public meeting to pay for her classmates' textbooks. Although she did not initially know English, she became an excellent student and graduated as valedictorian of her class. At fourteen, she attended high school while working part-time. At this point, her mother insisted that she should quit school and get married. Instead, Golda rebelled and bought a train ticket to Denver, Colorado to live with her married sister, Sheyna Korngold. While living with the Korngolds, she was exposed to Zionism literature, trade unionism, and other philosophies during many evening gatherings. These events played a significant role in solidifying her future convictions in life.

Golda returned to Milwaukee in 1913 and graduated from high school in 1915. She attended Milwaukee State Normal School Teachers College and subsequently taught in Milwaukee public schools. In 1917, Golda took a position at a Yiddish-speaking Folks Schule where she became a committed Labor Zionist. During this time, she met and began dating Morris Meyerson, a dedicated socialist. The two were married in December 1917, but on the precondition they would settle in Palestine. Having staunchly embraced Zionism, Golda immediately wanted to make *aliyah* (the immigration of Jews from scattered settlements outside of Palestine to the land of Israel, *Eretz Yisrael*).

The return to the Holy Land had been the deep aspiration of many Jews since the Babylonian Exile in 586 B.C. Golda's plans were disrupted, however, when all transatlantic passenger services were canceled due to the outbreak of World War I. In 1921, Golda and her husband eventually quit their jobs and along with her sister, Sheyna, moved to Palestine to join a *kibbutz* (a collective farm in Israel). Her initial duties included picking almonds, planting trees, working in the chicken coops, and running the kitchen. However, her leadership skills were soon recognized, and the kibbutz selected her to be its representative to the *Histadrut,* Israel's organization of trade unions.

In 1924, Golda and her husband left the kibbutz and resided briefly in Tel Aviv before settling in Jerusalem. They had two children during the next two years, a son Menachem (1924), and a daughter, Sarah (1926). By 1928, Golda was elected secretary of the Working Women's Council, which required her to return as an emissary to the United States for two years. She and her two children spent 1932–1934 in the United States, but Morris remained in Jerusalem. This separation caused the marriage to fail, but Golda and Morris never divorced. She returned from the United States in 1934 and continued to move up the ranks of the Executive Committee of the

Histadrut and ultimately became head of its Political Department. The latter proved to be excellent preparation for Golda's future role as Israel's leader.

Over the next ten years, Golda increasingly was selected to key leadership positions in several political areas. In July 1938, she was the Jewish observer from Palestine at the Évian Conference, called by U.S. President Franklin D. Roosevelt to discuss the question of Jewish refugees fleeing Nazi Germany. During the British crackdown on the Palestine Zionist movement in June 1946, Golda took over as acting head of the Political Department of the Jewish Agency. In this role, she became the principal negotiator between the Palestinian Jews and the British Mandatory authorities. In January 1948, Golda traveled to the United States and managed to raise $50 million to purchase arms in Europe for her emerging state. Just four days before the official establishment of the Jewish state on May 10, 1948, she is said to have traveled to Amman disguised as an Arab woman for a secret meeting with King Abdullah of Transjordan. Allegedly Golda urged him not to join the other Arab countries in attacking the Jews. Abdullah asked her not to hurry to proclaim a state. She is said to have replied

"We've been waiting for 2,000 years. Is that hurrying?"

The day after Israel was recognized as an official state, it was attacked by the joint armies of Egypt, Syria, Lebanon, Transjordan, and Iraq. Expeditionary forces from other Arab countries and Arab guerilla movements also joined in this 1948 Arab–Israeli War. Amazingly, Israel successfully repelled the combined Arab assault, then launched a series of its own military offensives and expanded its territorial holdings. As Israel grew as a state to be reckoned with, Golda served tirelessly in key positions with incredible determination, focus, and strength. To the world as well as her fellow Israelites, she was deeply revered and seemed to be held securely in the hand of Providence.

In 1949, Golda was elected to the Knesset (the legislative branch of the Israeli government) and served continuously until 1974. She served as Minister of Labor from 1949 to 1956. While serving in this role, she enacted new state welfare policies, orchestrated the integration of immigrants into Israel's workforce, and introduced major housing and road construction projects.

In 1956, she was selected to be Foreign Minister under Prime Minister David Ben-Gurion, and shortened her last name to "Meir." (Her husband, Morris Myerson, passed away in 1951.) Golda promoted ties with the newly established African states because she believed Israel could be a role model for shaking off foreign rule, becoming self-sufficient, and defending itself. Having lived on a kibbutz, she was especially confident in assisting Africans in reclaiming their land and making it highly productive.

In the early 1960s, Golda was diagnosed with lymphoma and retired in January 1966, but refused to remain on the sidelines. She soon returned to public service and devoted the last fifteen years of her life working to ensure the survival and viability of Israel in a rapidly changing world. The rigors of the office of Prime Minister, the wars, and many critical crises finally took their toll on Golda, and she resigned her position in April 1974. Her parting words were,

"It is beyond my strength to continue carrying this burden."

I sincerely wanted to visit Israel in hopes of personally meeting Golda Meir and other heroes of Israel, but it was not to be. There is, however, an interesting conclusion to my quest to visit Israel, the country for which Golda gave so much of her life. The paths of five top Israeli pilots and mine crossed in 1976 when I was a test pilot for the new F-15 Air Superiority jet fighter. As an American ally, Israel was allowed to send their top pilots to Arizona to learn first-hand about this jet that eventually would be provided for its defense. I had the privilege to help train these pilots and established a lasting personal and professional relationship.

Thirty-one years later, my wife, Peggy, daughter, Gail, and I fulfilled a long-held dream of visiting the Holy Land. I was able to locate retired Brigadier General Moshe Melnik, one of the five pilots who had trained at Luke AFB. By then, he was also the top ace of the Israeli Air Force. In May 2007, we met Moshe and his lovely wife, Raya in Tel Aviv, and they graciously hosted us for much of our trip.

One afternoon, Moshe and I stood high on the wind-swept pinnacle called the "Finger of Israel." It is wedged tightly between the borders of Lebanon and Syria, a stone's throw from each. From this high strategic lookout post, we experienced the quiet stillness of the Golan Heights, an area that had been contested by these three nations for many years. That day, unconstrained by racial, religious, or denominational differences, we stood in solemn wonder overlooking the hallowed ground that the Patriarch Abraham trod centuries ago. I couldn't help but think of Golda Meir and the many great heroes and heroines of Israel from biblical history. I remembered the admonition of Pastor Stills fifty years earlier, *"Pray for the peace of Jerusalem."* Now willingly, I silently prayed for the peace of Jerusalem and that Golda Meir was resting quietly in peace in the bosom of her precious Israel.

Coretta Scott King—An Amazing Intersection of Destinies

I began writing this section of the book August 28, 2013. It was the fiftieth anniversary of the iconic *"I have Dream"* speech delivered by Dr. Martin Luther King, Jr. at the Lincoln Memorial in Washington, DC. That speech has been credited with being the seminal catalyst that advanced the civil rights movement in America and led to the Civil Rights Act of 1964. As I reflect back on that historical day in August 1963, I never cease to be amazed at how God used women to propel man forward in His planned purpose for this world. History is replete with stories of women who played a vital role or who were intimately involved in the lives of great men—Sarah and Abraham; Anthony and Cleopatra; Queen Isabella of Spain and Columbus; and Sally Heming and Thomas Jefferson.

Dr. Martin Luther King, Jr. can be similarly paired with Coretta Scott King, the woman who helped shaped the course of his life. His mother, Alberta, gave him birth, but it was Coretta Scott King who had a profound impact on determining the path life would take. I didn't plan writing this portion of my book to coincide with such an historical moment. Yet an amazing intersection of destinies is anchored upon my meeting of Dr. King in 1957 and upon meeting his wife, Coretta, forty-one years later. Much has been written about

Dr. King and Coretta, and I dare not attempt to improve upon that. What follows is my effort to underscore how God used Coretta to significantly influence the man who became the moral conscience of a nation and the world.

Coretta Scott King (1927–2006), the widow of Dr. Martin Luther King, Jr., played a crucial role in her husband's life while he was alive. As a faithful wife, mother, and advisor, she weathered the storm of his fifteen-year career as a leader in the Civil Rights movement. These were often perilous times filled with life-threatening physical assaults, bombings, and unauthorized privacy invasions by the Federal Bureau of Investigation. Despite these trying times, the Kings were blessed with four children: Yolanda Denise (1955–2007), Martin Luther III (1957), Dexter Scott (1961), and Bernice Albertine (1963).

After Dr. King's assassination in 1968, Coretta became well-known in her own right as an activist, author, and civil rights advocate. In December 1968, she exhorted women to *"unite and form a solid block of women power to fight the three great evils of racism, poverty and war."* Later in life, she was at odds with one of her daughters, a cousin, several ministers, and other activists over certain social issues. Nevertheless, I believe her greatest accomplishments were the development of the Martin Luther King, Jr. Center for Nonviolent Social Change and the fight to establish the national holiday in his name. These landmark achievements ensured a permanent memorial for Dr. King's powerful legacy that continues to inspire the world to strive for human rights and racial equality. To better appreciate the innate character, determination, and fortitude of this great woman, a brief look at her early life will be instructive.

Coretta Scott King was born in the small town of Marion, Alabama, approximately twenty-five miles from the infamous city of Selma. She was the third of four children born to Obadiah "Obe" Scott and Bernice McMurray Scott. Three other children were born to this couple—two sisters and a brother; one sister died in childhood. Coretta's parents lived to be in their nineties, and her two siblings reached the age of their early eighties. The Scott family had owned a farm since shortly after the Civil War, and they survived the Great

Depression with the help of their children picking cotton. Later, Coretta's father became the first black person in Marion to own a truck. He was also a barber and owner of a lumber mill. His mill was destroyed by fire when he refused to sell it to a white logger.

Despite rigid segregation in the town and the constraints of time, the Scotts were determined to see that their children received a suitable education. The Scott children attended a one-room elementary school near their home and later were bused to Lincoln Normal School, the only black high school in Marion, Alabama. Coretta's mother, Bernice, was the local bus driver for all the black teenagers in Marion. Given the close supervision of concerned parents, Coretta graduated valedictorian of Lincoln Normal School in 1945. She was also a gifted musician who played both the trumpet and piano, sang in the chorus, and participated in school musicals.

After graduation from high school, she joined her older sister at Antioch College in Yellow Springs, Ohio. Antioch had an Interracial Education Program that recruited non-white students and provided them full scholarships in an attempt to diversify the historically white campus. Coretta studied music under Walter Anderson, the first African American chair of a department in any predominantly white institution of higher learning in the United States. By then she had become recognized as a talented young soprano singer.

The small number of black students at Antioch College still faced widespread racial discrimination in the community. During Coretta's second year, the local school board denied her request to do her practice teaching at Yellow Springs Public School in order to earn her teaching certificate. The Antioch College administration was either unable or unwilling to change the situation; however, they hired Coretta to work in Antioch's associated laboratory school during her second year. Undaunted, Coretta became politically active in the emerging Civil Rights movement. She also joined the Antioch chapter of the *National Association for the Advancement of Colored People* (NAACP) and the college's Race Relations and Civil Liberties Committees.

Coretta left Antioch College after winning a scholarship to the New England Conservatory of Music in Boston, Massachusetts. While studying in Boston, she met Martin Luther King, Jr. The courtship blossomed into a permanent relationship, and Coretta and Martin were married on June 18, 1953 at her home in Marion, Alabama. Although the ceremony was performed by Martin Jr.'s father, Martin Luther King, Sr., Coretta demonstrated the unusual independence of her own mind. She had the vow *"to obey her husband"* removed from the ceremony! Furthermore, she completed her degree in voice and piano at the New England Conservatory before moving to Montgomery, Alabama to be with her husband in September 1954.

In 1957, I was a student at Tuskegee Institute when the path of my life began its convergence with that of Coretta Scott King. On a warm night in September, I met her husband, Dr. Martin Luther King, Jr. I heard him speak and shook his hand. That encounter in itself changed my life. I saw Mrs. King for the first time in March 1965 as she participated in the historical march from Selma to Montgomery, Alabama. She was a beautiful and courageous woman, marching arm-in-arm with Dr. King and thousands of others destined to change the course of America. That unprecedented march helped forge the passage of the Voting Rights Act of 1965.

On the morning of April 4, 1968, while I was serving as a captain in the Air Force in Germany, the glaring news headlines announced:

"MARTIN LUTHER KING, JR.
ASSASSINATED IN MEMPHIS, TENNESSEE!"

My eyes clouded over in disbelief, and my hands shook so badly I could hardly read the print. That night, my young wife and I cried in despair as our country roiled in the violent aftermath of Dr. King's death. As we prayed, I asked God to one day allow me to help carry on Dr. King's work. As I grappled with this senseless tragedy, a deep and abiding resolve slowly emerged in my mind:

"Please don't hate! Maintain a positive attitude. Pursue excellence in all you are assigned, and be prepared to make whatever contribution you can when the opportunity comes."

Thirty years after the death of Dr. King, that opportunity came unexpectantly through Coretta Scott King! In 1998 I had retired after twenty-six years in the Air Force, worked for H. Ross Perot, and was serving on the Board of Regents at the University of New Mexico. Mrs. King was the keynote speaker for an event sponsored by the African American Studies Department. My wife and I were honored to share the stage with her, and I was asked to give remarks for the occasion. Thus, I met Coretta Scott King face-to-face after an odyssey that began forty-one years after the night I met her husband. Prior to giving our speeches, we shared many poignant experiences while living and serving in Alabama. The most incredulous moment came when we realized that our comments were taken from the same speech given by the great Negro statesman and orator, Fredrick Douglass in Rochester, New York in 1852! Afterwards, we both felt that a divine hand had placed us together for a yet undetermined cause.

Several weeks after Mrs. King's visit, Mr. Ross Perot called me to Dallas to listen in on a request by Martin Luther King III, the new president of Southern Christian Leadership Conference (SCLC). Having previously worked for Ross and having earned his confidence and trust, he subsequently hired me to assist Martin III and SCLC. The goal was to regain SCLC's relevance that was established forty years earlier by Dr. King and others and to chart a new course for the twenty-first century.

A local team was formed in Atlanta Georgia that included Martin III, Dexter, and former Ambassador and Atlanta mayor, Andrew Young, still a close friend to the King family. Mrs. King was consulted for her advice during the entire process. Later, I was scheduled to meet privately with Mrs. King to gather firsthand her views regarding the direction SCLC should take. We met one afternoon and spent over three hours in the very home Dr. King purchased while he was alive. This was an extraordinary experience as Mrs. King was a most beautiful and gracious host. She spoke at length about the beginning of SCLC, its growth and decline, and the need to be a Christ-centered outreach organization again. She reiterated the unwavering faith of her late husband in God and his profound love for family, his country, and the world. This love, she said, must be embraced by all who seek to make Dr. King's dream a reality. I listened intently to all that Mrs. King said and was awed by a pervasive truth: She still possessed a profound, unwavering love for her husband!

By mid-November, the Atlanta team completed a five-year plan that was presented to the SCLC Board of Directors for approval. Mrs. King had been a key participant in our success. My task was completed in early 1999, and I flew to Dallas to give Mr. Perot a final report. His generous support provided SCLC the "jump start" it needed and a realistic plan for the 21st Century and beyond. SCLC had a way forward; however, its success would depend upon the leadership of Martin III and the visionary support of the Board of Directors.

Thanks to Mrs. King, Martin III, and former Ambassador Young, I had a final opportunity to return to Atlanta. These three hosted a national educational initiative for disadvantaged children sponsored by the late philanthropist Theodore Joseph "Ted" Forstmann and the late John Thomas Walton of the Walton Foundation. Mrs. King was said to have been involved in identifying individuals from across America to gather in Atlanta to craft the program that benefited children nationwide. I was honored to have been involved. A formal dinner was held at the conclusion of the week. As I departed that night, I told Mrs. King what a joy and privilege it was to have been involved and thanked her for making it happen. As usual, she was very appreciative and gracious. It would be the last time we would meet. On January 30, 2006, the world received the shocking headlines:

"CORETTA SCOTT KING, THE WIDOW OF CIVIL RIGHTS LEADER, MARTIN LUTHER KING JR., DEAD AT 78"!

At times, I have been deeply saddened by the loss of someone I'd grown to love. In some cases, the news also caused the world to mourn the death of a phenomenal human being. Such was the case with Coretta Scott King. Her passing was particularly painful to me because I had been privileged to meet her husband and later to have worked with her. The amazing intersection of our lives was a divine orchestration that is very rare in anyone's lifetime. That I was so blessed is humbling and inexplicable; however, the impact of my experiences with the Kings will last for the rest of my life.

The funeral for Coretta Scott King lasted several hours. It attracted over 14,000 people to the New Birth Missionary Baptist Church in Lithonia, Georgia. These included U.S. Presidents George W. Bush, Bill Clinton, George H. W. Bush, Jimmy Carter, their wives, then U.S. Senator Barack Obama, and other dignitaries. Coretta's daughter, Bernice King, an elder at the mega-church, eulogized her mother. On November 20, 2006, friends and family gathered for the unveiling of a new mausoleum where Dr. and Mrs. King are interred.

Into the 21st Century

Looking back over my life, I can truly say that every experience I had with women has been beneficial for enrichment and growth. Some of these transited my life ever so fleetingly; others remained for a time, and some stayed for a lifetime. A few touched me intimately; but all had a significant impact in shaping me into the man that I am today. The foundation of my belief in the greatness of women in general was largely established from the influence of African American women. Yet, this experience enabled me to have a universal admiration, appreciation, respect, and sensitivity for all women wherever our paths crossed. My overall perception of women rises astronomically when I consider the greatness of multi-racial women throughout history and worldwide today. As I ponder the future, I am encouraged by what I have experienced and learned during the two-year journey in writing this book. Every woman to whom I have spoken or from whom I have received input has given me a resounding hope. The women of the 21st century will continue to make their marks and use their God-given abilities and gifts to further the advancement of humanity. For the sake of my granddaughters and great granddaughters, I am eternally grateful.

FOUR NOTABLE WOMEN OF THE 20TH CENTURY

Mary McLeod Bethune

Irene Sendler

Golda Meir

Coretta Scott King

Epilogue
Coming Full Circle
From Hagar to Miss Israel, Titi Aynaw

On March 2013, an historical event took place in Israel when US President Barack Obama, met Yityish Titi Aynaw, Miss Israel. During his first visit to Israel, President Obama had invited Miss Aynaw to attend a private gala with Shimon Peres, the President of the State of Israel. This notable gesture by the president may have been for political purposes since both President Obama and Miss Israel are black. However, this meeting has historical significance that dates back to over 4,000 years!

The epoch journey of Miss Aynaw, as well as that of President Obama, may be said to have begun in the days of Noah. It continued through one of Noah's three sons, Ham, the father of the Canaanites. The journey was benchmarked in Abraham's time through Hagar, the Egyptian handmaiden of Sarah, Abraham's wife. In despair over her inability to have children, Sarah gave Hagar to Abraham to bear children that she could call her own. This union resulted in Ishmael, who became the father of the Arab nation. Ishmael's descendants became the Midianites who later in Jewish history purchased Abraham's great grandson, Joseph, as a slave.

Joseph later became the second highest official in Egypt and married an Egyptian woman of color. The descendants of that union, Manasseh and Ephraim, were established in the historical twelve tribes of Israel. When the Israelites were eventually scattered to other parts of the world, some of them likely settled on the continent of Africa. In 1992, centuries later, Yityish Aynaw was born in a tiny village in Ethiopia. She was orphaned by the time she was eight years old when both her father and mother died. When she was twelve, an aunt brought her to Israel to live with her emigrant grandparents. In the years that followed, Yityish learned the culture and language of the Jews, completed high school, and served as a Lieutenant in the Military Police Corps of the Israel Defense Forces. By then, Yityish had grown into a beautiful, statuesque young Israeli model. At the urging of friends, she reluctantly entered the contest for Miss Israel.

In early 2013, Yityish Titi Aynaw won the title of Miss Israel. She is the first Ethiopian Jew to win the contest and the first black Miss Israel winner! In the backdrop of the great history of the Jews, this amazing historical event is a monumental milestone for Miss Aynaw and all of Israel. But it speaks more to the incredible work of God in His purpose for women of all ethnic origins. I no longer wonder about God's intentions for humanity because I am a humble, living recipient of His amazing grace. That's enough for me!

Appendix

Richard Toliver

Woman—A Great Creation

Interview Questionnaire

1. Woman, who art thou? (WHO ARE YOU?)!

2. What were the early experiences in your life that enabled you to know who you were or what you wanted to be?

3. Who or what influenced you the most in your early life?

4. When did you discover who you really were or who you really wanted to be?

5. How did you determine the path you wanted to take in life?

6. What were some of the obstacles, pitfalls, or mistakes that got in your way?

7. What would you consider to have been your greatest challenge?

8. What was/is your greatest achievement in life?

9. What are/were your goals/opinions regarding the establishment of personal and professional relationships?

10. Have you established or do you have the criteria whereby you allow personal or professional relationships to be developed?

11. What are/were your personal goals of marriage? Family? Children?

12. What value do you place upon the sanctity of life?

13. Why do you believe young women enter into poor or ill-advised relationships?

14. Why do you think women chose to have children out of wedlock?

15. Have there been or are there now unfulfilled ambitions or aspirations?

16. What do you plan to do about it?

17. What lessons in life have you learned that could be helpful to those seeking to know themselves?

18. What advice would you give young women today about life? Ambitions? Pitfalls?

Index

Biographical Names

Geographical Names

Organizations

Proper Nouns

About the Author

Richard Toliver retired from the Air Force as a Colonel after twenty-six years of dedicated service, including two combat tours in Southeast Asia. He is a protégé of the famed Tuskegee Airmen, where he was mentored, trained, and commissioned under their tutelage. Colonel Toliver has been married for over fifty-one years to the former Margaret A. Hairston of Baltimore, Maryland. The Tolivers have eight adult children, five of which are adopted or part of the family through acceptance, commitment, and love. This book was written to encourage women of all ages to better appreciate and embrace the truth that they were created by God for a great and noble purpose. As a father, grandfather, great grandfather, and combat veteran, Colonel Toliver's purpose is to **seek out** and **eradicate** the commonly held myth that women are the lesser of men.

Colonel Toliver continues to be in demand as a motivational speaker in the United States, Europe, and Southeast Asia.